WHAT PEOPLE ARE SAYING
ABOUT "MILLER TIME"

"The Millers are the pride of Pittsburgh and Beaver County, in particular. This book about their father will have Sean and Archie smiling — and will make all of western Pennsylvania stand up and cheer. What a great tribute to a great coach!"

-Tony Dorsett, Dallas Cowboys

"Basketball seems to flow in the bloodlines of the Miller household."

- Brian Reinhardt, NC State Pack Preview

"John Miller: Great Coach ... better man.
Miller Time is one of the best sports books of all time.
And in the Pratte Pack Gym it's always Miller Time!"

- Rob Pratte, CBS Pittsburgh, KDKA Radio

"It's no surprise both his sons Archie and Sean are big time college coaches.
John Miller's one of the best."

- Bucky Waters, NBC Sports

"Maybe one of the most important things that breed success is who you are around particularly at a young age. I u~~~~ ~~~~~~ ~~~~~ l Miller as a coach. Because of his passi~~~~ ~~~~~~ ~~~~ rs, benefited. This story tells how John's a ~~~~~ ~~~~~ ame work ethic. It is a remarkable story"
- Bob Davie, Head Coach, Univ~~~~~ ~~~~~~~~ ~~~iversity of New Mexico

"I have known Coach Miller for more than 40 years. In that time I've studied under him, I've watched him at work and I've been amazed at the wealth of basketball wisdom he possesses. You won't find a finer teacher of the game anywhere, at any level."

- John Calipari, Head Basketball Coach, University of Kentucky

"Coach Miller is a fantastic teacher and coach. I've been fortunate to get to know him through his sons, Sean and Archie. I can tell they've learned at the feet of a winner.
Miller Time tells their story."
— Thad Matta, Head Basketball Coach, Ohio State University

"Coach Miller's a basketball legend in Pennsylvania and he continues to teach the game the way it's meant to be played. When he conducts a clinic on campus, I make sure I'm there."
— Jamie Dixon, Head Basketball Coach, University of Pittsburgh (Former), Texas Christian University

"Regardless of your level, Coach Miller's instruction will help you reach your potential."
— The late Dean Smith, Former Head Basketball Coach, University of North Carolina

"Even if he weren't my dad, I would recommend his instruction to any young coach who is looking for a mentor. When it comes to training young players and developing their basketball skills, there's no one better. No one."
— Sean Miller, Head Basketball Coach, University of Arizona

"Though not old enough to be on the team, Coach Miller would let me participate in practices, and by doing so, he set me upon a path of athleticism and dedication to every sport or endeavor I would go on to attempt."
— Khalid West, HBO Sports

"These days there are a lot of basketball coaches, but very few can teach the game like John Miller. A great read for parents and coaches alike."
— Mike Hartsock, Broadcaster for the Dayton Flyers

MILLER TIME

COACH JOHN MILLER'S STORY

DAVID A. BURHENN

FOREWORD BY JOHN CALIPARI

WORD ASSOCIATION PUBLISHERS
www.wordassociation.com
1.800.827.7903

Printed in the United States of America.

ISBN: 978-1-63385-160-3

Library of Congress Control Number: 2016912310

Designed and published by

Word Association Publishers
205 Fifth Avenue
Tarentum, Pennsylvania 15084

www.wordassociation.com
1.800.827.7903

FOR BENNY AND BROOKE

ACKNOWLEDGMENTS

Dave would like to thank the following

John Miller, Barb Miller, Dard Miller, Ryan "Archie" Miller, Sean Miller, Lisa Miller Oak, Dana Miller Tapia, Tim Miller, John Calipari, Art Kunkle, Tim Kolodziej, Mark "Doc" Balbach, J.O. Stright, Benny Burhenn, Brooke Burhenn, Kristi Burhenn, Melissa and Donald Dunlap, Eleanor Burhenn, Boggs Family, Ryan Reynolds at the University of Arizona, Christina Trittschuh at the University of Dayton, Eric Lindsay at the University of Kentucky, Corey Evans, Tess Zufall, Phil Meanor, Johnny Carson Entertainment Group, Khalid West at HBO, Sally Maxon Photography, Tom Costello at Word Association, Susan Kauffman (copyediting). Thanks to April Urso (book design), Greg Suhayda, Kirk Haberman (proofreading), Leanne Thome (proofreading), Pittsburgh Post-Gazette, Beaver County Times, Leah Lindemann at the Blackhawk High School Library, Ed Olkowski, Dr. Brad Brown, Francis Essic, Dan Vander Wal, Dave Vettica, Dori Anderson Oldaker, Tom Richards, Tim McConnell, Tim Jones, Matt Ciciarelli, Dan Rosenberg, The Brighton Hot Dog Shoppe, Bob Maher, Dennis Maher, Rob Pratte, Bob Amalia, Blaine Cleckley, Ron Galbreath, Nick Aloi, Al Campton, Jeff Cheatham, Rob Davie, Diane Huston, Antoine Childs, Jack Fullen, Brandon Fuss Cheatham, LAMP Apparel, Ken Yonkee, Dante Calabria, Jason DeRose at Faster, "Sweet" Lou Dunbar, Stacie Leves, Gabe "Action" Jackson, Chris Pipkin, Rev. Rod Smith, Mark "Knobby" Walsh, Brenna Wise, Frank and Anna Huang at Taiwan 101, Rudy Flyer, Wilbur and Wilma Wildcat, Tom Lucchino, Lisa Latshaw, Jen Conforti, Tom Servo, Bednar family, Tara Rowan, Warren Jackson, Rich Thome, Bunny Dorsett, Jack Fullen, Brighton Hot Dog Shoppe, DeAngelis Donuts and Andy Shelby of Your Beaver County.

"Keep plugging. Look ahead. Something good is going to happen."
—Coach John C. Miller

TABLE OF CONTENTS

FOREWORD

"FAMILY"

By Coach John Calipari

Y ou can't pick your relatives. That's a common phrase I've heard people say over the years. And as far as John Miller goes, I don't even know if we really are blood related. In fact, my guess is that we are probably not. But for me, John Miller is the older "cousin" that I most definitely chose.

I have known Coach Miller for more than forty years. In that time I've studied under him, I've watched him at work, and I've been amazed at the wealth of basketball wisdom he possesses. You won't find a finer teacher of the game anywhere, at any level. His brother Tim and I are still good friends. Long ago in a place called Glenwillard, we were childhood buddies and teammates. I spent as much time at his mother's house as I did my own house. My high school coach Bill Sacco was teamed with John as an assistant coach when I was the ball boy for the Moon Tigers varsity team many "moons" ago. Before that, they were players on the same team at Moon High School. You could say that I more than looked up to them. By watching John, I couldn't help but fall in love with the game that has now become my life. In fact, while playing with his brother Tim, I spent many summer days growing up watching, mimicking, and learning from J. C., as he was called. He was one of the "big kids" and my best friend's big brother. As far as I'm concerned, we are more than family.

J. C. Miller was one of the first people that I looked up to, and I told myself, "I want to be like that guy." From his demeanor on the court as a player to the way he inspired his players from the bench, to the stellar reputation he had as a teacher, J. C. was the complete package. In the blue-collar neighborhood where we grew up, teachers were thought of as the professionals. They were known as the smartest and the best. And that's where I first set my sights. As a kid, my dream was to go to college and become a teacher and maybe even a high school coach like my cousin whom I respected and loved. I never considered being a college coach in the beginning.

But with John, it was always about making people, myself included, believe that they could do anything. You just had to work hard enough. When given the chance to be the head coach at UMass, I knew I could do it. I know now that much of the confidence I developed had come from lessons I had absorbed from John growing up in our "family."

Since the beginning, our lives, both basketball and personal, have been intertwined. In 1986, back in my days as an assistant at the University of Pittsburgh, I was champing at the bit to recruit a talented young man named Sean Miller. I knew where he got his magic. Nowadays, every March seems to be a Miller/Calipari family reunion in the NCAA tournament brackets. I can't help but scan over the bracket as the weeks go by to see which Miller, Sean or Archie, I might get matched up with to battle. So far the brackets have been kind, and we never had to face each other head to head, but I'm sure it will happen someday.

In 1988, I was honored to introduce J. C.'s *Drill for Skill* instructional video, which is as relevant today as it was then, and I am just as honored today to pen the foreword to this book about his life. I knew some of the stories Dave has gathered and written in the following pages, but much of it surprised and amazed me. Coach Miller's work ethic and stamina still astonish even a workaholic like me. His labors, though, have paid off in so many ways.

He affected innumerable lives as a teacher and as a coach. His many championships brought pride and upped the basketball I.Q. of an entire community. And personally, my family and I will always be deeply indebted to John Miller for the foundation that he laid in our lives. No one has worked harder for his players and his family. And maybe most importantly, his family and players have reaped the benefits of the daily grind that was and still is his way—the Miller Way.

WRITER'S INTRODUCTION

"If there's a book that you want to read, but it hasn't been written yet, you must write it."

—Toni Morrison, American novelist

I write this introduction while waiting in the parent observation area at the Drill for Skill Academy in Monaca, Pennsylvania. It sits unassumingly behind the Beaver Valley Auto Mall, a new and used car dealership. As one enters through the red, unmarked steel door of the academy, the surroundings turn from grey brick to a colorful open space filled with the sounds of basketballs being dribbled, athletic shoes squeaking on polished wood, and an occasional whistle followed by Coach Miller's instruction. You would wonder at first how all of these people heard about this place since there are no signs or advertising outside. But like a prohibition speakeasy, word has gotten around.

As I sit proudly watching my eight-year-old son Ben dribbling quickly through some orange traffic cones, I overhear another father talk about the real reason he takes his son for training at "Coach Miller's."

---

*The Miller boys with a camp coordinator and Larry Bird

Coach and Ben

Sitting back in a black folding chair and motioning with his hands, he states, "My boy is never going to be in the NBA. I come here because Coach is beyond a positive influence on these kids. Look, he takes as much time and effort with the little guys as he does the high school and college players that come in for training. He has an old school work ethic and just a manner about him that I hope will rub off on my son."

My reason for bringing my son, Ben, to the Drill for Skill Academy gym is a little stranger than that. In kindergarten, Ben's speech teacher at school suggested that he had a language disorder. He could speak well enough, but he had trouble processing what others were saying. Concerned, I asked the teacher what we could do to fix the problem. She suggested getting him involved in an activity that would make him do something physical when oral directions were given. This would force him to prove that he was listening and that he understood. At the time, Disney's *High School Musical* was all the rage, and little Ben liked to pretend that he was Troy Bolton, the lead character who loved to sing and play basketball for the East Side Wildcats. For whatever reason, I thought of Coach Miller immediately. Not because of the singing of course, but because of the basketball. Coach Miller was my gym teacher at Blackhawk High School, a few miles down the road in Beaver Falls, Pennsylvania. In high school, I was far from being an athlete, but he was able to get through to me and took the time to work with me. I was even able to juggle three balls when he was finished with me. It's been four years now since I first brought Ben to Drill for Skill. And after all is said and done, "Benny," as Coach Miller calls him, is no longer in speech classes. He's excelling at school and even recently went with Coach Miller to perform for a basketball coaches' clinic in front of about fifty local coaches from the Pittsburgh area. Even better, in the true Miller Way, Ben won the 2016 Knights of Columbus Pennsylvania State Free Throw crown for his age group. He has come a very long way, and I give a lot of the credit to John Miller.

Coach John C. Miller is a local legend. The most successful high school coach in western Pennsylvania high school basketball history, he retired in 2005 only to discover that he loved the game too much to just call it quits. It seemed that the sound that the ball makes as it catches nothing but net is just too sweet to the Coach to totally stop hearing it altogether. The solution was to open the Drill for Skill Academy. The place would turn out to be a basketball-training destination for western Pennsylvania's hardcore athletes and for those curious to see if the game is for them. A few months after its opening, it was billed as "Miller's Hoop Heaven" in a full-page article in the local newspaper, the *Beaver County Times.*

Almost immediately upon opening (which by the way was done with almost no fanfare or advertising), the Drill for Skill Academy was filled with promising local basketball players hoping to learn from the master. After all, it is common knowledge in the area that Miller's sons Sean and Archie both made it as standout NCAA players and are now Elite 8 coaches for the universities of Arizona and Dayton, respectively. His daughters Lisa and Dana made names for themselves in sports as well. Lisa was a point guard at Toledo and Elon Universities; Dana made tennis her sport of choice. People in western Pennsylvania still talk about Sean Miller being featured on ABC's *That's Incredible!* and NBC's *Tonight Show* with Johnny Carson when he was just 12 years old. Sean recently admitted that he tires of the questions about those days. Two weeks do not pass when someone doesn't insist that he revisits those days.

With all of this in mind, I faced the possibly embarrassing task of asking a coaching legend, John Miller, if he would be willing to teach my kindergartener to follow directions. Luckily, when it comes to my children, I will find the courage to do anything if it helps them. I found the number and placed the call. When I explained the situation over the phone, I expected a polite no from Coach Miller, maybe followed with the very real and understandable reason that he was too busy teaching real players to dominate the hardwood.

Boy, was I wrong. He agreed to help me right away. I believed he used his trademark, "Yeah, let's get him going, let's get him rolling," before ending the call. He scheduled my son for the next day and put his heart into getting Ben to dribble, shoot, pass, and, most importantly, talk and listen to directions. It showed me that even though Coach Miller eats, sleeps, and breathes competitive basketball, there are underlying values and ideals that he professes that transcend sport. Hard work, dedication, and doing the right things all are key in his teaching of basketball and, more than that, his philosophy of life. And it was pretty amazing. After a few sessions with Coach Miller, Ben became more businesslike when he practiced (well, as businesslike as a six-year-old can be). You could see in his eyes that he was hooked. After all, enthusiasm isn't taught; it's caught. And with the amount of enthusiasm toward basketball that John Miller has, a person can't help but be infected with it.

"Keep your head up." Coach shows Benny the two ball dribble.

But again, Miller's passion isn't solely about basketball. It's about doing things, all things, the right way. This life philosophy has certainly rubbed off on his family. Past teachers of his children were just as eager to mention how polite and caring the Miller kids were as they were to mention their fame or exploits on the court. His kids had every right to be cocky. But they weren't. Amazing.

Which leads us to the present. In 2015 and 2016, both of Miller's sons had their teams in the AP Top 25. During March Madness 2014, *Pittsburgh Post-Gazette* writer Mike White observed that, "John Miller has a dilemma, like no dad ever before. Go west to see No. 1 son, or south to see No. 2 son? That's a tough choice, but one sweet parental problem. How might that feel?"

The dilemma that Mr. White was addressing was that both the University of Arizona Wildcats' coach Sean Miller and the Dayton Flyers' coach Archie Miller had their teams in the Sweet 16 of the NCAA tournament. It was the first time in history that two coaching brothers have had their teams in the same Sweet 16. The next year, they would be the first brothers coaching teams in the Elite 8.

I was so intrigued at the question that Mr. White had posed. How did it feel to see both kids at the top like that? I knew I'd have to ask Coach Miller how he felt about it. And while I was at it, I might as well find out the rest of the story. I've read about people and seen people on television that seemed to have life all figured out, but this guy was sitting right in front of me.

So, I'm going to listen to Toni Morrison's advice and write that book that I'd like to read. I'm about to challenge Coach John Miller to share with me his key to success both at work and at home. Hopefully, we'll get to hear some great basketball stories along the way.

Enjoy,
DB

PREGAME SCOUTING REPORT:

JOHN MILLER AND FAMILY

Ask anyone who is remotely familiar with western Pennsylvania basketball what they know about Coach John Miller and they may respond with kind words such as "basketball genius," "dedicated," or "hardworking." Almost without exception, even people who have played or coached *against* Miller, without hesitation give John nothing but words of respect.

Western Pennsylvania hall of fame coaching legend Ed Olkowski described him as "one of, if not, *the* hardest working, relentless coaches I've ever known. If you let your intensity down even for a second, you might as well forget it. John had his guys trained so that they worked like a machine. Great coach—just great."

Another local hall of famer Gabe Jackson, a player for the rival New Brighton Lions, would go on to excel for the Robert Morris Colonials in college and overseas professional basketball. He remembers, "Man, that guy was the 'General,' a motivator. I never played for him, but just looking over at (Blackhawk's) bench you could tell that he had those kids in the palm of his hand. They would run through walls for him. He had what has now become known as the 'X Factor.' I mean it's hard to put into words how his presence and ball knowledge got into his players. Late in games, my team and I would think we'd have his Cougars tired and starting to give up. He'd take a timeout, and the next thing you'd know is they would come back on the court looking like it was the opening tip again. John Miller's thing was bringing the best out of you.

P·R·I·O·R·I·T·I·E·S

"A HUNDRED YEARS FROM NOW IT WILL NOT MATTER WHAT MY BANK ACCOUNT WAS,
THE SORT OF HOUSE I LIVED IN, OR THE KIND OF CAR I DROVE...BUT THE WORLD
MAY BE DIFFERENT BECAUSE I WAS IMPORTANT IN THE LIFE OF A CHILD."

Framed picture from Coach's desk

That's what he did. He brought the best out of his players. And five mediocre guys playing their best will beat three wannabe stars any day of the week."

Other people, however, aren't as friendly with their descriptions of the Coach. They use words like "cold," "task master," and "obsessed" to describe Coach Miller. More often than not, these descriptions come from people who have not had any significant success in the sport themselves. Jealousy has a way of affecting how you perceive someone right away. And talking negatively about that person seems to be a salve to help the hater and his fragile self-esteem.

True, Coach Miller does not go out of his way to be overly warm and fuzzy to anyone, especially his players. That's not his job as far as he's concerned. His task is to get the most work out of his players and to squeeze the very best effort out of them. And as far as school-age players go, his job is to make sure that, after all is said and done, they are better people for having played for him. This has held true when the player has happened to be his son or daughter—maybe even more so.

People should be aware that Coach Miller isn't (if truth be told) *just* the hard-nosed coach that people assume he is. He has a softer side. He, in fact, has cultivated relationships with his children and his players that are to be particularly admired in this day and age.

Chippewa United Methodist Church in the suburbs of Beaver Falls, Pennsylvania, has a beloved pastor named Reverend Rodney Smith. "Pastor Rod" as he is known had the not-so enviable task of being an assistant coach for a few post-Miller teams at Blackhawk. "It's not that they were terrible teams, but how do you follow a coaching legend?"

Reverend Smith cannot say enough about the Coach, the father, and the man. "Every time I run into him, he bubbles with pride and joy of his family. That speaks volumes. Sometime in the nineties, I coached against him once when I was an assistant at Ellwood City. He could have buried our team by seventy-five if he wanted to, but in his classy way, he made it look like we were still in the game until the end. When one of his players lost his mother at an early age, he came to me for some consolation. I could see the genuine hurt in his eyes. God sure knew what he was doing when he called out to John—Coach—and John responded. The rest is history. So many lives touched in such a positive way."

John's youngest daughter Lisa agrees. "He has such a knack for molding character. I'm pretty sure I am who I am because of our car rides together to and from practice, to and from Drill for Skill camps every summer, always instilling in me, in his subtle way, how to be successful, respected, how to kill 'em with kindness. I could go on and on."

Lisa's big sister Dana puts it this way: "He's just really laid back and level headed and has taught us that you can't change people that upset you. Just do your thing to the best of your ability and the rewards will come. You just have to keep chipping away at what you want every day no matter what the goal may be."

John Miller talks about his relationship with his sons Sean and Ryan ("Arch" as he calls him). "Especially when my boys call, the words that are exchanged aren't like sweet, syrupy words or whatever, but the connection is there. Sometimes conversations that consist of, 'don't worry. You're good. Just run a "Loyola" play instead of your normal attack at the zone,' says I love you more that anything."

Of course, people can judge, scoff, and wag their heads at how tough Coach Miller seemed to be on his players and especially on his own kids. They can also debate if the methods he used were too harsh or too extreme. What cannot be debated, however, are the results that came from all of the hard work. The following facts and stats are some examples of the fruits of his labors:

- Coach John Miller and his Blackhawk Cougars hold the record for western Pennsylvania's longest section winning streak at 111 victories.

- Coach Miller won more than 630 games during his career at Riverside and Blackhawk high schools in Beaver County, Pennsylvania.

- He led Blackhawk High School to four Pennsylvania state championships in 1992, 1995, 1996, and 1999 and was state runner-up in 2000.

- His teams won eight WPIAL Class AAA titles in 1986, 1990, 1991, 1992, 1996, 1999, 2000, and 2003.

- He has received Coach of the Year honors at the regional, state, and national levels.

- He was coach of the Dapper Dan Roundball Classic in 1988 and 1994.

- He has lectured at over 400 clinics in the United States, Europe, and Australia.

- Coach Miller has sent more than forty of his former players on to college careers

- He's also trained three of his children—Sean, Archie, and Lisa—to become Division I college basketball stars. Sean and Archie are now among the hottest NCAA coaches in the nation. John, Sean, and Archie Miller are members of the Beaver County Sports Hall of Fame.

- Lisa Miller won two WPIAL Championships and one Pennsylvania State championship in high school under Miller's personal direction and under the direction of his female coaching protégé Dori Anderson Oldaker. Lisa was the Pennsylvania player of the year in 1999.

- Son Archie Miller is now the head coach of the A-10's Dayton Flyers. His successes include back-to-back NCAA tournament appearances and an Elite 8 berth in 2013–2014. He already has over 100 wins at Dayton. In 2016, he led his Flyers to their first A-10 conference championship. Archie is a career college coach who worked his way up the ranks, returning to his alma mater (NC State) as an assistant alongside his brother Sean Miller. He then broke out on his own for two years at Ohio State only to reunite as an assistant under his sibling at Arizona.

"BIG TIME PROGRAMS": DAYTON AND ARIZONA

- Coach Miller's oldest son Sean has brought the Arizona Wildcats back to prominence since landing the high-profile coaching job back in 2009. The Miller-led Wildcats have amassed many honors including Elite 8 appearances in 2011, 2014, and 2015. Sean Miller's Wildcats made the Sweet 16 in 2013 and was named PAC-12 Champions in 2015. Previously, he made a name for himself coaching as an assistant at Wisconsin, Miami of Ohio, Pitt, NC State, and Xavier. It was at Xavier that he was promoted to his first head coaching position.

- Sean and his wife Amy have been dating since they both attended Blackhawk High School. They have three sons, Austin, Cameron, and Braden. John has spent time in all of the places that they have lived and it's no surprise that he built a small court in each of those places. When he visits, he works the boys out and teaches them to chart their progress. Each has played basketball since fourth grade. Austin is now a manager for his dad's Wildcats. Braden and Cameron play high school ball. Cameron, a senior in 2016-2017, is hoping to get an opportunity to play college ball next year.

- Some have called the Millers basketball's version of the football Harbaughs.

- John Miller's brother Tim was a highly decorated basketball player at Saint Vincent College and has coached five nationally ranked AAU teams. He now runs Drill for Skill Baltimore.

- Coach Miller's brother Joe (who passed away in 2014) was a hall of fame high school football coach in North Carolina.

- Coach Miller's younger cousin John Calipari began his love affair with basketball watching Miller and his teenage buddies play with a dedication that was unheard of for kids that age. Calipari himself says that he was partly raised by John's mother in those early days. World famous now, Calipari played Division I basketball and is now the head coach at the perennial Final Four favorite, the University of Kentucky Wildcats. He has taken his team to the Final Four many times and has won a national championship. He is a member of the Naismith Basketball Hall of Fame.

- Coach Miller's former students also included Dante Calabria, a standout at the University of North Carolina and a professional in Italy, Spain, and France for thirteen seasons. Calabria recently traveled to Taiwan and Thailand to help children using basketball as a vehicle to teach important skills.

- Miller's coaching has influenced several athletes who have gone on to play at the next level. The following is a brief list of some of Coach Miller's former players who went on to compete in basketball—and other sports—at the collegiate level and beyond.

  - ★ Dennis Bott, Thiel College Tomcats
  - ★ Dante Calabria, University of North Carolina Tar Heels
  - ★ Alex Cantamessa, John Carroll University Lobos
  - ★ Jim Cantamessa, Siena College St. Bernards
  - ★ Antoine Childs, Western Carolina University Catamounts
  - ★ Pat Cutshall, Mercyhurst University Lakers (baseball)
  - ★ Rich Dickinson, Slippery Rock University Rocks
  - ★ Steve Dickinson, University of Pittsburgh Panthers (baseball)
  - ★ Ryan Evanochko, University of Wisconsin at Green Bay Phoenix
  - ★ Dan Fortson, University of Cincinnati Bearcats, NBA
  - ★ Mark Franitti, Gannon University Knights
  - ★ Nick Franitti, La Roche College Red Hawks
  - ★ Pat Franitti, Geneva College Golden Tornadoes
  - ★ Brandon Fuss-Cheatham, Ohio State University Buckeyes
  - ★ Andy Gray, Waynesburg College Yellow Jackets
  - ★ Dane Helsing, Bucknell University Bison (football)
  - ★ Jeremy Huber, Geneva College Tornadoes
  - ★ Jay Irwin, Indiana University of Pennsylvania (IUP) Big Indians
  - ★ Mark Kinger, Rider College Broncos
  - ★ Hal Koenemund, Robert Morris University Colonials
  - ★ Jon Koenemund, Point Park College Pioneers
  - ★ Marc Lodovico, Waynesburg College Yellow Jackets
  - ★ Steve Lodovico, La Roche College Red Hawks
  - ★ Adin McCann, Notre Dame Fighting Irish
  - ★ Bobby Maher, University of Steubenville Barons
  - ★ John Maher, University of Pittsburgh at Johnstown Panthers
  - ★ Lisa Miller, Elon University Phoenix
  - ★ Sean Miller, University of Pittsburgh Panthers
  - ★ Ryan "Archie" Miller, North Carolina State Wolfpack
  - ★ LaVar Arrington, Penn State Nittany Lions, NFL
  - ★ Kenyon Martin, University of Cincinnati Bearcats, NBA
  - ★ Matt Moye, Old Dominion University Lions (baseball)

* Ken Newmann, Thiel College Tomcats
* Jim Peel, Ohio State University Buckeyes (football)
* Jim Peterson, Ohio University Bobcats
* Tom Richards, University of Pittsburgh Panthers
* Jason Stanchak, University of Virginia Cavaliers (football)
* Sam Stanchak, College of William & Mary Griffins (football)
* Jay Strosnider, US Naval Academy
* J.D. Campbell, Shippensburg University Big Red
* Jeff Weaver, Rutgers University Scarlet Knights (football)
* Rodney Thompson, Mercyhurst University Lakers (football)
* Darren Tielsch, Robert Morris University Colonials
* Tim Tirlia, Cameron University Aggies
* Dave Vetica, Florida State University Seminoles
* Scott Weaver, University of Illinois Illini (football)
* Rick Burdine, California University of Pennsylvania Vulcans
* Doug Yeager, Mercyhurst University Lakers (baseball)
* Micah Mason, Duquesne Dukes
* Danny Fortsen, Cincinnati Bearcats, NBA
* Rodney Thompson, California University Vulcans
* Chris Horne, Duquesne University Dukes
* Bobby Brannen, Cincinnati Bearcats
* Sam Breen, University of Dayton Flyers.
* Dontonio Wingfield Jr., Cincinnati Bearcats, NBA: Portland Trailblazers, Seattle Supersonics

• Coach Miller, even while being a member of three different halls of fame, is just as comfortable working with youngsters as he is with college and professional players.

Coaching staff of Team USA: Ed Cooley, Sean Miller, Archie Miller, and Justin Kokoskie

• Sean Miller, with his assistant, Archie, coached the U19 Team USA Men's Basketball, which received gold medals during the summer of 2015. In December of the same year Sean was named USA basketball's coach of the year.

• Dori Anderson Oldaker, another student of Coach Millers,

was the Girls U16 coach as well as a member of the Pennsylvania Sports Hall of Fame.

Being featured on a Brighton Hot Dog Shoppe cup means you've definitely made it in Beaver County, PA

• Coach Miller's appearance with his sons on a plastic souvenir cup from the locally loved Brighton Hot Dog Shoppe may be his biggest honor (Chris Bradford of the Beaver County Times wrote that this honor signifies that you've made it to the top in Beaver County).

Seriously though, through it all, everyone from Coach Miller's biggest fans to his most jaded naysayers agrees: His secret to success is actually no secret at all. He believes 100 percent in making a plan to succeed and then working to make that plan a reality. And the work has yet to stop. He has been called a legend by countless numbers of people. But Miller might agree with jazz great Miles Davis who was quoted saying, "A legend is an old man with a cane known for what he used to do. I'm still doing it."

Another recurring theme that was visited in the making of this book was that it is more important to be respected than liked. This does not mean treating people poorly to get what you want. Many times, if not most of the time, when you do the right thing, you will be ridiculed. Furthermore, if you go to war against John, you will have a real fight on your hands.

One of the reasons that John Miller agreed to the writing of this book is that he has a feeling that people think that they know who he is. Many of these people have no idea. As you read, you will discover that this man went through more in his boyhood than most people have gone through in a lifetime.

Archie backing up Sean at Arizona

CHAPTER 1

POLIO
(STARTING AT THE BASELINE)

"All my life I've been workin' them angels overtime."

—*Neil Peart*

- VILLAGE OF GLENWILLARD -
17 miles from Pittsburgh
1950

John Miller's earliest recollections of his life included a real life battle—a desperate fight—one that didn't look so good in the beginning.

Let's go back to the exact midpoint of the twentieth century. A six-year-old John Miller is lying in bed feeling miserable. He is burning with a persistent fever that continues to climb. His parents Joe and Catherine assume he's caught the flu or some other common childhood infection. The bad part is that even after waiting many days, the fever isn't going away. Days go by. A week, nearly two, go by. Finally his parents, first concerned and now worried sick, have had enough.

John's dad carefully lays him in the back of their Ford Prefect. His mom stares distantly out the car window as they drive through Glenwillard, the small, tough town they call home. Familiar buildings and houses pass by. Patti Page's "Tennessee Waltz" is playing on the radio. Joe switches it off, as no one is really listening anyway. Anxious thoughts go through everyone's heads. Mostly, "What could be wrong with John?"

Finally, they arrive to their destination, their family doctor's office. After a thorough examination, Dr. Robert D. Nix is confused and at a loss as to what the illness could be. A brilliant man, he was one of the doctors who worked with Dr. Jonas Salk to create the polio vaccine. He saw some signs that he didn't like, and he recommended that the Millers see some specialists at the nearby Sewickley Hospital.

It's only about an eight-minute drive that winds down Crescent Avenue along the Ohio River and across the Sewickley Bridge, but it seems much longer. When they finally reach their destination, the best doctors in the area check John. He is taken to an examination room further back in the hospital. Back in the waiting room, a newspaper sits unopened on the table. The sports page announces that pitcher Whitey Ford of the New York Yankees dominated the Philadelphia Phillies to win the 1950 World Series. But of course, Joe Miller, a normally fervent baseball fan, doesn't even care. The world is a serious, stark place right now. All attention is focused on one question, "What's taking them so long?" Joe and Catherine Miller are hoping for news from the doctors that will replace their worry with a rush of relief.

It isn't to be. Eventually, the doctor comes back with the terrible news. After a thorough examination and battery of tests, the conclusion is that John had the nightmare virus called polio. Paralytic poliomyelitis, or polio, is a virus that usually causes nerve damage in the spinal cord or brain stem. This damage can bring on paralysis in a person's legs and arms and the rest of the body.

The disease that kept President Roosevelt in a wheelchair was now destroying Joe and Catherine Miller's young son's muscles at a rate that would soon keep him confined to his bed or a wheelchair for an especially long time—maybe forever.

John was admitted immediately to the D. T. Watson Home for Crippled Children, also in Sewickley, for the best care possible at the time, but the prognosis was not encouraging. In the days to follow, John hopelessly and painfully would fall to the horrors that are the symptoms of the disease. Gradually, but steadily, he lost the use of both legs and his left arm. He would remain this way for a few months, and it looked like he may be restricted to a wheelchair forever.

Obviously, this is heart wrenching for any parent to see. For John's parents though, like many parents faced with a very sick child, with the pain came determination, a strong faith, and a will to do whatever it took to see their son walk again.

Under the hospital's instructions, the Watson Home staff began administering the best-known methods at the time. A considerable part of the treatments included a painstaking procedure known as the Kenny method. This method—developed by Sister Elizabeth Kenny, a chief nurse in the Australian military (the Australians gave the title of "sister" to military nurses)—completely changed the history of polio treatment.

Before Sister Kenny's method, doctors put splints and braces on affected limbs and used a respirator called an iron lung to help patients breathe. Noticing that patients' limbs were stiff but not permanently paralyzed, she thought it was best to use hot packs and encourage gentle movement rather than to restrict movements with splints and braces. Her method, in a way, taught patients how to use limbs again.

A female doctor—a rarity at the time—Jessie Wright was one of the most skilled at administering the treatment. At the beginning of each day, she instructed nurses to perform the following actions: All affected parts of the body must be heated right to the point just below a burn. This should be done either by applying just under scalding hot compresses or by submerging the patient into a hot whirlpool bath. Immediately following the moist heat, the muscles are to be worked vigorously by nurses.

The nurses dutifully performed this treatment once a day, and although there were days when it seemed that a muscle would twitch here and there, no real breakthroughs were seen. The answer to John's problem seemed to be nowhere in sight.

Many times in life a solution to a problem will come not from the person with the most intelligence, expertise, or experience; it will come from the person who cares the most about solving the problem. In the case of John Miller's polio, this was the situation. The real key to the eventual polio cure for Miller would not come from a nurse or someone with eight years of medical school. It would come from a hardworking blue-collar worker, Joe Miller.

A working-class man, Joe Miller worked jobs on the railroad and as a truck driver. Any downtime would be filled with building projects and odd jobs to help support his family.

After a few months of ineffective treatments, John's dad posed the seemingly obvious and sensible question to the doctor— a question that would eventually and miraculously end up being the missing piece to his son's recovery.

"If one treatment a day was good, wouldn't two or three be better?"

Surprisingly, the doctor answered yes.

Why, then, weren't they giving John more than one treatment a day? The doctor explained that there simply wasn't enough time in the day to schedule all of the children for more treatments. During the late 1940s and early 1950s, the Watson Home had a large influx of polio patients. "With all the beds full, and only so many nurses and whirlpools to go around, once a day was the best we can do," the staff explained.

At this, John's father and mother made the conscious and self-sacrificing decision to remove their son from the care of the hospital and its doctors. It wasn't that they weren't doing their jobs; they were. And Dr. Wright was the best the area could offer. But the hospital staff was overwhelmed with the influx of patients. What if someone was to focus the Kenny method on one patient, three times a day?

From that moment on, Joe Miller would be that someone. His life and his family's would revolve around his working night turn on the railroad and caring for his son. He created a whirlpool out of an inner tube, a tarp, an agitator modified from a broom, and a constant supply of steaming hot water delivered by John's mom. She would actually draw the water from a pump that was in the house, and it would then be boiled in huge pots one at a time.

Joe Miller would rub down his boy's affected muscles in a painstaking routine each morning. The entire process would be repeated again in the afternoon. After a quick meal and a few hours sleep, John's dad would give him one last treatment session and then head out for the night shift at the nearby Aliquippa and Southern Railroad Works.

This was life for the Miller family for thirteen wearisome months. Many would have lost faith and given up when nothing happened after a couple of months of this routine. But John's family did not give up. John's father created a regimen and a written schedule complete with charts for each part of the Kenny procedure and stuck to it. For hours, day after day, Joe worked toward his goal when others would have thrown in the towel, rationalizing that it was too much work and that the situation was hopeless.

This routine of scheduling, performing the task, and recording it on charts would resurface later in John's life in a much more enjoyable pursuit, basketball training. His father, in the hopes that John would walk again, unknowingly modeled the disciplined regimen in front of his son.

After a little over a year, a tiny pinprick of light appeared at the end of the long and dark tunnel. Faint glimmers of hope, almost abandoned, suddenly started to appear. John's leg muscles began to twitch and then move. The once-lame right arm would gain some limited motion. These movements restored hopes and reinvigorated the spirits of the whole family.

John reached another milestone when, with assistance, he was able to stand on his own. Finally, as his mother cried tears of joy, not devastation and dread, he took a few steps. It would be the late fall/early winter of 1952 when John began to walk again. The warm feeling of thankful relief finally replaced the family's constant underlying tension.

By the snowy month of January 1953, John wanted not only to walk; he was ready to get outside and play.

John asking, "Can I go play outside yet?" was a pretty common question that was heard around the house at that time. Finally, John's mom gave him, in his words, "the green light" and allowed him to go outside to play with his older brother Joe. She bundled up John in his winter gear and sent him out to sled ride. With this, it seemed that the Miller's nightmare had ended.

Younger brother Joe and John 1949

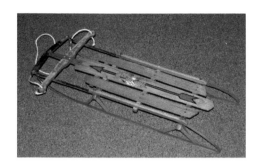

CHAPTER 2

MIRACLE ON ICE

"Do you believe in Miracles? Yes!"
—*Al Michaels, Lake Placid, 1980*

"God gives us only what we can handle.... Apparently God thinks I am a bad-ass."
—*Unknown*

▐▌ It's just a little hill around the way," John and his brother called back to their mother as they walked away from the house. "We'll be back before supper."

Miller recalls, "It was the perfect place to sled ride. I was having the time of my life ... beautiful winter day—not too cold—a little sunny even. The setup was perfect. A nice big hill would let the kids fly down to the bottom where it would level out at the base. You could gather yourself up, pick up your sled, and then cross the road. On the other side of the road was another hill you could go down. The neighborhood kids loved sledding there.

"First my brother goes down, then me. We were laughing and having a great time. It was my turn to go down again. I got a nice jump onto the sled and away I went. The next thing I tell you, you're not going to believe."

At this, Miller pauses, looks up, and begins again.

"A Pittsburgh Mercantile furniture truck, one of the big high backs, comes barreling down the road. My sled hits an icy patch and does not stop at the foot of the first hill, and I go skidding onto the pavement. My sled (with me on it) flies right under the truck and almost through to the other side. His back wheels run right over my lower body. My sled is smashed into the ice and pavement.

"The massive truck's brakes squeal down on the drums and the truck stops about thirty more feet down the road. The driver jumps down from his cab and runs towards me. I can still see the poor guy's face. He was in shock."

"Oh my God—where do you live?"

"I told him how to get to our house and he carried me the whole way with Joe following us. I knew that I was hurting pretty bad, but I didn't know how much damage was actually done.

"My mom and dad then rush me to Sewickley Hospital (again!) and they check me over.

"But the miracle was that nothing was broken. Nothing was that physically wrong. I have no idea how my legs weren't smashed. I had on thick leggings. Maybe that was it. Or I guess that my legs were so skinny and undeveloped from the polio that the truck just kind of zipped right over them. I'll never know, but it's a miracle I'm not talking to you from a wheelchair right now.

"Anyway, all that happened from me getting run over by a furniture truck was that I was laid up a few more weeks to recover, watching Roy Rogers and Superman on TV, and then I was on my way. After that stuff, I turned out to be a pretty tough kid. After getting out of bed that time, I never looked back."

John went on not only to walk but also to be a tremendous athlete in two sports. He would be a formidable competitor and an even more intimidating coach. His playing career would take him through college, and his coaching career spans nearly a half century and continues to this day with Drill for Skill Academy and Amateur Athletic Union (AAU) teams. The talent he continues to develop in others can be seen in current players such as Brenna Wise at Pitt, Micah Mason at Duquesne, and Shatori Walker-Kimbrough of the Maryland Terrapins.

As for the polio, all traces and reminders of the horrible disease and accompanying sled accident would be nonexistent for over fifty years. John was and still is the picture of health, but age would allow some benign signs to show up.

In 2003, Miller's brother Joe was visiting from North Carolina (he's a Hall of Fame North Carolina High School football coach, but that's a story for another day). He was watching John coach one of his final practices as coach of the Blackhawk High School Cougars. He noticed that his brother's right leg was a little skinnier than the left. He yelled over, "Hey John, what the hell's wrong with your leg?"

With a chuckle, Coach walked over and said, "That's the polio, man. I'm getting older and it's starting to show its signs."

Thankfully, it didn't have any real effect. He still, without a thought, gets down on the floor and shows the little guys at the gym the proper way to do push-ups. He still jumps rope and is in better shape than most forty-something couch potatoes of this era.

When one marvels at Miller's unlikely triumph over polio, which was largely a family secret, there is no doubt now where he learned his determination. It is no mystery where he picked up his patience and work ethic. It is no wonder now why he will plan, persist, and drill until his goals are met no matter the goal.

All of these admirable traits that he seems to possess must have come from enduring unspeakable pain and helplessness. These traits came from watching his father turn tragedy into triumph through hard work and self-sacrifice. They came from witnessing his family rally around him and sacrifice themselves for his good.

From his sickly youth, it seemed that John Miller almost immediately began a healthy obsession with strength, fitness, and sports. His younger sister, who was just a baby when her brother had polio, recalls that some of her earliest memories include her brother John. He'd be in the basement, on his own, working out with a small Joe Weider weight set. Another of John's favorite activities, according to his baby sister, was setting up Coke bottle obstacle courses in that same basement. "He would put those bottles and the wooden crates that they came in all over the place and dribble down there. I just remember my mother hearing the crashing of bottles and yelling from the top of the steps. 'That's enough now! That's enough!'"

But for John, when it came to sports and getting an edge on the other guy, it seemed like nothing was enough. All through high school and college, John continued with his own workout plans years before fitness and conditioning became the norm in scholastic sports. He would use every conceivable opportunity to make his body, especially his once shriveled legs, stronger. During college in the summers, he worked as a brakeman on the Aliquippa and Southern Railroad. The job involved jumping on and off railcars and applying a brake for each one as it stopped at the steel mill. The job might seem strenuous enough to most people, but John, now almost obsessed with making himself stronger, wore leg weights under his work pants. The other guys just shook their heads at the crazy college kid in their crew. They kiddingly busted his father's chops a little when they noticed the weights. "Hey Joe," they'd laugh and shout, "What's up with your son?"

Joe Miller didn't mind. He understandably relished the jokes maybe more than anyone. A few years prior, he dreamed that his son might someday walk. Now, for eight hours at a time, John was jumping off railcars and back on with ankle weights on.

Years later when John and his wife Barb were raising their own kids, they thankfully didn't have to show the kind of self-sacrifice that John's father, Joe, had to endure by nursing his son back from an illness. John showed his self-sacrifice in other ways. Miller states that he and Barb's goals in life were always "all about our four." They wanted their children to work to improve themselves at all times. This meant that, for most of the time, they did not have to worry about doing the traditional chores around the house. To put in the amount of hours needed for homework and "basketball homework," their mother Barb did nearly all of the work around the house.

John explains, "You know, I don't think we ever bought into the idea that we should show domination over them or make them do chores to show them who was boss. We (most especially, Barb) were happy to do the chores for them if they were doing something else productive— something that would help them reach their goals. I'm guessing they appreciated what she was doing even if nothing was ever said about it. That's how we were and still are."

And they didn't make a big deal of it. There wasn't scheduled out time assigned for "fun" and for "work" like many households do today. There were no chore charts or the like. There was just always something going on, and John was usually there working with them on their sports while Barb took care of the home. Miller puts it like this: "My family knows I'd go to the endth degree to make my teams win, so I'd sure as hell put at least as much effort to make sure they'd win in life. And Barb took care of everything to let us pursue our dreams."

So, as it stands, a newly recovered polio victim gets hit by a furniture truck and basically walks away. He goes on to lead his daughters to successful lives and his to sons to national coaching prominence, while making quite a name for himself. If that scenario were made up for a Hollywood movie, you could hear the crowd snickering, "Yeah right! Like that's going to happen." It would be called over the top and not believable. But it actually happened. For those people who believe in miracles or fate, this book will probably strengthen those beliefs.

CHAPTER 3

A 'SHORT' STOP IN BASEBALL

"People ask me what I do in winter when there's no baseball.
I'll tell you what I do.
I stare out the window and wait for spring."
—Rogers Hornsby

What does John Miller and Michael Jordan have in common? They can both dunk? Alas, no. Actually, they both were torn between baseball and basketball. Michael's problem was solved fairly easily when he failed miserably at America's pastime. His time with the Birmingham Barons, a minor league baseball team, was documented widely in the news and was even in the plotline of his movie *Space Jam*. Luckily for Michael Jordan, he had already established himself as a pretty okay basketball player. John Miller, on the other hand, was equally good at both sports and just starting out.

John made sports and fitness a priority as soon as he was able to walk again. He was quite right when he said, "After recovering from polio and the accident, I never looked back."

Not only did he rehab to the extent that he could walk and play like the rest of the kids. He began to play sports that required complex coordination and strength at a high level. John not only learned how to play sports but also learned the minute details of each game down to their smallest intricacies. And with basketball in particular, it would become his life's love and obsession.

His father taught all kinds of sports to John and his younger brother Joe Jr. Later on, baby brother Tim and little cousin John Calipari would be included in the fun. John realized later in life that the greatest gift his dad gave him after John's long battle with polio and the sled accident was to behave as if those things never happened at all. Those things were never brought up. His mom and dad very seldom talked about the polio in particular. It will never be known if this was a conscious decision or if it just happened that way. What John remembers, though, is that both his mom and his dad did not baby or coddle him in the least. It would have been very easy and almost natural to coddle a son that was almost confined to a chair for life.

But when springtime came, Joe Miller would address the boys all at once, asking them if they would like to catch ball with him in the backyard. Catherine would motion as if to say, "Go ahead, it's okay." If John fell down running to make a catch or got hit with the ball, no one rushed over frantically to see if he was all right. It must have taken some real restraint at first.

"That was the best thing for me really," explains John. "My dad was tough—real tough—on all of us, maybe most of all on me. And I know he wouldn't have done me any favors by taking it easy on me. The world doesn't take it easy on you. You should learn that fact early. Looking back, he wanted me to be prepared I think. He sure did his best to make sure I didn't get treated special because of what I'd been through with the disease and the accident. Kid gloves maybe would have stolen my desire to compete away from me."

So normalcy returned to the Miller family. As tragic and dramatic as life was in first grade with the illness, John's subsequent elementary years were blissfully uneventful. He went to school, played with the other kids, and did his homework. His parents demanded that he make good grades and always give his best, so that's what he did.

Like all school kids, he was exposed to all sorts of subjects in school like music, art, and the like, and though he was a little mischievous, he did his best to make sure he pleased his teachers. John's mother, trying to expand John's horizons with exposure to the arts, even signed him up for music lessons at a local instrument shop. But it soon became clear that John was not meant to be a Marvin Hamlisch.

"It's all kind of fuzzy to me, but I remember getting in the car to go to this music store for some piano or guitar lessons. Guitar, I think. Anyway I'm not sure why, but I know we never made it to the music store." Miller laughs as he continues, "We ended up at the softball fields in Ambridge and I was throwing ball with some other kids. Of course, right? I think there was a game being played at the main field. That's the last I heard about music lessons. They knew my heart was in sports."

That much was obvious. He wanted nothing else than to play and run. He loved playing ball games of any kind. He did not look like a prime physical specimen for sports, however. By middle school he was only about five feet four and kind of small compared to the rest of his peers. The long bout with polio may have had something to do with his size. It didn't matter much though, because John had the will to succeed and loved to work at his game. It didn't matter if the game was baseball, football, or basketball. He was going to compete, and competing in a piano recital wasn't going to cut it.

If you were betting on what John's first love was when it came to sports, the smart money would have been on basketball. But like most bets placed on sports, the gambler usually loses his cash in a hurry. John wasn't really interested in basketball when he was little. And his first attempts at ball handling weren't with the kind of ball that James Naismith invented for his gym back in Massachusetts. His sports heroes weren't in pro basketball at all. He, like most American boys of the time, was a fan of Willie Mays, Dick Groat, and Bill "Maz" Mazeroski. He wasn't concerned with whether Bob Pettit or Bill Russell would be the MVP of the NBA. He checked the sports pages more often to see whether Mickey Mantle or Roger Maris had beaten the bambino's home run record.

So in the beginning it seemed that John was destined to be a baseball player. His dad was good about throwing catch with him and his brother in the backyard. One vivid memory of John's was wearing out baseballs by throwing grounders on the road. Like the other kids, the Miller boys couldn't wait to sign up for little league. The only problem was that Glenwillard was so small (and so poor) that they didn't have a field good enough to play on, let alone a little league system in place. So John started playing on nearby Coraopolis little league teams in fourth grade, some pony league ball in Sewickley when he was a little older, and by junior high school age, he was strong and talented enough to make the Moon Area High School varsity team as a second baseman. By tenth grade he was a starter, and his position was shortstop. In fact, during a solid four years in high school, John was a premier baseball player. There was no doubt as to who would be Moon High's starting shortstop each and every game. It was number three, John Miller.

Miller gained valuable experience and had plenty of fun playing baseball, and in the 1960s, basketball was not even particularly on the radar for Pittsburgh sports fans. So how did Miller become so interested in hoops to be known as a basketball specialist?

The sport did have a decent following in the Three Rivers area. There were the college hoops teams such as the Pitt Panthers and the Duquesne Dukes. They competed in the annual "City Game" that was a pretty big deal in Pittsburgh at the time. And the only professional teams around during the 1960s were the clubs known as the Pittsburgh Rens of the American Basketball League and the Pittsburgh Pipers from the American Basketball Association. The Rens were a transplanted New York franchise bought from the Harlem Globetrotters mogul Abe Saperstein. Saperstein was the commissioner of the American Basketball League, which he founded in 1961 after repeatedly being denied an NBA expansion franchise. In an effort to promote the new league, Saperstein introduced the three-point shot.

His team, the Rens, was originally named for the legendary Renaissance Ballroom in Harlem (hence, the purposely incorrect spelling of "wrens"), where the team played

its games in New York. The name still fit the then dirty, smoky city of Pittsburgh because of the first urban renewal attempt going on at the time, called the "Pittsburgh Renaissance." The Rens, in fact, was the first basketball team to play in the brand new Civic Arena, sharing the bill that first season with touring acts the Skyliners, Judy Garland, Fats Domino, the Coasters, and Smokey Robinson. That being said, the Rens time in the steel city only lasted three short years.

The Pittsburgh Pipers had a little more success. It was the first ABA champion in the inaugural 1967 season. To this day, the Pipers remain the only Pittsburgh professional basketball team that has won a league championship.

But, at that time, the Pittsburgh sports scene was all about baseball and the Pirates. After decades of losing, the Battlin' Bucs just had come off a World Series win thanks to Miller's hero Bill Mazaroski and his moonshot over Yogi Berra's head at Forbes Field.

Furthermore, the now beloved Steelers was still a perennial loser back then. The only Steeler cheer was "S.O.S" or "Same Old Steelers." And as for hockey, well, as Pittsburghers at the time would say, the only people that cared about that was them "Canadians n'at." The now beloved Penguins didn't even exist until 1967. Mario Lemieux wasn't even born yet.

So in this land of Pirates, Steelers, and Penguins, how did Miller get turned on to the game of basketball? Of course like the rest of this remarkable story, the truth is stranger than fiction. John's love of basketball wasn't from the admiration of a six foot six star player or by watching highlights of the mighty Boston Celtics dynasty on television.

The source of inspiration would come from a stocky middle-aged hardware store owner from Glenwillard, Pennsylvania, named Mr. Mytinger.

CHAPTER 4

THE RUCKER PARK OF GLENWILLARD

OR THE DIRT COURT GANG

"This is my most special place in all the world, Ray. Once a place touches you like this, the wind never blows so cold again. You feel for it, like it was your child."

—Dr. Archibald "Moonlight" Graham

John Miller today describes Glenwillard, Pennsylvania as "not quite poverty, but not really a lot going on there." Right down by the banks of the Ohio River was where John's early years were spent. John admits it was "pretty rough." In junior high, though, the family moved to a nicer place in Glenwillard thanks to his father's hard work and scraping. He was still working two jobs along with building houses on the side. John vividly remembers he and his brother Joe helping his dad build the houses as soon as they could manage the work. It was real "man's work" that consisted of mixing mortar, carrying loads of bricks, and running loads of shingles back and forth. To John, his father's idea of fun was work. It seemed that he enjoyed the hard work kind of like a challenging game. Having grown up on a farm near a place in Hopewell, Pennsylvania, called Five Points, John's dad was used to the backbreaking labor and took pride in his ability to do it. Where John's mother Catherine was the disciplinarian and the organizer of the home, his dad's role was just simply to work.

And that constant work paid off when he could move to a slightly better neighborhood. But still, even in this new neighborhood, there were not many places where the kids could really play in a welcoming surrounding. A playground was nonexistent. But thanks to a well-meaning stranger, the boys in the neighborhood were about to receive a wonderful, albeit hard-earned, gift of sorts. A few years later, a young John Calipari would play on the court with John's brother Tim.

When John Miller was about 11 years old, his neighbor Bob Mytinger (always Mr. Mytinger to young John) and his brother owned a nearby hardware store called Mytinger and Co. It was located a little ways away on Merchant Street, the main drag in nearby Ambridge, Pennsylvania. Like the old company towns, Ambridge was named for the American Bridge Company that supplied the livelihood to the people of the area. Bob Mytinger had a son a year younger than John. His name was Denny, and he was always tagging along with Miller's gang of friends in Glenwillard.

"Me and about six other guys from the neighborhood were always playing some kind of game on the street outside Denny's house," explains John. "When his kid was out playing, more often than not, Denny's dad was sitting on the porch checking out what was going on with the happenings in the neighborhood. Thankfully Bob Mytinger wasn't the type of father that would get annoyed. You know, not the 'You kids get off my lawn' guy. He loved to watch us play whatever sport we were doing at the moment. Well, somehow one of the guys got their hands on an old, raggedy basketball. The only problem was we didn't have a hoop.

"Maybe it was because his son was playing with us, maybe it was just a charitable feeling he had at the time, I'll never know, but for some reason Mr. Mytinger decides that he's going to help us. He had a little side property and he had, of course, access to supplies from the hardware store. We were so excited when we realized that we were going to have a 'real basketball court' to play on. It was going to be a dirt court, not concrete or anything, but we didn't care. We were going to have a court with real hoops to play on. The whole idea was tremendous to us.

Mytinger hardware building today

"My buddies and I were more than willing to help Mr. Mytinger get this thing built. We each grabbed some shovels from the hardware store's truck bed and started to dig a hole that would be deep enough to support a pole for the hoop. Talk about sweat and blisters! But we didn't care. The whole time we could just imagine what it was going be like to run and shoot on this thing. The hole for the pole needed to be almost six feet down. We each took turns at the digging and the removal of the dirt. By the end we could stand in this hole we had dug. Or maybe it just seemed so big 'cause we were little. It was big anyway!

"After one hole was dug, we were dead tired, but happy. We started to walk towards home and waved back to Mr. Mytinger.

"At that point, he teasingly shouted over to us with this weird smile, 'Where are you guys going? I thought you were going to help me!! There's still one more hole to dig at the other end of the lot!'

"Are you kidding me? This thing was going to be full court! I mean we were pumped! We, of course, didn't dig the other hole that night, but we were back the next day with more energy than ever."

The vital lesson here is the joy that comes from building something; the satisfaction that can only come from working hard to get something that you want. Modern America seems to rob this from our kids every day. We buy and buy and buy to make our kids happy. They would appreciate more of what they have if we made them work a little for it. We have more "stuff" than ever yet have never been more medicated. It just doesn't add up. The court and the game would not have meant nearly the same to Miller and his buddies if Mr. Mytinger or someone's dad would have brought home two brand new hoops and paid to get a concrete court made. This was something that they did and that Mr. Mytinger allowed them to feel like they owned. It seemed like they earned that court, and that made them appreciate it more. But it was going to take a ton of work and hours to get it.

And the work had only just begun. Miller explains, "Now that we had the holes dug out, it was time to make the goals to put in them. We didn't buy anything; we couldn't afford to anyway. We wanted to get on the court as soon as possible because we were so excited." Miller laughs as he remembers, "One of my buddies tried to look for a short cut. He went to Sol's Sporting Goods downtown and priced out some basketball hoops.

"When he returned, he shook his head and laughed, 'Never mind, we better keep on building our own backboards!' Mr. Mytinger helped us create everything from overstock from the hardware store. He brought home some hardwood flooring to use for the backboards. These things were heavy duty. We painted them red and white (our school's colors) with a clear topcoat. Once we saw the finished products, we knew that they were better than the ones from Sol's Sporting Goods. Anyway, we screwed those backboards to the poles heavy duty like and screwed on the iron hoops, and we were good to go.

"The next thing we see is this big truck with Mytinger & Co. painted on the side roll in. I can still hear KDKA radio crackling out from its open windows. We somehow unloaded the goals and placed them in the ground. We filled the dirt in, packed it, and it was game time! I mean we were in Heaven. We tried out the court and loved it.

"It was probably about fifty feet long, and made of dirt, but to us kids, it was Madison Square Garden. Half of the court was still covered with grass, but it didn't take long for us to dribble that grass into submission. Mr. Mytinger would come around every once in a while to spray something (some kind of oil) on the ground that kept the dust at bay. We would just play on this thing so much, the ground would turn to dust. My friend Bill Sacco and me would have contests and write the results on the back of Mr. Mytinger's garage door (he didn't mind). By the end of the summer, the door was all covered in stats and our personal records.

"A few weeks later, Mr. Mytinger had one more surprise that was over the top and no one expected. 'How would you boys like to play at night? I've got some outdoor flood lights down at the store.'"

Miller explains, "The look on our faces must have been priceless. To this day, I get a kick out of that. So, with that, it was definitely going to be the coolest spot to play outside of a real gym. We even dug a trench about a half a block long to bury a cord that stretched from the court around the corner to an electrical outlet on Mr. Mytinger's porch. I mean it was awesome. To this day, it's one of the most exciting things to happen to me. Especially since we kids weren't used to having much of anything. I'll never forget that guy."

Just around a decade later, John and Bill Sacco would work together as assistant coaches at Moon under Milan "Skip" Tatala. The Moon Tigers ball boy was none other than little John Calipari (when he wasn't hanging out at Miller's mother's house). Bob Davie, former Notre Dame football coach, was on that team as well. It's hard to think of any other time when so many future big-time coaches were together as kids and young adults. It would be similar to Ted Williams, Babe Ruth, and Willie Mays hanging out on the same corner as kids.

- SATURDAY MORNING LEAGUE -

Bob Mytinger had a brother named Ken. He was an assistant basketball coach at nearby Ambridge High School and ran a Saturday morning league for the little kids in the area. There, the kids were divided into teams that would be scheduled to play each other. It was kind of like a little league for basketball. The teams were given the names of colleges. The idea was that it would be more fun for the kids to say, "Hey, mom, we're playing Villanova this week," instead of "Team number three" or the "Red Team."

Mr. Mytinger saw how much the neighborhood kids were playing on their dirt court and noticed their improving skills. He observed that Miller and his buddies weren't just fooling around, they were coming up with plays and actually learning the game and its rules. He had one more great idea up his sleeve that ultimately opened Miller's eyes to what might be possible in basketball and a yet unseen wider world. He arranged for them to go to Economy Junior High School to play against one of his brother's Saturday morning teams. When Miller and his gang heard this, they practiced extra hard all week. When Saturday rolled around, they played a close game against "UCLA" and, in the end, shocked them by beating them by four points. It wasn't the real UCLA, but to the dirt court kids, it may as well have been. As far as confidence and self-esteem went, these kids from the lower end of town were on top of the world.

What a difference a simple court made in the lives of those kids from Glenwillard. In a bigger sense, you never know how your actions, whether bad or good, big or small, can have an effect on the future.

To illustrate, if hardware store owner Bob Mytinger would have looked out his window at the kids playing in the street with disdain or apathy, Blackhawk High School basketball would most likely not have the mountain of WPIAL championships or hold the record for consecutive section wins. If Bob Mytinger told the kids outside his house to go play somewhere else, would Arizona and Dayton be competing in the Elite 8 at the same time in 2014? Who knows what Sean and Archie Miller would be doing today had Bob Mytinger not gone the extra mile to help his son and the neighborhood kids back in 1956? Luckily, for the faithful fans of the Wildcats and Flyers, Mr. Mytinger did go the extra mile.

Obviously, his kindness and charity toward kids who could never repay him paid off for many people in many ways in years to come. In addition to affecting Miller and, by association, his sons, there were others of note who helped build the dirt court. About five years later a little sprout named John Calipari would learn the game in part from John Miller and his brother Tim on the very same poles and hoops that were by then transported to Tim's backyard. Has anyone heard of him? Would John Calipari's Wildcats be national champions in 2012 had it not been for the mighty dirt court? Would he be in the National Basketball Hall of Fame? That young boy saw John Miller (who was a late teenager by the time he played on the dirt court) as someone to look up to and emulate. John Calipari would naturally imitate John's moves and work ethic on that same dirt court that Mr. Mytinger made possible.

John's younger brother Tim also benefited from the dirt court in Glenwillard. In basketball circles, he has gained national recognition for his dedication to the game. His coaching, like his brother's, has influenced hundreds of athletes that have gone on to college ball and the pros. He was a highly decorated player at St. Vincent College and has coached five nationally ranked AAU teams. He now runs the Baltimore branch of the Drill for Skill Academy and uses the same tried and true techniques that his older brother made famous. The dirt court gang also included John Calipari's coach at Moon High School, Bill Sacco. Coach Sacco is about the same age as John Miller. He still coaches today at Cornell

High School near the Pittsburgh International Airport. Sacco coached John Vlasic, who was Coach Miller's assistant for a time at the Drill for Skill Academy. The connections and loyalties between the people and places in the Miller basketball "tree" are strong and fiercely held. If the tree didn't have a place to begin its growth, it would have never grown to such heights.

The dirt court is gone now—a victim of time, weather, and the further decline of the Glenwillard area. The court and its parts lived on in many other ways though. Like a generous organ donor, the parts of the decrepit court wound up helping new people after its time in Glenwillard was done. The poles that held the backboards and hoops ended up in Tim Miller's backyard. The other hoop went in John Miller's backyard in Ellwood City and was used to train his sons.

Many years later the spirit, form, and design of the dirt court would rise again in a different location. If you visit Blackhawk Intermediate School in Beaver Falls, Pennsylvania, today, you will find a modern school building, complete with a brick-and-stone entrance where children over the years have climbed to fit in the square-shaped openings in the wall to sit and read awhile. The school is nestled between the Methodist church, the woods, and the baseball fields. It has a butterfly garden and an all-new playground. The McCarter Bus Company has its line, complete with yellow school busses and big tour busses with their trademark Clydesdale emblazoned on the sides, parked side by side to complete the scene. If you stand in the middle of it all and peek over the hill next to the ball fields, you will notice a rugged looking, amply lit basketball court. The lighting system is connected through an underground trench to a nearby building. A timer is used to light the court for four hours each evening. The hoops are mounted on steel poles that are set deep in the ground.

Mytinger's backboards reborn in Chippewa.

If you inspect the backboards closely, you will notice that they are not store bought; they are made from hardwood flooring, painted white with a black square for bank shots. Though the court is constructed on the hardtop surface of an abandoned tennis facility, it has the heart and soul of the old dirt court that was once in Glenwillard. When students and friends helped John Miller build it in the 1980s, maintenance men and even administrators joked that delinquent kids and the elements would destroy it within a few years.

Today, Miller laughs. "These guys didn't understand. I was good at building stuff, and I was going to build it strong like the Glenwillard court. These hoops would hold up to conditions that the even roughest neighborhoods could dish out." As of 2016, over thirty years have passed, and it's still there and still looks like it's just a few years old.

There is no debate whether the effect that the dirt court had was immeasurable for John Miller. In those days all of the neighborhood kids would play for an hour or so on that court every day. John and the select few mentioned earlier would always stay an hour or two more by themselves.

Miller reminisces, "Many a day, I can remember dragging along a snow shovel to clear off a place enough so that I could get some shots in. Some kids have a hard time deciding what to do in life. I knew that this was my thing. The world of sports was where I was meant to be. I really didn't know in what form it would take, but I would be in sports in one way or another."

Once again, Miller never looked back.

CHAPTER 5

THINKING FORWARD:

THE COURT OR THE DIAMOND?

"Think Pforward."

—Pfeiffer University Motto

At Moon High School, John Miller was an exceptional baseball player for all of the years that he played. He was a member of the varsity team his freshman year.

Basketball for Miller at Moon was a little different. The accomplishments that eventually would overtake his baseball success would take significantly more work and patience to achieve in basketball. He didn't begin to even sniff at the chance to start until tenth grade. He played junior varsity basketball, but the coaches could tell he wasn't ready in his freshman and sophomore years to play as a varsity Tiger. Finally, in his junior year, one of the starters got in trouble at school, and the coach benched him. Miller jumped at the chance to start, and his play was elevated to a new level. A fire was lit under him when he realized that there was a spot for him in the starting lineup.

For Miller, the theme of hard work comes back again and again. In a two year period, John went from not even coming close to starting to being named Most Valuable Player in the league in his senior year. Plus, the whole team improved too. They came literally seconds from winning the section title. Their biggest rival, the Montour Spartans, beat them in double overtime in the final game. Back then it crushed Miller and his team, but by giving it a little time, he could see what his accomplishments actually were. They improved so much in such a short amount of time, and that's what he looks back on with pride.

Miller uses those life experiences to teach his players now. He explains, "It was one of those stories where I can tell kids I teach and coach now, 'No matter what you're trying to do, you have to just keep working. You just have to keep banging away. If it's meant to be, it'll come. I wish there was more to it than that [keeping a positive attitude and working hard], but there's not. That's it.' There's no 'give up' in me because that's what I've done all my life. I've proven it to myself. Maybe I'm wrong, but there's never, ever been a time in my life where a goal wasn't met when I've had that attitude. Sure, I've lost games in the championship where I tried to prepare my team the best I could, but at the end of the day, I was satisfied because I truly knew that we did all that we could. At the time it hurts, but when you look back, you're still proud of what you and your team did. It's the same way with life."

Obviously, this way of thinking does not ensure that you will never lose. It's more about ensuring that regrets and second-guesses will become a rarity. If you constantly prepare and set goals to improve yourself, you're not competing against someone you don't know. You're competing against your former self. Fighter "Irish" Micky Ward echoes this theme, "I never lost a fight because I wasn't in shape or because I wasn't ready. I lost because I was either beaten by a man better than me or because it wasn't my night. That's a lot easier to take in the morning."

John was surely hooked on athletic competition by the end of high school. With the success he had in sports at Moon, there was no doubt in his mind that athletics were going to be his future in one form or another. The exact sport and the nature of the job were still in question though. To sort out these issues, Miller planned on going to Morehead State to study education and to play on their basketball team. As it turned out, something happened with the assistant coach at Morehead who was recruiting Miller. When he checked on the situation, suddenly the assistant didn't work there anymore. He didn't know if he got sick or something. All he knew was that he was gone, and Miller would have to try to find somewhere else to go.

"My coach at Moon took me aside and told me that he had some connections at a college called Wingate [wing-it] University in Wingate, North Carolina. It was a two-year school, but I figured 'What do I have to lose?' I registered for the fall semester and went down to try out for the basketball team, the Bulldogs.

Johnny Miller

"They had a really good team. So I go to the try out, and I thought I did pretty well, but for whatever reason, I didn't make the team. I remember that there were so many guys trying out. I must have blended in. I remember making all these free throws in a row and seeing that the coach's back was turned while they were going in.

"So at that point, I just figured I'd try out next time and just go to class and focus on that. Well, thanksgiving break rolls around, and I was home. It ends up that I bumped into my old coach at Moon. He asked me how it was going. So I told him I got cut. Without me knowing anything, coach wrote this guy a letter supporting me. When I went back down to school, there was a letter in my mailbox asking me to report to the athletic department to see the coach. He gave me another tryout and put me on the team. My guess still is that I must've just blended in. I mean I'm not six foot eight or anything and I think he kind of already had his team picked out. Within a few weeks though, I was starting. I played as a Wingate Bulldog for two years. We had a good team, and we won a lot of games."

There would be more school and more hoops on the horizon for John Miller. A coach named Francis Essic from the four-year university team called the Pfeiffer Falcons was about to swoop in and grab Miller for himself. As transistor radios blared Del Shannon's hit song "Runaway" across the country, Essic made an attempt to run away with Wingate's point guard. He needed a speedy point guard with the skills that John had. The Pfeiffer Falcons were a struggling basketball team that needed to get their talons into some new talent to compete in its Division II section.

Pfeiffer Head Coach
Francis Essic

Coach Essic sealed the deal with Miller in the spring of 1963, landing Miller a full scholarship to play basketball for the Pfeiffer University Falcons in the town of Misenheimer, North Carolina. Even though the scholarship was for basketball, the Pfeiffer Falcons would be eager to see what John could do on the baseball diamond as well. Coach Essic recognized that John was an all-around good athlete.

Johnny Miller
Guard

Pfeiffer University

Essic and the university weren't disappointed. John Miller shined on the diamond and the basketball court like few ever had before at Pfeiffer. Despite being only five foot eight, he was able to excel at the guard position, so much so that he was named to the All-Carolina Conference All-Star Team and to the All-Southern Regional Team. He was even the team's captain and Most Valuable Player in his senior year. Years later, Miller was inducted to Pfeiffer Hall of Fame in 2003. Always turning challenges into advantages, Miller was quoted saying, "I really thought as a player that my size [or lack of it] helped me because the other guy always underestimated me."

At the Pfeiffer Hall of Fame induction ceremony, deputy athletic directory and 1974 graduate of Pfeiffer, Jack Ingram remembered, "John was one of the most outstanding student athletes to ever play at Pfeiffer. He was a leader on the basketball court and a star shortstop on the baseball diamond. He took the knowledge he gained in the classroom and in competition and has shared it with many people since."

A little giant: #3, John Miller

He had a full four years at Wingate and Pfeiffer as a player and as a student. During his junior year though, John experienced a nasty injury on the baseball field that would allow him to savor only one more year as a baseball player. It was curse turned into a blessing; it would introduce him to coaching basketball for the first time.

Miller explains, "So, we were playing against the Catawba College Indians and we were batting. I had hit a triple and when our next guy was up, I had a pretty good lead off of third base. The batter was a lefty and he could really smoke the ball. He got his pitch and sent one screaming over the third base bag. The fielder leaped for the ball and caught it. Just as I was lunging back to touch the bag with my hand, down the big third baseman comes with his spikes. Boom! Like that, they went a good way through my hand. I still have the scars and my fingers are a little misshapen now. Hurt like hell, but it ended up being a little bit of a blessing in disguise."

The typical pessimist would have looked at the spiking and seen only negatives. Miller didn't. He looked into the situation and found that there was a chance of bigger and better prospects hidden in that painful injury. Patience paid off when the spiking injury paved the way to an exceptional opportunity.

Miller recalls, "The way the whole thing worked out was that because of the time the injury took from my scholarship, I was eligible to play baseball for the Falcons for another year. And when Pfeiffer University secured me for that, they offered me a chance to be the assistant coach for the Pfeiffer basketball team under head coach Francis Essic. This guy was a real professional and a wonderful teacher to the players on the team and to me as his assistant. He was definitely a mentor."

Coach Essic returns the love. When asked about the Millers, in his southern drawl, he replies, "Ah yes. John's my 'basketball son' and boys Sean and Archie are my 'basketball' gran'kids. I'm so proud. So proud of them."

Being the assistant coach to Francis Essic was the experience that would lift the curtain on Miller's true aspiration—to be a basketball coach.

By the time April 1964 rolled around, the Beatles had the numbers one through five most popular songs on the Billboard charts in the same week. Meanwhile at Pfeiffer, the basketball team was a hit with the college kids like never before. Ask Coach Essic today and he'll give a good portion of the credit for the Pfeiffer Falcons' breakout season of 1964 to Miller.

"He energized the guys and they truly listened to him. They knew he could play, and you could tell straight away that he had a great basketball mind. You could tell even back then. It was my fourth year as head coach, and my first winning season. We went 21 and 7. The student body loved what we were doing and was coming out to support us like never before. John was in reality still considered a student, but I always give him the title of 'assistant coach' because that was what he was. He had a knack to inspire people. If somebody wasn't getting the job done on the floor, he didn't make any bones about it. He told the guy, and in the long run, they respected him for it."

That year, Miller realized more than ever that coaching was what he was meant to do. Under Coach Essic, not only did he prove that he was a quality assistant coach but also he was noticed by some as being ready to take his coaching career to the next level. After his one and only season as the Pfeiffer Falcons assistant coach, offers at the collegiate level came calling. The offers were flattering, but returning home was looking more and more attractive to him. This was especially true because his future wife, Barb was there. After many hours of thought, prayer, and meditation, it became clear what John knew all along. He knew his future was with Barb, and John didn't feel that she was ready to head south, away from home. So, he decided that the best thing to do was to make coaching high school ball close to home his next goal.

Besides personal reasons for wanting to move closer to home for a job, it was also a smart move financially. Because of strong unions, a public school teacher in Pennsylvania made more money and had more benefits than a southern counterpart. Because of this, teaching jobs were coveted and were few and far between. Teaching positions that included a basketball coaching position were even more difficult to come by. For every teaching vacancy, there were hundreds of applicants. Fortunately, John didn't have to substitute teach like most teachers waiting for a chance at a permanent job. Moon Area High School had a physical education position open in the Junior High, and it included the job of junior high basketball coach. Because of the good reputation that he earned as a student at Moon and at college, John was hired immediately. It was the perfect place for him to hone his coaching skills and try out anything and everything he came up with as a new young coach. The Moon Area Junior High Tigers became guinea pigs for what would become known as the Miller Way. That team is proud to have been taught how to play by John Miller, long before Sean and Archie would take the court.

Describing himself as "the original guinea pig for the Miller Way," Tom Richards credits his time learning from Coach Miller as one of biggest reasons for his eventual success on the court and off. And what a success he has become. Tom is now the chairman and CEO of CDW, a $13 billion corporation headquartered in Vernon Hills, Illinois. It is a provider of technology products and services for businesses, government, and education. In his heart, Tom has always been a hoops junkie. But his skills as a basketball player first started taking off when he met his junior high basketball coach, John Miller. About a decade after their first meeting, Richards would find himself playing as the starter for the next four years for the Pittsburgh Panthers. Many predicted he would go to the NBA had it not been for a hand injury during his senior year. He'd never be the same after that. Fortunately though, the lessons about basketball that he learned at an early age from Miller transferred nicely to the real world. And he always kept involved in basketball in one way or another. He speaks at camps and has passed the ball to his son Jason and his daughter Lindsay. He calls them "second generation Miller guinea pigs."

In 2008, Jason played for Davidson University with Steph Curry and led the NCAA in assists. He signed with the Miami Heat but was forced to retire after enduring multiple ACL injuries. Currently, he is the video coordinator and director of analytics for the Pitt Panthers. Lindsay was on the first ever McDonald's All American Team and is now the Pitt Lady Panther's assistant coach.

CEO and Pitt guard Tom Richards

But back in 1967, Tom was a member of the first team that Miller ever coached, the Moon Junior High Tigers. In 1966, he was a seventh grader that made the ninth grade team. That year they lost 18 of the 20 games that they played. When Miller was hired, Tom and his friends began to experience a whole new way of learning the game. There were two-hour practices held almost every day in the summertime at Robert Morris University. To make a long story short, that season his team won 16 of 20, and the year after, the record would be 19 and 1. After experiencing this turnaround, Tom had found his basketball idol. He would do anything for John. Tom didn't realize that the true value of John's teaching wouldn't just be the forgotten records of a sixties junior high basketball team.

At Miller's retirement in 2005, Tom's teammate Phil Meanor would report that out of that first team at Moon, two of the team players would become CEOs, at least three multimillionaires, one chief of police, one pharmacist, and one a master chef. Phil himself has a master's degree in statistics and is the senior manager for the SAS Institute Inc., a computer software company. Could that have happened by accident?

Tom remembered Coach Miller always preaching, "Gotta put in the hours." All of the guys realized that that phrase related to more than just basketball. From Coach Miller, Tom learned a repetitive, routine-oriented, disciplined approach to the game and to life. He credits Miller with creating a stellar work ethic in all his players. He remembers his routine of getting up for school, putting on ankle weights as part of his outfit for the day, and dribbling a ball to the school. He'd drop the ball off in the gym office and pick it up after school. From there, he'd strap the ankle weights back on and dribble the ball all the way home. It was like that every day. "We'd fill out these big 'shot charts' that were all over the gym. We'd chart their number of shots compared to the number of shots made. Everyday the guys would see their improvement bit by bit." Phil Meanor proudly boasts that he was Miller's first point guard and his team was "the original." Phil would run the plays that would, much of the time, involve getting the ball to the big guys, Tom Richards or Joe Bags, who was another star of the team.

Tom Richards' family had always been a basketball family. Tom was admittedly obsessed with the sport before meeting Miller. So, when he got to know John as a coach, it was like pouring gasoline on a bonfire. "I drank in every thing that he could tell me and show me. He would take me as an eighth grader and another couple kids that were probably in sixth or fifth to these playgrounds all over the place to play against high school kids. And we would win—because of John. We could shoot from anywhere. These 'big' kids were stunned. I still think I learned then more about the game as a junior high school kid more than I would learn over the entire rest of my playing career from anyone else."

Meanwhile, unbeknown to Tom, during this time in the late sixties, his beloved coach was still looking around for what he really wanted—a high school coaching job. After only a few years waiting, coaching, and teaching physical education at Moon, the opening that Miller was waiting for came to be. Finally, there was an advertisement in the paper for a physical education teaching position at the nearby Riverside High School. It came with the duties of high school basketball coach. John applied for the job, and because of his experience and background coaching in college and at Moon, he was called in for an interview.

Nervous but poised, Miller walked into the district office where the interviews were being conducted. The superintendent at the time was Kenneth Yonkee. He knew exactly the type of teacher/coach that he was looking for. He didn't want a yes man. He wanted someone who was principled and firm, even if his decisions were not popular. With this in mind, he hatched a plan to find just that type of person. But how can one determine if someone is a yes man? Yonkee surmised that he needed to find someone who didn't have any problems saying no to anyone. And it is especially difficult for a yes man to disagree with the very person that he is trying to schmooze in an interview.

Yonkee began the interview pleasantly. Smiles and handshakes were exchanged; however, about halfway into the interview, he switched gears and began acting. He played the part of a George Steinbrenner-esque boss who liked to manage from the press box. He began to lecture Miller on the ins and outs of certain defenses that he should use and how practices should be conducted. At first Miller listened politely and nodded as if to agree. In reality, he vehemently disagreed with almost all that Yonkee was saying. Miller responded just as Yonkee had hoped. John told him that (make no mistake about it) if he were hired, he would do the job his way. He went on and talked a little basketball and gave an outline of his coaching philosophy. The two then shook hands and Miller went on his way.

When John returned home after the interview, he told his wife that he had blown the interview and that there was no chance that he would get the job. They obviously were looking for something different. Unbeknown to Miller, Yonkee had already made a decision to hire him immediately.

John Miller landed his first real head-coaching job. He was on his way.

Again, the lucky high school that Miller was hired to teach and coach at was a smallish country school. The district was located within a small municipality called Ellwood City in Lawrence County, Pennsylvania. Ellwood was about a forty-five-minute drive from Moon, and for the next few months, John would gladly make the commute to be the coach of a high school team.

The team that he would be leading was the Panthers. The players were struggling at the time, especially because they were in a particularly good division. The Riverside Panthers was a perennial second and third place finisher and was in dire need of some guidance. The story of John Miller, Pennsylvania's premier high school basketball coach, was about to begin.

Although Tom Richards may have thought that this was the end of his days of learning from Coach Miller, it was far from it. John saw so much talent in the kid that he asked him if he would like to make the trip with him each day in the summertime to Riverside High School to practice with his new team. It would be a win-win for everyone. John could use Tom to demonstrate the drills and techniques, and Tom would still get to be coached by his idol even if it was not for his high school team.

The best part about it for Tom, though, may have been the forty-five-minute car rides to the practices. "Just think of it," Tom says today, "I was riding in a little Volkswagen with the Obi Wan Kenobi of basketball. I had him all to myself. I picked his brain the whole way there and back. His wife, Barb, even packed my lunch for the day! It was great. I was like the demo guy. He would have me show the rest of the team all the stuff he taught me. He knew I was the hardest working kid around and we just fed off of each other."

On those drives, Tom was taught so many lessons about competing and what it takes to be a great leader. As the CEO of software giant CDW, he says today he still uses quotes from John Miller to motivate guys under him. Tom's favorite Miller quote that he uses all the time was meant for basketball but relates to almost all endeavors in life. "As good as you are today, somebody, somewhere, will be practicing just as hard. What are you going to do to be prepared when you meet that person somewhere down the road?" That stuck with Tom more than anything else that Coach Miller taught him and he thinks of it daily. He also points to other lessons that John taught him.

"When John played, he never gestured or said a word. He just *looked* like he knew he was the best player on the court. It was intimidating to the opponent. It didn't matter that he wasn't the biggest guy on the court. And that's how he taught his players to be. You never whine about calls. You never celebrate on the court. And you retrieve the ball for the referee with respect even if he is the worst referee in the world. You hold yourself responsible no matter what. No excuses."

As far as the secret to becoming a success in any endeavor, Richards translates the Miller Way like this: "From a leadership perspective, people that are successful, no matter what they do, really have a clear vision of what they want to accomplish. But more importantly than the vision, they must have the self-discipline to build a very *prescriptive* plan to get there. So many people have dreams and aspirations for greatness, but few people have the discipline to go through the rigors to get there. That means not only knowing what you want to do, it means planning it out step by step and following through religiously with those plans *every single day.*

"In basketball it meant doing all of the drills in the book *every* day at the same level that you would play against your most hated rival. It meant shooting 1,000 shots and charting them every, single day. It was and is no more complicated than that. It worked for me in basketball, and I know for a fact that it works for me in my duties as a vice president of a fortune 500 company."

CHAPTER 6

HOME COURT ADVANTAGE

"My parents are my backbone. Still are. They're the only group who will support you if you score zero or you score forty."

−Kobe Bryant

It may seem oversimplistic and trite to compare the Miller family to one of John Miller's basketball teams, but the similarities are impossible to ignore. The dictionary definition of a team is simply "a group of people that work together to reach a common goal." Is that not what a successful family is as well? When each player puts the team ahead of individual wants, the team is bound to succeed. This is the way each member of the Miller family, to an extent, describes growing up and how they have now chosen to raise their own families. Everyone put the family ahead of their own personal wants.

John's youngest daughter, Lisa Miller Oak, expresses gratitude. "One thing about my dad and our family that no one knows or ever thinks about is the endless work and support of my mom. How my dad was able to be so passionate about basketball, his teams, our teams, training his own kids and thousands of others year round was because my mom ran the ship. All credit of chores, cleanup, meals, all our wants and needs off the court she took care of. The endless hours we dedicated to basketball

★ Barb and John Miller

were possible because she was at home taking care of everything. Mom was always one step ahead of us. Ask my dad about her, he will tell you she's his number one teammate."

John Miller himself says that his wife was the ideal person to complement him. "She is the perfect person to keep me grounded and to keep our ship afloat. She's a very unselfish person for sure. She was always great at keeping the kids looking right, eating right, and keeping everything running smooth. She made sure that everything had its place. That way, we weren't wasting time looking for things."

John fondly puts it this way: "She's always wanted her kids to look their best and be their best. She handles the things that I'm not good at. She wears her heart on her sleeve, where I tend to hold things in. I guess we use each other's strengths to make things work."

The Miller's oldest daughter, Dana Miller Tapia, a great tennis player in high school, never really felt compelled to dedicate herself to sports like her siblings. A success in her own right, she was a flight attendant and now lives in the city of Spring, Texas. She describes her dad by saying, "He seems like a throwback to a more simple time. But it works. I get the same question time and time again when I meet someone and they realize whom my brothers are or whom my dad is. 'With Sean, Archie, and even your sister Lisa going so far in sports, wasn't your dad upset that you didn't choose to go that route too?'

Dana Miller and friend Megan Moretti (Calabria)

"And my answer usually surprises them. My dad honestly didn't care if we played sports or not. What mattered to him is that we chose to do something that we loved and that whatever it was we put in one hundred percent. He taught us the importance of choices. A common question was, 'What do you want?' And then it would always be followed up with a talk about the work and sacrifices that would have to be put in to achieve what we wanted. It was about making a choice that was right for you and then giving that choice (whatever it was) the best that you had."

That statement brings to mind a lesson often repeated by Capuchin Franciscan friar Father Scott Seethaler in his lessons to people who come to hear him. "It is very simple. Your life is the sum of the choices that you make. The outcome of our lives depends on the choices we make and how we deal with those choices." John Miller would agree with that statement fully.

Dana and her "little" sister Lisa both agree that once they made their choice to do something, their parents would help them and encourage them to do their very best at whatever they chose. This included school, relationships with people, and everything else in life. The family's philosophy seems to be that if you choose to have kids, you'd better be putting one hundred percent effort into raising those kids. "That's surely what my parents did," Dana explains. "I mean we had a good unit. All of us were so lucky to have two parents both working towards the same goal—the success and happiness of all of us. In June 2016 they celebrate their fiftieth wedding anniversary. They've been together and worked for us together all those years. They've been together since they were in high school."

People at the highest levels of play have acknowledged John as a veritable master of his craft. Even so, he chose to stay coaching at the high school level even when the opportunity was clearly there for success at the college level and beyond. He knew that this decision would allow him to be home every night. In the end, he traded fame and money for a closer relationship with his children.

John could have moved to get a bigger spotlight on himself, and Barb could have gone for a career, but instead they *chose* to make parenting their highest priority. Once the children were old enough to engage in conversation, Miller chose to make sure late nights in the office were rare. Dana remembers that no matter how busy, Dad would be sure to sit down with the family for dinner. He made the *choice* to make it a priority.

Dana continues, "I need to say this again. My dad's 'give one hundred percent, do your ultimate best' attitude wasn't just about sports, as some would believe. It was mostly about his family. That's where people get him wrong." Dana couldn't help but laugh as she added, "My siblings all liked running around in a gym getting sweaty. That wasn't my thing. I made the tennis team, and I was pretty good. I liked to play and practice, but no one forced me to drill tennis like crazy so that I was like a tennis star. It wasn't like that, and people should know that."

Back when Dana was in high school, John Miller acknowledged this idea in a news article from 1990. "When she was small, she followed Sean around. She played basketball in junior high, but I guess she didn't have the aggressiveness it takes to be a basketball player. She thought that she would give tennis a try. She's made me into a tennis fan." After seeing Dana play in United States Tennis Association tournaments, her coach James Paisley even said that she had enough game to play in college.

Weeks before I spoke to Dana about her dad, John interrupted one of his basketball stories and, out of nowhere, offered this sentiment about her: "I want people to know that I'm so appreciative to my daughter Dana. I think she was a big help to both of us when it came to attending to the two little ones,

Young Dana with a pillow basketball

Ryan (aka Archie) and Lisa, when I was off with Sean doing clinics. Our schedule was beyond crazy, and she kind of naturally was involved in helping her younger brother and sister. It just kind of happened that way. We didn't have to twist her arm to get her to help. She never complained about it. She just started pitching in. I already told you that my wife Barb was selfless. Well, Dana was that way too."

Dana Miller heard people talk and had seen articles that claimed that while growing up her family never went on vacation. Dispelling some rumors, Dana explains, "Well, that's both true and not true. We went all over the place, but it was never a matter of 'Let's sit down and schedule a trip to Disney or the beach.' But in the summer especially, if my dad were taking Sean or Archie to a clinic in North Carolina, we would sometimes come too. My uncle lived there, so we would get to go places with my mom and his family. Or if the basketball destination had a beach or some other attraction there, we'd get to go. Or even if we just hung around where he was, it was always fun. He'd find stuff for us to do and play on while he did his thing. I never felt cheated in the least. He was just a busy guy, and we all knew that he wasn't busy for himself. It was all about the family and getting us to where we wanted to be."

Miller shows the extent of how demanding his schedule once was. "I just saw one of my old neighbors from the old days when I coached at Riverside and lived in Ellwood City. He was laughing as he said, 'Man, I can still remember seeing you jump out of the car from school or some practice, an hour or so would go by, and then the next thing I'd see is you up on a ladder fixing the roof or some siding or whatever on your house. And then you and Sean would be waving and jumping back in the car off to some game or clinic. That was almost every day. I don't know how you did it!' Well, looking back, I don't know how I did it either. I just had so much energy and with everyone at home backing me, there was nothing else really that I wanted to do. I didn't want to sit around and watch TV. So instead, I did the whole house's aluminum siding! I just think, 'How did I do that?? And that was before Starbucks and energy drinks!'"

Dana and Lisa share how powerful an example their parents' work ethic was. "After seeing both of them work so hard, we never wanted to disappoint them. It was obvious to us even at a younger age that these guys cared so much for us and did so much for us. We didn't want to let them down. Plus we kind of knew, as we grew older that some people had placed a target on my dad's back especially. It seemed like people couldn't wait to find something wrong with what we were doing and report it to him. It's the same now with my brothers. It's as if people want you to do well, but they don't want you to do better than them. Once that happens, they try to tear you down. We all knew that people—not all, but some—were waiting for us to mess up and to take the news back to him. They loved it when there would be a controversy or something to gossip about. But I guess that's just the nature of people. So anyway, we respected my dad enough not to want to embarrass him."

Joe, John, and Lisa after a game at Elon University

All of the pep talks and bits of advice about working hard and doing the right thing would have surely fallen on deaf ears had John and Barb Miller not lived out this ethic. But they did. After speaking to each of the Miller adult children, they all seemed to have grown up believing that hard work and dedication toward what you believed in was just *normal*, and so it became normal for them. It may be as simple as that.

The Miller Grandchildren

Top: Archie's Leah, Lisa's Neely and Jackson.
Bottom: Sean's Cameron, Austin and Braden, Dana's Alexa, Jaden and Adrian

CHAPTER 7

LEARNING TO DREAM ON THE WAY

"All those cars were once a dream in someone's head."

—Peter Gabriel

For the Miller kids, with all of the activity and time constraints involved, the best time to talk to their father was on the way to or from a practice, game, or clinic. Miller's kids all mention his car ride talks. With the demands of his schedule, sometimes it was the only place to talk, so they cherished the opportunity. They knew that both parents worked so very hard and could approach mom at home. But if they wanted dad, more often than not, in the quiet and contained car was the place to be.

"As we pulled out of the driveway," Dana Miller remembers, "that was when I got to really know my dad. He was first and foremost an exemplary teacher. He had a way of teaching you lessons about life. And even when you messed up, he had a way of calmly dealing with it. It was more effective than any amount of yelling."

Younger sister Lisa agrees. "You know, my dad never yelled at us. I can't remember a time when he screamed or anything. I think we saw how hard he worked at everything, and we just didn't ever want to let him down."

He taught his kids how to handle stress by example. One of the sayings that he was famous for in his household (especially with the girls) was, "Don't let it get you down. The sun will come up tomorrow." He repeated this phrase to his kids following bad games, bad losses, injuries, and even personal matters. He told them that it was no use crying over a situation. Amnesia is a common trait of successful people; you fail, you process it, you learn, and you forget it.

Lisa Miller explains, "It was ok to feel bad directly after a loss. But a short time later, usually less than an hour, we began to prepare for the next game. We didn't flip out over a loss during the season. We would prepare for the next game. We didn't stew over losing a play-off game or a championship. We would wait for the sun to come up and then we'd prepare for next year. This wasn't just a flowery phrase he would repeat to us, this is what he *showed* to us. When he'd lose a WPIAL Championship for example, sure he'd be down that night, but the next morning, you'd see him figuring out his team for next year. If I had an injury, the injury wouldn't be the focus. *Rehabbing* the injury would be the focus."

Lisa scrambles for a loose ball

Archie Miller fondly remembers those times with his dad. "Car rides home after practice, driving from camp to camp? My dad was really teaching you how to be a coach, and you didn't even realize it. He knew what hard work was. He knew what dedication was. He knew what preparation was. He knew how to communicate. It starts to come naturally to you. It's all you do. It's all you're around, and it's all you talk about. It is ultimately who you naturally become. You become a coach. There's no faking it."

It was the same for Sean. "I'd be riding in the car with him back even in fourth or fifth grade, and him talking about the game we just played. Because of the exchange of information and being around the game day in and day out, it just became a part of me. My dad always had time for me. It was never a problem for me to go with him on the team bus or to be with him when he was scouting." Sean remembered riding with his father in cars even as far back as elementary school, and John talking about the game Sean had just played. It wasn't just the score or key plays. He found a way to break down the ins and outs of the game to make his kid, no matter how young, understand.

Sean doesn't remember his youth as anything extraordinary and compares it to the households of less spotlighted professions. "It's no different than if you grow up in the house of a doctor or a businessman; you seem to follow the profession of your father or whoever you grew up around. Not only is he a basketball coach, he probably has as much passion for the sport as any person standing. Because of that, not only did I grow around basketball as a player, but also, ultimately, coaching just seemed to be in my blood from the beginning. Because of the exchange of information and being around the game day in and day out, it just became a part of me, like a natural thing."

John recently reflected on all of that. "I really don't even look at it as being so much different than what goes on in all good homes. I just led by example, nothing special, it just was that."

The Miller kids remember another lesson that they learned in the car: It didn't matter so much your size or your talents, the cream was going to rise to the top. None of the Miller children ever grew to be very much over six feet tall—Archie was only five feet nine. Yet they all could play. They weren't the fastest either, but they prepared and practiced more than anyone. They were taught to ask the question, "Did I practice longer and harder than all of my competitors?" before calling it a day. If the answer was no or even maybe, then it was back to the line.

Lisa Miller said, "A lot of people know the saying that whoever works the hardest comes out on top. I mean the things that he taught us were like old adages that everyone knows, but I think that the difference was that he actually practiced what he preached. And that kind of enthusiasm was catchy. As hard as it may be to believe, I, for one, couldn't wait to go practice. When people say that Sean or Archie or I were good at basketball because we were forced, I just laugh. For one, my sister Dana didn't even choose basketball, and Dad couldn't care less. She always did her best at what she chose. That's all that mattered in his mind. I was a college basketball player, but in fact, in the beginning, I was a cheerleader of all things! I didn't even want to play basketball. I thought that it was a 'brute' boy sport at that time. I liked getting dressed up and going to the mall like any other girl my age. What started my interest in basketball for me surprisingly wasn't my dad or brothers. It happened that one of my girlfriends from cheerleading told me that she was going to be in Little Cougar Basketball and that her dad was going to coach. She kept asking me if I wanted to join so that we could play together. That's why I wanted to play. Not because of Sean or Archie or my dad was forcing me. That's all in people's heads."

Lisa and Dana Miller both talk about not just what was said in the car, but about how it was said. They both stated almost verbatim that he was always so intense about what he was saying. He gripped the steering wheel in a way where you knew that he was totally focused and enthusiastic about what he was saying.

Lisa laughs as she says, "And when it came to sports, my dad infected us with a disease called 'Hate to Lose.' More than loving to win, my dad just hated to lose. It's that way with all of us now. It's that sick feeling you get in your stomach leaving the gym. Ugh! It's awful! That's where I think we are a little different from a lot of people. For instance in school if I was just playing in an open gym and normal kids would just be having fun joking around or being silly. I literally couldn't be like that! I tried to win every time. It must be in my blood." It must have been. In high school, Lisa racked up quite a number of impressive accomplishments. There, at Blackhawk, she averaged sixteen points, eight assists, and six steals per game. She helped her team win a WPIAL and a state championship. She was an Associated Press Player of the Year and was named to the all-section team. Like her brothers, she too was a member of the *Pittsburgh Post-Gazette*'s Fab Five in her junior and senior years.

Dori Anderson Oldaker was the 2015 Team USA women's coach of the year. In 1999, she was Lisa Miller's coach at Blackhawk when they won the Pennsylvania state championship. At that time, Dori saw John's passion come through in Lisa's attitude and play all the time. She was a fan of John's even before she got to coach Lisa. She admits that she would go to the boys games, not to watch the game, but to watch John Miller coach. She would pay attention to how he worked the game and how he interacted with his players, the other players, and the officials. "His attitude, his presence, and his intensity were contagious to his players and anyone else that happened to be watching. Every quarter that you watched was better than reading any book on how to coach. He was a man of few words, but when he did speak up to express his opinions, the conversation would often be life altering.

"I'll never forget his words to me once after I received a technical foul in a game. During that game, something happened, and under my breath I said, 'You're crazy,' meaning the referee. The ref heard me, and the next thing I knew the whistle blew and I was busted. Coach Miller wasn't at the game, but somehow he heard about it. He called me to his office and offered some advice about always playing with class and composure. He told me the obvious reasons, but beyond that, you never knew when you would encounter the same referee again. He said that it was his experience that these guys had great memories, and you wouldn't want to sway their opinions of you in a bad way. I never forgot his advice and I would never again receive a technical foul. I am a pretty accomplished coach I think, and I have to give credit where credit is due. If you walk in on one of my practices, you will find that it is set up the Miller Way.

"And as far as Lisa Miller, when she played, you could tell it was *his* blood that was in her veins. She was the ultimate competitor. She had that look in her eyes just like her dad. You could tell that, to her, it wasn't just a game. It was serious business. And her basketball IQ had to come from being around her dad."

Lisa Miller

Lisa Miller relates the lessons that her dad taught her to real life. She goes on, "I carried that attitude over when I was in sales. I thought of making the sale like a win. It feels good to win, but losing is the worst. But you have to take it for what it is. No one is sick. No one is dying. After the initial bad feelings, you can't let it affect you or get you down more than it should. He always told me that if losing happens, it happens, but you don't want to leave the gym or the situation feeling like *you* are a loser. Maybe you take the next day off, but realize that it was a game or whatever, it was a learning experience, and you take the good out of it and start planning for the next one."

Back in the car, as the kids would pull into the parking lot of the destination, the last words would often be a reminder to look everyone in the eye, say hello, and be friendly. It seems like a simple thing, but it is almost a forgotten thing today. It is proven to be vital in making positive first impressions. How can you have any success with people if you do not establish a connection?

In the study "To Be Looked at as Though Air: Civil Attention Matters," published in 2012 in *Psychological Science*, the lead author Eric D. Wesselmann, a psychology professor at Purdue University, explained that when approaching new people or strangers on the street, "The people who were given an 'air gaze' [or no eye contact] felt the most disconnected. On the other hand, the people who received eye contact and a smile felt the least disconnected of anyone studied. I wonder if you add a 'hello' to the smile if it would lower the feeling of disconnection even more. Either way, it seems that even the smallest gestures to connect toward strangers can bring about a sense of community. That's good for human health." And that's what Miller conveyed to his kids before they got out of the car. Let people know you're friendly. Let people know you care. Mostly though, let them know that you are there.

The lessons in the car weren't just exclusive to Coach's children. Ohio State Buckeye Brandon Fuss-Cheatham was Miller's point guard from 1997 to 2001. He too remembers Coach Miller teaching him life lessons and basketball lessons in the car. This was made possible partly because Miller would have to drive him around to various clinics and basketball events. Brandon remembers, "Coach was always teaching. That's his real gift. He is a teacher first before anything else. An opportunity would not go by where if Coach thought he could make you better, he would do so. He was the best at using the right words and the right slang even to help you remember what you were taught. It didn't matter if it was basketball, driving, or life. Coach had a way of simplifying what was being taught and giving it a catch phrase so that you could use what you learned right when you needed it."

If you're around Coach Miller for any period of time, you begin to notice the catchy, captivating patter of his speech. His language is part Pittsburghese and part faux-street, mixed in with a professor who really knows his stuff.

Brandon expands, "Like in basketball, he wouldn't just say to 'stop' in front of your defender. He'd yell 'Put on the brakes!' It seems so simple, but I know that when I'd be in a game situation, I could hear him in my head saying his things like 'Put on the brakes' or 'you gotta be a tough hombre' or 'You have to *drive* past your defender. I don't think the points he made would have stuck as well had he not talked the way he did. 'Keep it inside the railroad tracks,' for instance, meant to keep your dribble tight and controlled."

Brandon in his own way echoes what his Miller's adult children told me over and over. "He was so smart and such a hard-working, good guy. You just wanted to go out of your way to get his approval. More than that, we didn't want to disappoint him. That was the worst."

Dana Miller remarks, "Having your dad being prominent where you lived and also being a teacher in my high school, we had to make decisions as kids growing up that would not tarnish his reputation or disappoint him in any way. You would always know that just about every week there would be an article on him, his team, or Sean in the paper, so there was always a target kind of on our backs, so we kept in line for ourselves, but we mostly kept in line so that he wouldn't have to hear about it."

CHAPTER 8

A PANTHER TRAINER

"And we carved our love in a heart on the witness tree
And swore we'd raise our kids in Ellwood City"
                                    —Donnie Iris and the Cruisers

In 1975, the movie *One Flew Over the Cuckoo's Nest* was brand new in Theatres. In a famous scene in the film, Jack Nicholson tried in vain to instruct a fellow insane asylum patient named Chief on the finer points of playing "an old Indian game called put the ball in the hole." Simultaneously, Coach Miller was trying to teach the same game to his new players, and it seemed, at first anyway, that he was having about the same amount of success as Nicholson. Miller still kept positive though, and he summed up his attitude perfectly following a relatively rare victory against the Rochester Rams in 1975: "We take them one at a time, and we don't look ahead."

As dominating and legendary as it would become, John Miller's high school coaching career had an auspicious beginning to be sure. When he was hired to coach at Riverside School District, its basketball team, the Panthers, was good, but in no shape to compete with the great teams in its class. In fact, Riverside's division contained some of the best hoops teams in the area. Class B, as it was called in those days before the A-AAAA system of dividing schools, was loaded with great teams.

The division included the state champion Midland Leopards, the state runner-up Monaca Indians, the Freedom Bulldogs, and the Rochester Rams.

Miller's Riverside Panthers

All of the schools in the division were really good, but the Midland Leopards, in particular, was the Goliath compared to Miller's David in Riverside. Coach Miller welcomed the challenge.

Midland, though having a small enrollment, was big on talent and had a hall of fame coach to boot. Coach Ed Olkowski led the blue and gold Leopards to four state titles in the 1970s. In a 2015 popular news blog, *Your Beaver County*, an article was posted about the top five Beaver County basketball coaches of all time. The post pointed out that, with one runner up and seven WPIAL titles, Olkowski is the only coach in the county who can boast a similar resume to John Miller. In fact, many note that if it hadn't been for Olkowski's dominant coaching presence in the seventies, Miller would have had no trouble claiming some of Midland's WPIAL and PIAA championships for himself and the Riverside Panthers.

In a 2015 interview, Coach Olkowski remembers, "No one—and I mean *no one* worked harder than John at getting his guys ready. He ate, slept, and breathed basketball. He still does, I've heard. He infused his enthusiasm and hard work into that Riverside squad."

I tend to believe that Ed Olkowski knows what he's talking about. In the early and middle seventies, his Leopards owned western Pennsylvania basketball. You sensed a changing of the guard when Miller's green and black Riverside Panthers would go on to shock everyone by beating Olkowski's state champion Leopards twice.

Miller stated, "When you look back at it now, you just think to yourself, 'How did little Riverside beat Midland? I mean, these guys were the state champs.' But we worked hard, and when you do that, things tend to bounce your way. That's why you play the games as an underdog. You know, Maz hits that homerun sometimes."

Losses never go down easily for warriors, especially when they were favored to win. Even many years after that win, Coach Olkowski only half jokes that one of those wins happened because he benched some of his best players. He, in his own words, "just wanted to take some of the cocky players down a few notches." He grudgingly acknowledges that Miller was destined for greatness. The respect was and is clearly there.

Experience Plus
Riverside head coach John Miller, kneeling at right, has four starters and six lettermen back from last year's 15-7 team. Starters returning include Mike LaFratto, kneeling, and standing from left Joe Bell, Dave Yeles and Art Kunkle.

Stories like these go to show what fierce competitors the two were and still are. And it reinforces the idea of what a big influence Coach Olkowski was on John Miller. It's still evident how losses in that competitive division were tough pills to swallow. The value that comes with fierce and healthy competition is measureable growth and excellence. Both coaches hold each other in very high regard because they witnessed greatness in each other years ago—even if that greatness showed itself when each was trying to defeat the other.

There's a little known story about Coach Olkowski to illustrate that he would do anything to prove that his teams would win the *right* way and that there would be no doubt in the legitimacy of those wins. According to Ed Olkowski, he was coaching an important game during which the opposing coach—not Miller—was having a meltdown on the sidelines because he felt that Midland had been given a call that should have gone the other way. This display went on for what seemed like forever (probably a minute or two) when Coach Olkowski walked calmly to the scorer's table and pushed the button connected to the scoreboard so that it boosted the other team's score by ten points!

Next, he called over to the irate coach of the opposition and posed the question, "Is that enough now?" This display wasn't just for show. Coach Olkowski insisted that the points be left on the board. As if to add an exclamation point to the whole thing, Olkowski's Leopards still went on to win by fourteen, proving that no bad call would determine the outcome of the game.

It's no wonder that John Miller, without hesitation, names Coach Olkowski as the person who taught him most about coaching. "I studied everything he did when I was at Riverside. I just think so much of that guy. I mean he was intense. I know I patterned much of what I do from what I saw in him."

In a January 1976 interview following a 69–54 loss to Olkowski and his Leopards, Miller didn't hesitate to voice his respect of Ed Olkowski. "What do I blame for our loss? What beat us? The Midland Legend, that's what did it to us tonight. The kids came out tight and as a result we didn't shoot well. The Midland legend beat us."

Even though there were no championships brought back by the Riverside Panthers during Miller's time there, he insists that the teams from 1972 to 1976 were arguably *the* hardest working teams he's ever coached in his thirty plus year career. "They had no quit in them and would work relentlessly to get better as a team unit and to be the best conditioned teams around."

One premier member of these Riverside teams was Beaver County Sports Hall of Fame 2015 inductee Dr. Brad Brown. A dentist now, he played for Coach Miller at Riverside High School and at the Ivy League school Columbia back in the late seventies. At Columbia he was able to play against some star players, including Isaiah Thomas and Chris Mullin. He even helped none other than President Barrack Obama with his jump shot. Obama spent his junior year of college at Columbia. Brad Brown

Brad Brown

always jokes that in politics and with his game, Barrack always "went to the left."

As far as Coach Miller, Brown remembers, "To play basketball for Coach Miller, one had to have the mindset that it wasn't just a winter sport. It was a yearlong commitment. He didn't just announce, 'Hey guys, you'd better practice during the summer,' he'd be right there with us. He was involved and 'all in' all the time."

In 2015, Brad says, "He was almost a third parent for me when I think back on it. Coach Miller had the driveways all over Riverside buzzing with activity. This was back when gyms with the automatic ball return 'guns' didn't exist. So it took three of us working as a team to shoot, rebound, and return. We were practicing our shots and drills, it seemed, like everyday from 7:00 a.m. until noon. We'd each get in one thousand shots every day. Imagine high school kids getting up every day that early to do that. There were honestly almost no days off. Coach had a way of making you believe that it was the only way to get to be a great shooter. And for those that bought in, that wanted to be great shooters, it became like a religion."

Coach Miller's teaching wasn't just restricted to repetitive drills and repetitive shooting. He taught his players to be smarter than the opponent and outthink them. For example, many of Miller's best players were small guys. Conventional strategies would have ensured loss upon loss against taller and faster opponents. Brad Brown comments, "You know, I'm a small player. I'm only five feet nine. Why did I pick basketball? It was because of the success that Coach Miller showed me that I could have if I used my brain along with the physical training. He taught all of us, small guys especially, to create space between you and the guy guarding you. It was all about changing your speed constantly and stopping on a dime. Once you fooled the opponent with misdirection, you could take that open shot. It didn't matter how tall you were."

In 2016, complicated ball handling maneuvers—through the legs and around the back—is commonplace and an accepted, almost necessary part of the game. This was absolutely not true in Miller's early coaching days. Back then, most people saw ball handling tricks in a game and wagged their heads, dismissing them as showboating and flash. This was not the case with John Miller. Ahead of his time, he taught his players that dribbling the ball between your legs had a purpose. It created a barrier between you and the defender. Likewise, behind-the-back dribbling and no-look passing can be purposeful. If your body is between you and the defender, the ball is unlikely to be stolen. Any way to mislead your opponent can be used to get yourself open, and when you're open, you're going to make your shot.

Dave Vetica, Tom Bentley, Joe Bell, Art Kunkle, Mark Stronider, Mike LaPenta

Again, these skills took hours upon hours of drills to perfect. It took a special kind of commitment that Coach Miller required from his players. Beyond basketball, that kind of dedication forced them to restructure and become experts at managing time. His players are astounded when they look at what has become of them. "Looking back now," says Brad Brown, "it's astounding how many of his players that I know have become doctors and six, seven figure salary guys. That's from the lessons he taught us about responsibility, work ethic, and time management. More than that, maybe it was seeing his constant march towards excellence that got us going in the right direction."

Riverside's Dave Vetica

Another example of a success story out of Riverside that credits "Miller and my father" would be Dave Vetica. When John Miller retired as Blackhawk High School basketball coach in 2005, he was asked to name some of the best players he ever coached. His first mention was Dave Vetica.

He was one of the most prolific scorers in Beaver County basketball history. He graduated from Riverside as the school's all-time scoring leader (1,536 points), averaging 14 points per game as a sophomore, 23 as a junior, and 34 as a senior, when he led the state in scoring. As a senior, he set Riverside's scoring records for a season with 718 points and in a game with 52 points. And again, during this time you must remember that Dave amassed all of these points before the three-point line.

Dave went on to accept a scholarship at Florida State University and played there for one season before transferring to Cameron University, a NAIA school in Oklahoma. There, Dave switched to point guard, and by his junior year, he'd helped the Aggies win the NAIA title. His coach called him the smartest basketball mind he had ever coached. Dave now owns and runs the county's oldest golf course, Beaver Valley Golf Course in Patterson Heights.

Dave, without hesitation credits all of his knowledge and skill on the court to John Miller. He believes that, with or without the high school prefix, he is one of the best basketball coaches in the country. Without even a hint of levity, Dave poses the question, "Can you imagine what LeBron and the Cavs could have done in those finals against the Warriors if Miller was coaching them? The man is a master of motivation. That was his forte. He would bring confidence. He could make you believe that they could do things that you previously thought were impossible. He was just energizing. I never felt that way with any coach in college or anywhere else. He just had a way about him. Yeah, he would yell at us all the time, but he somehow made it fun after it was all over. When you accomplish something, he didn't have to tell you that he was happy with you. You just knew it."

In 2007, Dave was honored by Riverside High School for his basketball accomplishments, and his old coach, John, presented him with the plaque.

To help his players at Riverside achieve their goal and his goal of becoming the best that they could be, John Miller discovered a way to condition some of his guys that was kind of unconditional, but definitely effective. In those days, most teachers did summer jobs to make ends meet. Since John helped his dad with building projects all through his teen years, he became a pretty good builder, and he was no stranger to physical labor.

Fast forward to 1972. Teaching was a respectable profession, but when summer came, the paychecks stopped for a few months. John knew that, like his father, he could get jobs roofing, siding, painting, and the like and make pretty good money to get him through the summer. Many of his players needed some work for the summer months, too. Those comments were all Miller needed to hear. He offered his players the chance to work with him on building projects around Lawrence and Beaver counties and to make some extra cash in the process. The unspoken, understood bonus when the kids signed up with Miller Roofing and Siding was that roofing houses in the summer could definitely lend itself to becoming stronger and leaner in a hurry.

Brad Brown remembers, "His crew was made up of all the guys on the basketball team. He would put me and another kid on one side of a roof and the brothers Tim and Tom Tirlia on the other side. Miller being Miller, all the work was made into an athletic contest. He would have us race to see who could get their side of the house roofed first. We couldn't just slap the work together though. Steep time deductions were added on to our totals if he saw shoddy work, so our jobs were done fast, but more importantly, they were done right. The winner would get a free lunch at the Brighton Hot Dog Shoppe courtesy of Coach. Everything was a competition in those days. It's funny what you remember. I can still hear 'It's Too Late' from Carole King playing below from a sunbather's radio while all this was going on. It was kind of appropriate for what we were doing."

A typical summer workday for John Miller and his "crew" would be as follows: In the early morning, Coach Miller would meet the guys from the team at the site where they were to work. All through the day in the blazing heat they would work together roofing, painting, and siding these houses. Miller and the kids made relatively good money to boot. Construction definitely paid better than a summer job at McDonald's or the car wash. After a day of work, the kids would then go home for a shower and some supper. Next up was a summer league basketball game. Miller notes, "By the time fall was in the air, and the school sports seasons rolled around, these guys were big and strong—I mean, these guys were in shape. They were monsters. There wasn't any further conditioning needed. Those teams were a joy to coach and I'll always remember those guys. We learned so much from each other."

While the summer may have ended, the rigorous conditioning did not. It can't be overstated, though, that once the kids bought into the Miller Way, they needed no further convincing or prodding to work hard. On that, the entire Riverside team agrees.

Brad Brown remembers, "Miller wasn't holding a gun to any of our heads. He had us believing that we were on the track to greatness if we just stayed the course and kept working everyday. The work ethic couldn't help but spill over into our schoolwork and our daily lives. For example, we would all work extra hard to get good grades so that the school would allow us to shoot hoops in the gym during study halls. By the time practice after school rolled around, a lot of the guys would have three hundred shots in already.

"Everyone on the team could shoot. Everyone on the team had great ball handling skills. That's a trademark of Miller teams. On other teams, maybe two or three guys have good 'handles.' Everyone else just uses rudimentary dribbling to get by. On John Miller's teams, everyone down to the last sub has great ball handling skills. You can take that to the bank."

And again, crossovers—being able to dribble between the legs and behind the back—weren't at all for show. Coach Miller made sure that the players knew that when they were dribbling between the legs, it looked impressive, but it was, more importantly, placing a barrier between the ball and their defender. When they crossed over, it was misdirecting their opponent. His players worked for hours mastering these moves and many others.

It didn't seem to matter that Miller was a new coach. He came off as genuinely confident. Just being in the same room, you could tell that he was self-assured and believed 100 percent that what he was doing and what he was preaching were the most important things in the world to him. Brad Brown recalls, "You have to remember that I knew him before all of the championships, all of the records, all of the accolades. I'm telling you, he had the same swagger and the same edge to him that he has now. I think it subconsciously made everyone around him want to attain that level of confidence."

Art Kunkle, one of Miller's best players, lives in Memphis, Tennessee. He is now the vice president of Radian, a safety products company. He remembers that John affected his life much more than just a basketball coach or a teacher. "Miller as a subject is a personal matter to me. My father is eighty-four. He was drafted into the Marine Corps in 1951 and served on active duty until 1954. I think he stayed in the reserves until fifty-six or fifty-eight. He ran the Marine Corps Marathon at sixty-seven and remains healthy today. He has several USMC t-shirts and continues to wear them proudly. Not until I was quite a bit past forty did I hear stories about Parris Island and his service experience, but I learned that Boot Camp was one of the most intense periods of his life.

He formed habits and friendships during that stretch that left the most lasting impression in a lifetime.

"It may seem extreme to say, but to a degree, Riverside basketball and Coach Miller's drilling was the closest thing to military experience in my life. I was a little too young for Vietnam, and thankfully I faced no other kind of hardship or adversity severe enough to be more influential."

To compare adjusting to Miller's coaching style to serving in Vietnam may be a bit over the top, but his extremely high demands on his players' time and effort are indeed legendary. But in all fairness, he made it clear from the beginning that this is what he was all about. By the end of the first practice, the kids fell into two categories: the kids who recognized Miller's obsessive dedication and bought in, or the kids who recognized Miller's obsessive dedication and called it quits. It was no mystery. It got difficult sometimes because some parents thought of basketball as just a fun after-school activity.

Miller thought of it as a way of life and demanded the same from his players. Some parents shook their heads in disbelief. They believed what he was doing wasn't right. They believed that he was robbing the kids of their high school years because of all of the work. But when speaking now to his former players, they tell a different story.

Brad Brown says, "You can look back at all the players that 'got' what he was trying to do. They are all successful now. The message to be responsible, work harder and smarter than the next guy. Everyone kind of knows that as an adult. But to get that message early and realize that it was the way to go in your teen years? That lesson was invaluable to us that played for him. Forget Miller's 'stars.' I'm talking his day-to-day players. There's a very disproportionate amount that are wealthy and have successful families in 2015. His lessons translated to life and business so seamlessly. It's all about drive and time management. He was teaching basketball, but the lessons learned cost a pretty penny at business seminars around the world. He wanted everyone to be ahead of the competition mentally and physically. That's what all his charts were about. The numbers proved that you outworked the other guy. He firmly believed that if his team significantly out-prepared the other, only a crazy set of circumstances would cause the other team to win. And of course, that way of thinking works wonders in the work world, too. "

Longtime Miller friend Bob Maher tells of a stack of cards that Miller carried seemingly everywhere. These cards had a different basketball drill or play on each one. The stack was so impressive, Maher began calling it the "rolodex." Maher laughs, "I swear, he had a card for every situation."

Former Miller player Art Kunkle concurs, "His preparation made him and us ready for anything. One of the observations that time and distance helped me to make about Miller was that he was committed to us and to the goal of being excellent. He believed in and practiced preparation as a way of life."

Dave Vetica jokes about the vast amount of time and preparation those Miller teams put in. "Brut was big back then. You know, those big green bottles of aftershave. Brut: by Faberge. Half the time, we never had time to go home after summer practices to shower before some event that night. So the next best thing was Brut. We always thought that we kept that company in business. You never wanted to leave until that number on your chart was bigger than the one you put up the day before."

A player from decades later, Ohio State and Blackhawk point guard Brandon Fuss-Cheatham, remembers the value of charting. "Those charts were golden to a basketball player who played for him. He didn't want you to just believe that you were getting better; he wanted you to actually *see* that you were getting better. Preparation for the game *was* the game to him, and the charts made everything clear for all of us."

For Miller, the charts were a tangible reminder of the work that his players were putting in. The charts told the players not only how much they did but also what gains were made from the work.

Yes, Miller believed in being overprepared. To prepare that much required the discipline to work even when you didn't feel like it. The word "discipline" comes from the Latin *disciplina* and means instruction or knowledge. That is why a disciple is one who seeks to learn. He believed the outcome in most games was largely determined by the time warm-ups were underway. The players, coach, and team that prepared had the advantage, and only a very unlikely set of developments could rescue the underprepared from their fate.

Art Kunkle, though from a completely different era, tells the same tales as Brandon Fuss-Cheatham. "We practiced summers as well as seasons. We were physically conditioned as much or more than our opponents, and as a result, started most games with an advantage."

The only way Kunkle can explain the tenacity and endurance needed to survive the frequency of his workouts is with a story. "I heard a story once of a young man working on his car. It was on jack stands in his driveway. Through some unplanned development, the car moved, the jack stands tipped, and the young man was pinned beneath the car. Hearing the commotion, the grandmother emerged from the house. Seeing the circumstance, and not knowing what to do, she grabbed the bumper and lifted. She was able to move the car enough to allow her grandson to wriggle free. Desperation and a jolt of adrenaline allowed her to save a life. 'What the mind wills, the body can do.'

Riverside Panthers: Dan Weil, Joe Bell, and Art Kunkle

"Take that jolt of adrenaline to the start line of a marathon. It will carry the average person about a hundred yards, but preparation carries you to the finish line. Our coach not only jolted us to perform at the beginning, but he also used preparation to carry us to the finish line, no matter how far off that line seemed to be."

John Miller prepared his team months in advance of an upcoming season. One way to do this was to find out which players had hoops in their driveways or in their neighborhoods. The remaining players would be dispersed among those driveways and neighborhoods. Each would have rotating jobs like shooter, rebounder, and passer. By the end of a summer morning, each player would have hundreds of shots in. This happened every day.

Art Kunkle remembers, "We worked on skills. We worked batteries of drills to develop dribbling, passing, defending, shooting, free throws, and skills that were specific to our positions on the team. If you think about basketball and list the core skills, there are only eight or ten. The winning team does those eight or ten things better than the losing team. Half of summer work was dedicated to making individual players better and more prepared in those skills than players on other teams."

The other half of summers was dedicated to exposure to all kinds of competition and toughness. The community around Riverside was mostly sedate suburbia, insulated middle class. Miller saw his players defer or show fear to players from tougher, more urban or scrappy communities. Two or three nights a week, Miller took rides with his players to grittier urban neighborhoods that often scared them to death. By the time the regular season rolled around, nothing could scare them. They were conditioned to see no player, team, or gym as intimidating. Add to those things the fact that Miller had a better mind for tactics, and his success boiled down to better preparation, better player development, and the ability to apply the best of the current offensive and defensive schemes.

One characteristic of Coach Miller's that was shared by famed USA Hockey coach Herb Brooks was his sometimes puzzling, sometime funny sayings. When these words of wisdom were spoken using his deeply embedded Pittsburgh accent, they made quite a unique and long lasting impression. One of Herb Brook's most remembered expressions Miller used when criticizing a player was, "Johnson, you get worse every day, and right now you are playing like the middle of next week!" Miller had a few of those, and his guys used to take great pleasure in repeating them in the showers or locker room.

One remarkable player who made an impression on Miller was a young man named Mike LaPenta. Miller remembers him as a live wire, and other players who were interviewed all concur that Mike had an ornery streak in him and could have gone down the wrong path. He was beginning to be a discipline problem at school when he gave basketball a try. His former teammates all give John Miller and his discipline techniques credit for steering the LaPenta in the right direction. This is just one example of how Miller's method of having a goal and focusing almost all energy toward reaching the goal can teach anyone how to succeed in the game and then, in turn, succeed in life.

The following is an excerpt of a memoriam for Mike LaPenta memorial service, written in 2006 by former teammate Art Kunkle. It illustrates John Miller's role in LaPenta's life.

To say that Mike's high school career was colorful would be an understatement of monumental proportions. Mike was an average student. He had a nose for trouble and seemed to enjoy finding it. He excelled at baseball as a catcher, and at basketball as a point guard. Mike was small. He seemed always to be in the shadow of teammates with more apparent gifts of talent and ability.

Mike LaPenta

Under certain circumstances it is customary to be generous in characterizations, even to exaggerate. In reflecting on LaPenta's athletic or 'extra curricular' activities, I can say with a complete sense of objectivity that no superlative seems quite sufficient. He was unequivocally the most fearless and most tenacious athlete I have ever seen.

In high school years we spent much of our summers together, under the careful guidance of basketball coach Miller, drilling in the mornings and finding playground games in the evenings. It was often the case that the places with the best playground competition were the most dangerous. I remember quietly praying on many evenings that Mike would take this factor into account. He never did. No opponent was too big, and no challenge was left unanswered. Although I was 9 inches taller and 30 pounds heavier, in the most perilous of circumstances, the guy I followed to safety was always Mike. No teammate of Mike's ever faced trouble alone. For the risks he took on my account I will always be grateful.

(We) lost a distinguished man on January 8, 2006. Mike died suddenly and unexpectedly of a heart attack while working with youth at his church.

This memoriam hints at what everyone remembers about Mike LaPenta. He was a prime example of what special teachers and coaches do for at-risk kids. Mike LaPenta had an overabundance of energy and a mischievous nature that could have had him easily end up as a statistic. But when redirected by dedicated and unselfish people like John Miller, the problem child can end up being an inspiration.

Miller remembers, "LaPenta loved to run. He was one of those guys that would miss the line on a 'suicide' drill on purpose so that they would all have to run it again. And as fate would have it, we lost him too soon. He died of a sudden heart attack doing, of all things, running a marathon with his son."

When John began coaching, he wasn't just a new coach, he was a relatively new father. His first son, Sean, was born in 1968, and in 1971, he was a very active toddler. And as any new parent of a toddler knows, demands are sky high when it comes to the amount of time and energy the little one demands. Luckily for this little one, his dad had energy by the bucket load and didn't mind taking his son with him to practice to give mom a break at home.

Some modifications and adjustments had to be made to make this happen, but they didn't interfere with practice whatsoever. The gymnasium at Riverside High School had retractable bleachers, and when they were pushed back, they were flush against the gym wall. Coach Miller had come into possession of a fan-shaped backboard and rim and attached it to ropes. The hoop could be lowered all the way to the ground and raised almost to the rafters by a pulley system behind the bleachers. Coach's high school players never used that hoop. It was reserved for little Sean. As JV and Varsity Panther practices were in full swing, three-year-old Sean was content to shoot basket after basket off to the side. All the while, he would be taking in all of the sights and sounds of what would one day be his chosen profession and obsession. One would surmise that a toddler would tire of this routine after awhile, but Sean never did. This early fascination with basketball would be one the first signs that John had something special on his hands.

Toddler Sean Miller sinking shot after shot on his sideline hoop wasn't the only happy memory from the Riverside Panther days. The teams that Miller coached were a source of pride and joy to him year after year. "Those Riverside teams gave their all and would almost to a man end up successes off the court later in life."

But as rewarding as those successful seasons at Riverside High School were, Miller knew that he would not coach there forever. The one constant in John Miller's philosophy is to set your goals as high as possible and to avoid complacency. "As soon as you get comfortable, you're in danger of missing chances for future success and experiences. 'You can achieve your dreams' is a cliché for a reason. It's a cliché because it is true. But you have to both believe in yourself and, most importantly, put in the work. If any one part of that formula is missing, the goal won't be met."

Upon leaving Pfeiffer for a teaching and coaching job up north, John Miller set a real, attainable goal. In his thoughts and in his beliefs, it was a real goal, albeit a lofty one. In his coaching career, he was going to be the best, and not just for one year. He thought of the teams and coaches he idolized and set out to pass what they had accomplished. He vowed to create a perennial winner in a competitive high school section. Simply put, he wanted to beat the best.

Miller looked around him. He loved the guys he was coaching, but they weren't going to be around forever. The section had some great teams in it, but was Riverside ever actually going to be able to compete for a championship? The talent pool of athletes at Riverside just wasn't going to be able to produce the athletes John needed. As difficult as it may have been, a move needed to be made. But where would he go? What would that next step be?

Kneeling: P. Troia, B. Beck, R. Capozza. Standing: Coach John Miller, M. Langhel, P. Frazzini, J. Panner, B. Kelly, M. Rimbey, T. Lipp, B. Jarvito, M. Sutton.

CHAPTER 9

THAT NEXT STEP

"If you're not going to go all the way, why go at all?"
−*Beaver Falls Native and Super Bowl MVP, "Broadway" Joe Namath*

Fortunately for Coach Miller, he wouldn't have to look too far for a place that both wanted him and would supply him with talent and opportunity for years to come. Just next door to Ellwood City was Beaver County. It is just west of Pittsburgh and nestled up against the Ohio line. Named for the Delaware Indian Chief known as King Beaver, Beaver County had been the site of the impressive Fort McIntosh during the American Revolution. With the industrial revolution came Andrew Carnegie's steel city of Pittsburgh. And on Pittsburgh's coattails rode its neighbor, Beaver County. Its two biggest areas (Beaver Falls and Aliquippa) were populated enough to be classified as cities in the Hammond atlas. Smaller towns like New Brighton, Rochester, and Freedom gathered around these little cities. Though its people were mostly of European descent, it was a true melting pot with every imaginable ethnicity being represented. And even with these small towns and cities, it had large rural and suburban stretches of land. The area's pride and power came from the steel mills that dotted almost every corner of the valley. Every night at precisely eleven o'clock in Aliquippa, the monster steel mill named Jones and Laughlin turned the night sky a bright orange when the slag would be dumped. You could set your watch by the luminous sight. This was the area's equal to the Arctic's Northern Lights. Along with the light show, J&L also brought the intertwined towns of Beaver

County decades upon decades of prosperity and growth. It seemed that most of the remaining pride came from area sports teams. Competition was in the blood of the residents of the area. Yet unborn in the 1960s, John Miller's youngest son Archie understood this and explained it in a quote from 1999 when he was at North Carolina State. "The place I came from is just that type of area that is a very competitive town. My high school team always won, and that is why I think I'm able to play at this level right now, because of where I came from."

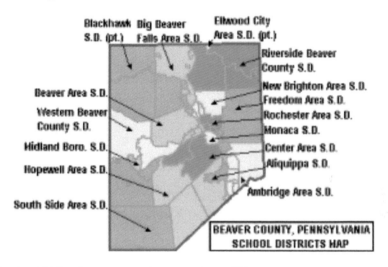

Blackhawk S.D. (pt.)   Big Beaver Falls Area S.D.   Elwood City Area S.D. (pt.)

Riverside Beaver County S.D.
New Brighton Area S.D.
Freedom Area S.D.
Rochester Area S.D.
Monaca S.D.
Center Area S.D.
Aliquippa S.D.
Ambridge Area S.D.

Beaver Area S.D.
Western Beaver County S.D.
Midland Boro. S.D.
Hopewell Area S.D.
South Side Area S.D.

BEAVER COUNTY, PENNSYLVANIA SCHOOL DISTRICTS MAP

In the 1970s, the area was just coming off its most prosperous time in history. The booming steel industry had produced an affluent middle class in the "Valley" since the turn of the century, but with Japanese steel becoming cheaper and flooding the market, the good times were about to change. The steel town, blue-collar work ethic would be soon tested. Mills closed in rapid succession in the early 1980s. These tough times would shape the demeanor and the strength of a generation of athletes who could rival competitors from anywhere in the world. As Bachman Turner Overdrive's anthem "Taking Care of Business" blared in local bars, businesses were shutting their doors all over the steel-dependent county. The only place, people realized, that business could truly be "taken care of" was on the fields and courts of their local sports teams. The collapse of the international steel market was confusing and scary, but the gridiron or court, well, that you could control and understand.

So, it makes sense that when John Miller looked around western Pennsylvania and Beaver County in particular, there were many schools to choose from that had a rich, athletic history. John had established himself enough by this time that he knew that he could begin to search for schools that needed a coach and could also provide him talent to work with and mold for years to come. The surrounding gritty steel towns that spewed ash into the air also lavished the sports' fields and courts with legendary players. By the time that Miller was scanning the area for a place to continue and advance his coaching career, many sports legends had already sprung from the area. Nationally known sports stars such as Tito Francona, Norm Van Lear, Joe Walton, Tony Dorsett, Ty Law, Sean Gilbert, "Pistol" Pete Maravich, "Iron" Mike Ditka, and "Broadway" Joe Namath were just a few pro luminaries who were also members of the talented Beaver County Sports Hall of Fame.

JOE NAMATH
In his high school days

#24 Joe Namath wasn't just the QB at Beaver Falls.

There were two basketball programs that Miller coveted, and they were the powerhouses of the region: the Quips of the Aliquippa School District and the Beaver Falls Tigers. The Dallas Cowboys' megastar Tony Dorsett, Da Bears' near-deified Mike Ditka, and the freak of nature that was LSU's Pete Maravich were just three of the talents that would spring from the hardworking steel town of Aliquippa, Pennsylvania. As far as a talent pool, the nearby Aliquippa Quips had an ocean of talent that replenished itself every year.

Beaver Falls was a more complicated story. Beaver Fall's huge claims to fame at the time were football coach Larry Bruno and most famously, his

Mike Ditka visits
modern day Quips.

understudy, Super Bowl Champion "Broadway" Joe Namath of the New York Jets.

However, during the early 1970s, more and more people were moving out of Beaver Falls and into the suburbs of Chippewa and Patterson Heights. Rather than bus all of these kids into the city, it was decided that a new district should come into existence. The area that Beaver Falls controlled would be split into two. The first area would be the urban Big Beaver Falls School District and the second was the more suburban and rural areas of Chippewa, Darlington, and West Mayfield. These areas would make up the new district. There were some people who alleged racism, expressing concern that the district only existed because the white people didn't want their kids to go to school at the more minority-heavy Beaver Falls. Nevertheless, the decision was made and the newly christened Blackhawk would come into existence.

The district was located in the northwestern part of Beaver County. It encompassed the communities of Chippewa, Darlington, Enon Valley in Lawrence County, Patterson, South Beaver, and West Mayfield. Over 17,000 people lived in the 65 square miles of the district.

A big portion of what Beaver Falls used to draw its student body from would now be handed to Blackhawk. The new green and gold Cougars of Blackhawk was destined to be able to compete with the big boys right away. The area was country strong and blue collar and had portions that were affluent, too.

Looking at the area today, it is difficult to imagine just how country it was back in the early 1970s. Route 60 in Chippewa today is pretty much filled on both sides with shopping plazas featuring super Walmart, K-Mart, the big Pittsburgh-based grocery store Giant Eagle, and a wide variety of gas stations and restaurants. Back then, though, the road cut through mostly woods and maybe a gas station and a couple of restaurants and places to stop. One of the most memorable was Harold's Ice Cream. But no one called it that. It was known simply as the Cow thanks to a life-sized plaster version of the animal bolted to the roof.

John Miller's gut told him that Blackhawk was going to be able to provide him with enough talent to reach his goal of building one or more championship teams. In fact, by the time John Miller set his sights on the Blackhawk basketball job, though barely in existence, the Cougars had just narrowly been defeated in the WPIAL Championship for football. This was indeed a good sign. The Western Pennsylvania Interscholastic Athletic League Championship (locally known as the WPIAL and pronounced "whippial" by donut shop sports gurus) was what every team in the county strived for. Miller knew that landing a coaching position at either Aliquippa or Blackhawk would make his chances for a WPIAL Championship astronomically improve.

High school sports fans noticed that something special happened to Riverside Panthers basketball since Coach Miller was hired. And it was no secret that Aliquippa and Blackhawk administration had noticed too and would inevitably try to land the coach. Both schools would be an excellent fit for Coach Miller. All there was to do now was to wait for an opportunity to bring his basketball mind to either of these schools.

Aliquippa High School would have been the obvious choice. It was already established and had a more than decent basketball program in place. And "Quip town" was already well represented as far as alumni in professional sports went. It was more hoops oriented than Blackhawk and would definitely supply the talent that Miller would need to reap championships year after year. And the hiring almost happened. After the showing that the coach made with the underdog Riverside Panthers, rumors swirled that Aliquippa was very interested in hiring Miller as their next head coach. In fact, members of the Aliquippa school board quietly let Miller know that if it were brought to a vote, the job would be his nine to one. But it wasn't to be.

School politics in Beaver County are just as touchy or maybe even more so as anywhere else. As things turned out, being the next basketball coach for Aliquippa wouldn't be in the cards for Coach Miller. Because of a budget cut and enrollment issues, the Aliquippa School District had to furlough about twenty teachers that year. It would now be political suicide for any school board member to vote to hire a new teacher just so he could coach the basketball team.

At the other end of the financial spectrum was Blackhawk School District. There were no layoffs in its foreseeable future. It was one of the few districts in the declining steel county that was growing and was in a favorable position to land the new coach. People were moving into the district at a steady clip, unlike the slowly dying steel town that the Aliquippa School District drew its students from.

As you look back now, the success story of John Miller and his family may not have been as intriguing had Miller been hired in Quip town. With the caliber of players he would have coached every year, the victories may have come too easy. John still jokes, "If I would have had the personnel that Quip produces year after year, I would have more championships with half the work that it took to do what I achieved at Blackhawk High School."

Simple success without the work wouldn't have fit his style anyway. The Miller Way is about the drills, the grind, and the constant, earnest work. Area basketball fans agree that Miller coaching at Aliquippa would have just been unfair for everyone involved, and the basketball team would've rolled over people.

So it seemed that Blackhawk High School was the place that Miller was destined to go. The school board and the superintendent of the new district knew the importance and the significant impact that scholastic sports had on the overall success of a school district. Everything seemed set for Blackhawk to make not only an academic splash but also one in the WPIAL sports record books.

You must realize that football is the king of sports in western Pennsylvania, and that was especially true during the era of the super Steelers of the 1970s. So, of course, before any other coaches were hired, the district first secured the position that was in the front of everyone's minds—the football coach. In 1977, they hired Joe Hamilton. This decision would prove to pay off as the years passed. Coach Hamilton, who only recently retired in 2015, would lead the Blackhawk Cougars to four WPIAL football championships and be elected to the Beaver County Sports Hall of Fame in 2009. Though the district was excited to have the opportunity to hire John Miller, the basketball coach was somewhat of an afterthought. It wasn't football, after all. Still, Blackhawk wanted quality at the position of head basketball coach.

Once word got out that the Aliquippa basketball job was up in smoke, the Blackhawk school board wasted no time offering Miller a social studies teaching position that happened to come with the head varsity basketball coaching job. As if to make sure the catch wouldn't get away, Blackhawk even offered the coach a choice of starting in January of the 1976–1977 school year or at the beginning of the next one. When Miller looked over the returning players on his roster, he had five athletic juniors to work with starting in January. John decided to jump right in. So, as Jimmy Carter was moving into the White House, John Miller was moving in to his office in the bowels of Blackhawk High School's lower locker room. Fortunately for John Miller, his tenure would outlast Carter's by twenty-two years and would eventually be thought of as much more of a success. The first four years of Miller's tenure at Blackhawk, however, would be filled with almost as much stress and drama as was found in the Carter White House.

So it was done. On a handshake, Miller was made the new basketball coach. To make the hiring official though, Blackhawk had to wait until one door closed to open the other. Back in Lawrence County, the Riverside School District still hadn't accepted Miller's resignation. Once the Riverside's board of education received Miller's formal letter of resignation, many on that board and in the community cried foul. Riverside had recently lost a few teachers and coaches to the up and coming Blackhawk School District and wasn't going to lose its favorite coach without a fight. It was at the school board meeting when John's resignation papers were presented that many members of the board voiced their disapproval publicly. The proceedings became heated at times. "We will not put up with this type of action in the future," charged Kenneth Bollinger, board president. "This is the fifth person we've lost to Blackhawk in recent years. This 'Hawk' is really picking us clean. This puts us in a really difficult position."

In Miller's resignation letter, he admitted that working for a bigger school like Blackhawk would be another step toward his goal of coaching at the college level. Time would not allow this goal to happen the way he envisioned it, but in a way, his dream would come true through his sons Sean and Archie.

The Riverside school board, in a last ditch effort of protest, also wrote a letter to Riverside superintendent Dr. Francis Mauka calling the move "immoral" and "unethical." A copy of the letter was sent to Blackhawk's school board and superintendent as well. The words in that letter, of course, fell on deaf ears.

Others on the Riverside board saw the reality of the situation and realized that Coach Miller just wasn't going to spend his prime in Riverside. After first refusing to accept the coach's resignation, a five to one majority finally gave way. School director James Cunningham was the main voice of reason, explaining that "holding him will only compound our problem, especially with basketball season approaching. We need to get over this and get on to the business of hiring a new basketball coach."

And so it began. Coach Miller was released from his job as physical education teacher and the coach of the Riverside Panthers. This new position would put him where he wanted to be to create a high school basketball superpower. His hall of fame coaching career was off and running.

John Miller would end up coaching for nearly thirty years at Blackhawk, where he won nearly six hundred games, seven WPIAL titles, and four state titles. He would be the third most winning coach in WPIAL history with 657 total wins between Riverside and Blackhawk.

But no one knew that yet. He had some bumpy years ahead when he would have to battle on the court and off to achieve his eventual success.

CHAPTER 10

THE PROVING GROUND

(PLAYING AT HALF COURT)

"The best way to predict the future is to create it."

—Abraham Lincoln

If turning around the Riverside Panthers got Coach Miller's foot in the door as far as being a revered coach, then his years at Blackhawk smashed that door down. But it wasn't going to be easy or instant by any stretch. Miller would have to endure some slaps in the face before he finally got the respect he was after.

Racecar builder Enzo Ferrari once told a man, "You may be able to drive a tractor but you will never be able to handle a Ferrari properly." The man was so enraged that he vowed to create the perfect car. The man's name was Ferruccio Lamborghini. In a way, Coach Miller would be trying to build a different type of racecar from scratch. One with, as Coach Norman Dale in the film *Hoosiers* describes, "five pistons firing all together. Five players on the floor functioning as one single unit: team, team, team—no one more important than the other."

And it wasn't just a new team that Coach Miller was going to have to mold into a winner. He had to train himself for a new teaching position.

★ Blackhawk High School, Beaver Falls, Pennsylvania

Going to a new town and a new job is almost always a challenge, and for John Miller, it was no different. He wasn't just facing a challenge as a new coach but also as a new teacher. At Riverside High School, Miller was the driver's education and physical education teacher in addition to coaching hoops. At Blackhawk, the teaching end of the job would be much more academically challenging. The course titles on Miller's syllabus would include Ancient Cultures II and Introduction to Anthropology.

"I'm sure there were those licking their chops waiting for the complaints to roll in that the new coach they brought in doesn't know anything about teaching anything more substantial than kickball," Miller recalls. Many people still feel that, in the words of Jack Black's slacker character Dewey Finn in the comedy film *School of Rock*, "Those who can't do, teach. Those who can't teach, teach gym."

And it wasn't just the students and parents John was worried about. He was about to find out that fitting in with the faculty was going to be a little bit of a challenge as well. At the time, the Blackhawk High School social studies department was a close-knit bunch that included (of all people) the exiting former Blackhawk basketball coach John Nace whom Miller was about to replace. To make matters worse, Mr. Nace was known to all as a gregarious, pleasant man, who everyone liked and respected. The transition would have been so much easier had Nace been a jerk that no one liked. To make matters touchier, besides being well liked, Mr. Nace was sort of unceremoniously moved out of the basketball position when news arrived that Miller was available to coach. This added a little tension to an already potentially uncomfortable situation in the teacher's lounge. Though nothing outwardly nasty was done on the coach's entrance into the social studies department meeting, it was a bit awkward at first. Everyone on the faculty was cordial and as welcoming as could be expected, but Miller knew his teaching would be under the microscope and that he would have to prove himself. He would have to show evidence of his abilities in the classroom before he even thought about enjoying success in the gym.

Though Miller had an idea about some of the dissent, his ideas were solidified one day when he was about to enter a conference room at the school. One veteran teacher was overheard commenting, "Well, this goes to show that sports come first. Big surprise." John knew this opinion wasn't held by just her and took it as a challenge.

Miller states, "I'm the type of guy that if you tell me I can't do something, then you might as well accept that it will be done. No problem. I will show up and put in the work to prove you wrong." And that's just what happened. Miller had a challenge in front of him, so he went straight to work.

Learning the material just a few chapters ahead of the students, Miller dove into the study of anthropology and ancient cultures. He embraced the subjects and made his teaching lively and fun. He infused games and humor into these subjects that could be quite bland if taught by the wrong type of teacher. This approach earned the new "hoops guy" some respect. Once the students were learning and having fun and engaged in a class, the parents and, in turn, the school district were soon pleased with Miller as well. No one, including parents, administration, the social studies department, or the rest of the faculty could say anything disparaging once they saw how Miller worked. Despite preconceived notions about how a coach taught, he wasn't going to be one of those guys who handed out ditto worksheets and drew up plays while his class did busy work and watched movies every day.

So all that year he grinded through and made sure he was a success as a teacher first and as a coach second. Though totally against his nature, he knew that basketball had to be a little in the background at the beginning. He also knew that his credibility would be on the line if he didn't show that he was a quality teacher right from the start. Once his anthropology and ancient cultures classes were being touted as solid learning experiences by teachers and parents alike, he could turn his attention to the place where he truly felt the most comfortable and at home: the green and gold painted hardwood of the newly built Blackhawk High School gymnasium.

But unexpected problems were about to surface with the basketball team. John had his plays ready to go. He had a practice regimen for the team written out and in place. He was ready to start practicing with his guys to get ready for a first season. His hopes were that his inaugural season as coach would include many wins. He planned to make a big splash in his debut. But the big splash came in the form of a cold glass of water to the face. When he checked the sign up sheet for the basketball team, he noticed that none of the four quality juniors who were members of the 1976 team were going out for basketball. With that, the chances of the basketball team having any success just plummeted before Miller's eyes.

The peculiar thing was that all of the student athletes who dropped basketball were football players in the fall. It seemed that they had all been convinced somehow that it would benefit them to focus their attention solely on one sport, but why? At this time the football team was rolling. Under new coach Joe Hamilton, the football Cougars were headed to Pitt Stadium. It was the site of the WPIAL AAAA championship that was held there each year. Though the Cougars would ultimately lose in that championship to the Penn Hills Indians, this was an awesome season for Cougar football and for new coach Joe Hamilton. This increased the popularity of football at Blackhawk even further and drove home the fact that it was still priority one. And as for the quality juniors that Coach Miller was counting on for basketball, they were (for some mysterious reason) off limits.

On getting the news that his expected starting team wasn't going to show that year, Miller looked at the dark situation. It felt like he was at the base of a giant mountain looking up at an insurmountable task. How could he possibly make a decent showing against the mighty teams of Section 3? In the mid-seventies, that section was arguably *the* best section in the entire state of Pennsylvania. It included big high school powerhouses like the Farrell Steelers, the Sharon Tigers, and the fearsome New Castle Hurricanes. And this list wouldn't be near complete without including the local Beaver County competition: the Ambridge Bridgers, the Aliquippa Quips and Blackhawk's built-in rivals, the Beaver Falls Tigers.

There would be no amazing Cinderella story here. The results of year one were predictable and disastrous. The Cougars would go 1–21 in 1977, Miller's first year. The writers for the school yearbook pulled no punches in the small blurb it included with the team photo. "A Very Discouraging Season" was the tag line. "For the Cougar varsity basketball team under the new head coach John Miller. The Cougars ended their season with a lowly 1–21 record in coach Miller's first year in a rough section three." The short article goes on to give nod to what was going on though. "With only three senior members, the biggest part of the team will return next season to try to improve on their record."

The coach knew that something needed to be done. He needed to build his team from scratch. To begin this, John sat at his desk alone. His thoughts returned to the days of his youth for inspiration. He remembered how he got hooked on the game early in his life. He remembered the Saturday morning league at Moon. He remembered how devastated he would be if any of those games were cancelled because of bad weather. Playing Saturday morning basketball with his friends had such a positive effect on him. He recalled how the competition at that young age helped him focus on getting better. With his competitive nature, he loved to measure himself against the other kids on a weekly basis and so did many others in the league. Maybe he could set up the same type of situation here at Blackhawk to get little kids interested in roundball. He could build them up from there.

"Back in those Moon basketball Saturdays, we were so young," explained Miller. Unlike high school guys, we didn't have girlfriends or final exams to worry about. I got so much better at basketball when I was that age. I guess it's because we could focus. No distractions. It was just fun and basketball. I thought that maybe if I could make a new league like the one from my childhood, I could get some homegrown players of my own. It would take a few years to see benefits, but after that, it would be like a minor league system. Something to that effect."

With these memories in mind, the Little Cougars basketball program was born. "When the rug got pulled out from under my program like that, I had to try to focus on what I had and not what I didn't have. What I *did* have was a quality fifth grade Bantam Team [named for miniature fighting chickens from the town of Bantam, Indonesia]. I noticed how good these little guys were when they were brought over to play against the Riverside Bantams. Fast forward back to Blackhawk—I didn't have much as far as talent went in the high school. So, why should I focus on what I *didn't* have? Another level of burgeoning talents that I could cultivate myself were the third and fourth grade guys at Northwestern and Chippewa [elementary schools] who just loved to play. Who knows what talents could be hiding there? Why not use youth to build my dream program? After all, I was expecting to be in this for the long haul."

And that's what happened. The Bantam youth programs were shut down. The kids who previously played in the Bantam program or could play at that level would focus on in-house play and development for the future. The high school basketball players who were particularly talented would be offered a chance to coach the in-house teams. To them, this was a big honor. The teams of Little Cougars would play each other and have practices each week. These practices and even the games served to teach the players the ins and outs of the game. These little guys, whether they realized it or not, were being transformed little by little, year after year, into experts of basketball fundamentals and proper shooting techniques. And from there, they were ready to be molded by Coach Miller himself in high school.

A little ahead of his time, Coach Miller got a little good-natured needling from some of the men in the athletic department because he welcomed girls to the Little Cougars program just as fast as he would welcome the boys. It's not that Miller was trying to be a supporter and proponent of girls' basketball. At first, he admits that he had a more selfish reason for being so accommodating. With a smirk and a smile, Miller reasons, "Well, most of these girls got brothers, don't they? They're going to want to play too. Sign 'em up and then we'll get their brothers too. You never know."

He surely didn't know that in the decades to come, girls' basketball would explode in popularity. In fact, in 1996 and 1997, Coach Dori Anderson Oldaker, who calls John Miller her biggest influence, won back-to-back WPIAL championships for the girls. She would repeat this feat again in 1999 and 2000, taking the state title in both years as well. Lisa Miller would star on the first three of those teams. And in March 2015, the Blackhawk girls' team sealed the deal on another set of back-to-back Pennsylvania state titles. In a way, this championship can also be traced back to John Miller's Little Cougar basketball program that happened to allow girls to play. Bob Amalia, who was John Miller's assistant coach for sixteen years, now assists the Blackhawk Lady Cougars' coach Steve Lodovico. Steve played on Miller's powerhouse Cougar teams in the 1990s. Trace the roots back and it all leads to girls being allowed to participate in the Little Cougars basketball program over thirty years prior.

Currently, John's girls AAU program is one of the best in the nation. Drill for Skill Academy is littered with innumerable trophies and medals, and they are mostly from his girl teams. Shatori Walker-Kimbrough of the Maryland Terrapins, and Brenna Wise, a new recruit of the Pitt Lady Panthers, are just a couple of the girls who have trained with Drill for Skill. Corey Evans, senior editor of *Hoopseen.com*, credits his start to Miller and the experience he got running Drill for Skill girls' teams and working at camps. "There's nothing he really said that affected me and got me inspired. I just was blown away from observing him. He was always hungry. Here's a guy that's seventy years old with mountains of accomplishments and he's still looking around saying, 'How can I get better?' That was his mantra. He was always trying to improve Drill For Skill, the girls on the teams, and himself. We'd go on these AAU trips with the Drill For Skill teams. I'd get up early and go to the gym thinking I was doing good, and I'd have to rub my eyes to make sure I wasn't seeing things. But there he was already working out on the elliptical."

Back to 1978, during the first year of Little Cougars, about 100 third through sixth graders came out to play, and yes, some were girls. The kids would be split into two divisions. Third and fourth graders would play together as would the fifth and sixth graders. The stars in the eyes of these little players were the high school basketball players who were now their coaches.

All were encouraged to help, and dads volunteered to help round out the coaching staffs. The elementary kids already admired the older boys like Mark Kinger (Rider College) and the Dickinson brothers. Later on, Rich Dickinson would go on to play college hoops for Slippery Rock and his brother Steve would belt homeruns for the Pitt Panther baseball team. These "big" Cougars were like celebrities to the Little Cougars that they were training.

Coach Miller used this celebrity aspect to his advantage in the technique of the big kids helping the little ones to make the Little Cougars program succeed. The elementary listened to the high school student-coaches more than they would their own dads. The other side of the coin was that the high school players were benefiting too. Like every effective, experienced teacher knows, the best way to learn something by heart is to have to teach it to someone else. The high school kids learned the game better than ever because they had to teach it to their elementary-aged players who were assigned to them. They couldn't teach sharp fundamentals if they couldn't do them at a high level themselves. Point guard Dan Vander Wal remembers how much coaching a team helped him learn the game. "You think you know how to play, but you never really learn the ins and outs until you have to explain it to a little kid." Cooperative learning succeeds in the classroom. Why shouldn't it succeed in the gym?

Of course, there were doubters and detractors at first. Parents couldn't understand why their sons on the bantam team were suddenly playing in-house instead of traveling to play other schools, but it all became clear that the madness was working the very next season.

The core team of the 1977 Blackhawk Cougars erupted for fourteen wins in Miller's second season as coach. The squad missed the play-offs by only one game. This turn of events immediately stopped the chirping that the coach didn't know what he was doing. And as if to slam the door on John Miller's detractors, the yearbook tag line went from "A Very Discouraging Season" in 1977 to "Best Season Ever" in the 1978 edition of the school yearbook, the Ohyesia. Of course, the yearbook staff couldn't have known what was going on behind the scenes, but in hind site, the polar opposite statements used for the those respective tag lines illustrated the overwhelming effect Miller had on his team.

Obviously no new talent was found in the Little Cougar system just yet—at least none so great that they could affect the varsity level. But the high school players involved in coaching the Little Cougars sure seemed to know the game and, hence, play the game at a more advanced level. And when the teammates were brought together, it made them a stronger team as a whole. Additionally, John Miller introduced a much more rigorous practice schedule that year. As Miller's classroom became a well-oiled machine, more attention could be afforded to the basketball team. Stars began to emerge from the team in the 1977–1978 campaign. Miller's top player Bob Maher was awarded All-Section First Team honors. Dave Angle and Tom Feyka both earned All-Section Honorable Mentions. The team's future looked even more promising with much of the team returning for a go in 1977–1978.

As far as the "farm system," the Little Cougars program was tweaked as the years went by and a transition league was put in. Between Little

Cougars and regular school basketball, there was a middle school program called Highland Jump Shot League and, later, Cougar Jump Shot League. Wearing a t-shirt with the Highland Jump Shot League logo on it was an instant pass into the "cool" table in the Highland Middle School lunchroom. As a kid, you felt like you were part of the high school program, and in a way, you were. "The best part of the Little Cougar/Highland Jump Shot League," as Ohio State's Brandon Fuss-Cheatham attests to "was that the basics were taught to the little guys, but by middle school, plays were being taught. These plays were the same ones that were used in JV or varsity. By the time you were in high school, you were already trained in the system. It was just a matter of polishing by then."

Not only were the players and the coaches learning lessons, but Coach Miller was learning some things as well. Miller grasped that you didn't need a team of superstars to succeed. He could use the guys he had available in creative and effective ways that showed results. This "everyone has a part to play" mentality also fostered a more team-oriented approach. Everyone knew that he had to perform his role at a high level for the whole machine to work properly. Upon his retirement in 2003, Miller was quoted saying, "You know, I never really had that many great talents year after year. What I was able to do was really form great teams from good talent. It's been quite a ride."

Plus by now, some real talent was starting to emerge and come on board. After a relatively successful year two, more kids were starting to come on board. Future Pittsburgh Steeler Greg Best was a key piece of the 1978–1979 team. Along with scrappy Brian Harsh, Dave Angle, Tom Feyka, and Bob Maher, the Cougar basketball team was no longer something to scoff at. In the beginning, many of the best athletes at the school were pure football. For many western Pennsylvanians, basketball takes a clear backseat to football. So they didn't fully buy into Miller's program in year one. Because of the positivity, hard work, and dedication the coach projected in the classroom and his new reputation as a coach, many decided to go out for the hoops squad despite the whispered advise of boosters and others. They would stick with it for the remainder of their high school careers.

The beginning of a new era for the coach was at hand. Miller, who was embarrassed, ridiculed, and laughed at because of a 1–21 start to his career at Blackhawk High School, would never suffer such a lopsided losing season again. There would be tough seasons to come but none in which the Cougars couldn't at least compete to win with anyone on the schedule.

The unexpected success of the basketball program suddenly began to win over those athletes who had been going to other sports. And if they had an interest in basketball, they were able to dismiss the whispered criticisms that had dogged the program in Miller's first two years. In fact, forty years later, one player thought enough to call Miller from Maryland expressing regret for listening to people who swayed him not to go out for the team when Miller first arrived. He congratulated John on not only his success but also for the national success that sons Archie and Sean are enjoying in the college basketball scene. Miller explains, "That really meant a lot to me. Sometimes the fruits of your labor and the benefits of your toils don't make their appearance until years later. If you trust what you are doing is right, you can't allow yourself to be swayed by the negative messages that are being thrust at you every day."

So as it would turn out, as year three rolled around, even more kids on the football team realized that it might be a positive athletic experience to join the basketball team too. Things were looking up when the talented quarterback Dirk Yonkee and a six foot three, two hundred twenty pound tight end named Dave Dever played for the hoop team. With the addition of these two, Miller was looking forward to more success right away.

But, again, the coach wasn't going to be able to count on good fortune just yet. Just before the 1978 basketball campaign, one of his best players Dave Dever ripped up his knee during one of the last football games. He'd be out for the year. And to add insult to injury (or maybe the other way around), would-be point guard Dirk Yonkee followed suit with a bad shoulder injury. Because of these injuries and other factors, the Cougars would still be far from contending for any championships that year. The 1978 team would only garner eight wins that season, but the improvement continued. Most encouraging, a way of playing was starting to immerge; a system was beginning to evolve. The Miller Way, as it became known, would attract players to the program for decades to come.

And later in his coaching career, when a few players from the Pittsburgh area began selling homes and moving to Blackhawk, his detractors accused the coach of recruiting. Those accusations were no concern to Miller. "I had my blinders on, and I was setting my sights on the goal. My system was in place, and it worked. I wasn't going to try to go out of my way to recruit. If someone thinks enough of your program to sell his house and move into your district, what are you going to do? It's a free country." And the facts support what he is saying. If you look at the players who he coached over the years, there aren't many Division I guys. There are a lot of players who maybe went Division II or hung up their Converses or Nikes after high school.

Dan Vander Wal, a point guard from one of the early Blackhawk teams, touches on this. "The season was rough, but with Coach Miller directing things, it wasn't as much about the results as it was the work that you put in. The guys on his team just kept their heads up and just kind of knew that more victories were on their way. Even though we didn't have any real stat players in their group, they all felt that they were going to eventually succeed. That's how it was over the years. Miller teams are not teams where you have a star and build around him. They were teams where everyone has a part to play to make the machine work."

One of the most widely recognized names that John Miller coached was North Carolina University Tar Heels guard Dante Calabria. He responds to those who accuse John Miller of recruiting high school players even more directly. "You know why everyone hates the Floyd Mayweather, the Yankees and the Patriots? It's because they consistently win. It seemed for a while that they won everything every year. It was like that with us [the Cougars] I guess, but in a smaller, county setting. Every great sports dynasty gets accused of cheating."

"They accused Coach Miller of recruiting me. I went to Blackhawk since Kindergarten. I guess a rumor gets started, and it's much easier just to accept it and spread it than to look into its validity. It's also very hard for some people to accept that you can get that winning percentage from simply working hard and having a detailed plan. He outworked everyone. We outworked everyone. We weren't exceptional athletes, but we worked harder than the exceptional athletes that the other teams had. We didn't have guys jumping higher than the rim. So what did we do? We became the best shooters around. We handled the ball. We could pressure you. We worked on getting guys open. Putting the ball inside to cause the defense to react and then throwing it back out there and lighting up a three. We worked on that stuff. That was our thing. That part of the game takes an extreme amount of practice and sweat to make it work. But that's exactly what it was. Coach knew how to work. He knew how to motivate us. And he knew how to create a plan better than anyone else. It was as simple as that. There was no magic formula. It was just years of sweat and labor. That's why a lot of Miller's players went to colleges to play. They were taught a work ethic and a system that worked, and they bought into it. It worked for us back then and it serves player after player now in their business and personal lives.

"He's someone to look up to. I look up to him just like I looked up to Dean Smith when he coached me at North Carolina. You didn't want to disappoint either of those guys. He doesn't deserve in any way shape or form the illegal recruiting talk. It's way out of line.

Calabria also made mention of the Little Cougars program when trying to find the key to all the winning that would take place in the late 1980s and all throughout the 1990s. And it's true. The early years at Blackhawk and the Little Cougars program were part of a gradual building process that would become a record-breaking winning machine in a few years to come.

And in Miller's bubble of basketball and concentration, everything seemed like it was going well. The kids were definitely on board. And if you follow scholastic sports, you cannot help but notice that the athletic programs in schools are usually run fairly, sportsmanship is the rule, and problems are few especially when it comes to the students. The adult members of the community are usually another story. It is usually only when adults, like overzealous parents, boosters, and old letterman jacket has-beens get involved that ugly situations tend to occur. For Miller's varsity basketball program, this was starting to become the case. The students at Blackhawk High School were on board with football, basketball, and other programs sharing the spotlight. For the kids, it's almost always about having fun.

The football staff also seemed to want nothing but the best for the basketball team as well as all other sports. Unfortunately, football parents and boosters didn't always share the football program's public encouragement. It certainly wasn't the majority of them, but many stirred the pot in the community a bit, hinting that John Miller wasn't what was best for the school.

With some injuries that occurred and the lackluster number of wins during the 1978 basketball season, some of the adults of Blackhawk began to turn on the coach. They were not afraid to voice their negative opinions in the community. Some came right out and said that Miller's program was "crazy," and it was stealing players and, therefore, wins away from the most important sport in their eyes,—football. The goal by some of these people was simply to find a way to get rid of the coach. Around the community, the rumors and accusations began to circulate.

And every Wednesday night, the football boosters, known as the Quarterback Club, would hold their meetings. In those days, the smoky Corsi's Restaurant & Bar was the location for the meetings. In addition to the showing of films of the previous weeks' football games, card games and BS sessions broke out. Friends of Miller who were present at these meetings informed him that if his ears weren't ringing every Wednesday night, they should have been.

Meanwhile, Miller was taken aback and a little hurt because he thought that he was doing his best to support the football program. He knew that the football program kept student athletes in shape and interested in competition all year long. Specializing in one sport was not nearly as common in those days as it is today, and students would try to letter in several sports. Plus, multisport players would serve him well when basketball season rolled around. Many exercises and drills used in one sport can help develop the muscles and thought processes in another. Miller voices his stance by stating, "It was up to players and their parents whether or not they should play more than one sport. I didn't have time to call people and force them to just play basketball. These people had too much spare time as far as I was concerned. The kids wanted to play and improve. The moms and dads seemed to care more about the wins and losses than their kids did."

At first, Miller attempted to offer an olive branch to disparagers. To wish the football coaches well and hopefully gain some friends, John would make a point to attend the football games each Friday night. He would journey up the steep steps to the press box rising above the fields of corn and the football field at Northwestern Stadium to shake hands and try to be friendly. It seemed, though, that many of the football crowd didn't reciprocate Miller's gestures of goodwill and cooperation.

Another hurdle that the basketball program constantly had to overcome was that the players practiced in half of the high school gym. Ill intent was never proven, and it may have just been an oversight by the athletic department, but it was just strange that the basketball team didn't even have access to the entire high school gym. That year's Cougar basketball team was resigned to using half of the court while the wrestling team, gymnastics team, and others worked out behind a partition at half court. Plus, off-season football players were using the adjacent weight room, the water fountain, and the locker room.

The distraction became unbearable. Being teenage boys, the passing athletes from other sports would shout good-natured jabs at their buddies on the basketball team. Miller would have to constantly shoo these guys away each time practice was interrupted. This combined with having the team practice on half a court while the competition ran their practice plays on a full court put Coach Miller's Cougars at a distinct disadvantage as far as he was concerned.

Miller's first instinct was to try to simply work with the situation he had. He didn't want to appear demanding by making a big deal out of it. After all, he was relatively new at the school, and he was still in his early thirties at this time. His brain told him that going with the flow of things for now was the right thing to do. His heart, however, couldn't contain his feelings after the next two games went down the way that they did. Matters came to a head when Miller's Cougars lost by one point to the Sharon Tigers and by two to the Farrell Steelers. Directly following the second last minute loss, all Coach Miller could think about was that both Farrell and Sharon high schools prepared for their games in full court gyms while he was holding his practices on half of a court behind a partition.

A reporter from the *Beaver Falls News-Tribune* approached Miller following the loss to Farrell. In the heat of the moment, he let his guard down and spoke his mind. The coach let it be known in no uncertain terms that if he had been working his team out on a full court like everyone else, the score would have probably fallen in Cougars' favor. Now that the cat was out of the bag, he went on to say that it was the football team and the wrestling team that was using half the court when the basketball team should have been using the full court.

Miller expected a backlash once the words were printed. He didn't have to wait long.

CHAPTER 11

RESPECT

"I firmly believe that respect is a lot more important than popularity."
— "Dr. J" Julius Erving

One prominent powerful member of the community was quite unhappy with Miller's postgame venting. This person was also on the school board. To make matters even more delicate and potentially explosive, this board member happened to have a son not only on the wrestling team but also on the football team. He called the school and left a message for Miller to contact him as soon as possible to discuss the matter.

Naturally, Miller was a little surprised and intimidated when he was summoned to this man's office. He swallowed hard, straightened up, climbed into his Volkswagen, and decided to face the music. In an office building a few towns away, sitting behind an imposing oak desk, the school board member let it be known that he didn't appreciate what was said in the *News Tribune* article. He came right out and told Miller that he had humiliated the district by implying that they were playing favorites with the various programs. Miller's reaction to all of this would serve as a turning point in his career.

Miller recalls with honesty and satisfaction, "Right then and there, I had had enough. I decided that it was going to be better for me to be respected than liked. If I didn't stand up for myself and speak up right

★ Jay Irwin (51), Coach Miller, and Dennis Maher (21)

then, I would be walked on for as long as I coached at the school, and at this rate that might not be too long. After all, I believed that I was the one being taken advantage of. If I was in the right, what was I afraid of? I was the one whose job was at stake at this point. I don't know if I gathered my courage, or just blurted out to him that I wasn't going down without a fight and that I wouldn't be pushed around by anyone, no matter what position he held or whom he knew. At the time I don't think this guy was buying what I was selling and I could see that he was burning up, but as I walked out of the office, I could tell by the new tone of his voice that I had earned a little respect that day."

That wasn't the only bit of negativity swirling around John Miller in the third and fourth years at Blackhawk. Like the eye of a hurricane, though, the coach decided to keep calm, rumors and negativity be damned. What made him such a target right now, right or wrong, was the fact that the team was losing, so it made sense that the only thing that would shut these people up would be for his teams to become champions. He dove headlong into the study of the game. He devised new plays and researched the ways of Ed Olkowski, Francis Essic, Farrell coach Ed McClusky, and other successful programs near and far. He designed his team around promoting the strengths that they already had. He ignored the naysayers, avoided reading the sports pages, and set himself to toiling over game film sent to him from all over. The extreme effort in the gym, the film room, and the classroom would eventually have a big payoff, but for now it was easy to get discouraged if he lost focus. He had to force himself to keep positive and only concentrate on the day's tasks ahead of him and his team. A small sign on his metal desk in the gym office declared, "Look in the mirror. That's your only competition." At this point he would have been overwhelmed to think of all of the different problems coming at him. He had to train himself to be calm and focused, no matter what happened.

This keep calm, "eye of the hurricane" attitude served the coach well all through his coaching years. Unless he was actually on the bench trying to motivate his players, Coach Miller could be depended on to be level headed, even when the world around him seemed to be going crazy. The eye of the hurricane concept is usually a figurative one, but on one occasion it became quite literal. Fast forward to the summer of 1998. Coach Miller's assistant at the time was current Seton-La Salle coach Mark "Knobby" Walsh. It's a tale of inspirational calm during a natural disaster that had all others panicked. "We had sixty little dribblers at a camp near Pittsburgh in the summer," explains Walsh. "The sky looked kind of weird going in with this yellow look. Anyway it was hot, real hot. And we had all these kids in this rec center. The air condition goes out (of course) and we're thinking of maybe calling the program off for the day because the temperatures in the gym were getting pretty crazy. Meanwhile, more and more people are coming in. But when they do come in they're talking about how the rain is going *sideways*. I look outside and they're right: sideways. So there's no cancelling this thing now.

Miller disciple Mark "Knobby" Walsh distributing WPIAL medals.

"We just get underway, and I mean you could hear it really rumbling outside. I open the door and the trees are bending like in that scene with the little boy in *Close Encounters of the Third Kind*. To make matters crazier, there is, no lie, a trailer park right next to the rec center, and all those people get the idea that they need to move into the gym before their homes blow away. So in they come carrying blankets and what not. I look over at coach expecting him to be panicked or whatever, but no, he's chomping on his gum like usual talking to a kid about keeping his head up while he's dribbling.

"But at the moment the gym is getting closer and closer to being a fire hazard because of all the people coming in. Miller, though, has his blinders on and is still running his camp. He tells me to take some of the kids into the other workout area to give them some more room. But lo and behold, this workout area is actually someone's office. It's this little office.

"So I move the desk and chairs over and start working with the kids that I brought in. By now, it's hot! I swear that the tiles were starting to come up because the glue was letting go. I'm a lot better now as far as nerves, but back then I was more likely to get rattled. I thought I'd better go talk to the coach.

"I say, 'Coach, shouldn't we just hunker down and hope the storm passes? What's all this dribbling about? We're going to die here. The tiles are starting to come up.'

"And just so matter of fact, Coach looks at me and says, 'We can glue the tiles back down.' And then he pulls me aside and tells me, 'The storms going to do what it's going to do. These kids are better off focusing on playing ball.'

"Wow. Right there, he just gave his philosophy of life. And right up from behind comes this little kid from the trailer park. He had to have been about five. He tugs on John's shirt and says so cute like, 'There's a tornado out there!'

"And in typical Miller fashion, John puts his hand on the kid's shoulder, kneels down to his level and says, 'Hey man, we're doing hoops, buddy. Let the weatherman take care of that! We'll be okay, here take a ball!'

"And that was the perfect picture of him. Focus on what you can do. Ignore the things that you have no control over. The rest will take care of itself."

From 1989 to 1993 the Blackhawk point guard was Dante Calabria. He tells another story that illustrates just how focused on the task at hand Coach Miller was. "I was playing professional basketball over in Italy, and I injured my leg. I was back home rehabbing it, and I thought that I should pay a visit to my old coach. I came in the gym and started up conversation with Mr. Balbach, coach's long-time partner in physical education. It was the Friday before the Super Bowl, so of course our talk gravitated towards the big game. Coach was over on the side working on his plan for the next basketball game. I called over to him. 'Hey Coach, who do you got in the Super Bowl?'

"His response? 'Who's playing?'

"It's funny, but it was very typical of him. He was all basketball, and he focused on what he could control. Nothing else."

So staying focused on what you can control is the go-to plan for John Miller. At times, you can address problems directly by speaking up and standing up for yourself when you can, but day to day, the best thing that Coach Miller could do as far as getting the respect he needed was to simply focus and win. Point guard Dan Vander Wal, now a coach at the Calvin Christian Lady Squires in Michigan, came to Blackhawk in

1979. His father got hired as a professor at nearby Geneva College. He loved basketball already on arrival but says that he had no idea what he was getting into when he signed on with Miller's Cougars. Some of the first friends he made at school were on the basketball team, but he didn't realize at first that basketball wasn't really a big thing in western Pennsylvania. He mentioned that, when lifting weights at the school became sort of a problem as far as room availability, Coach Miller just found another weight room for his team to use.

Dan explains, "Luckily for us, the assistant coach Bob Amalia had a workout room set up at his parents' house in Patterson. At the time, I felt like if you weren't football at that school, you weren't worth anything. Which was hard coming from Michigan where football was big, but basketball was an equal sport. I mean it was extreme. When a school newspaper kid asked me how I thought we could beat Beaver Falls at football, I answered back that I thought a certain kid should be starting at quarterback instead of the one who was actually starting. Four smashed mailboxes later and a report that my name was used as motivational tool in the huddle, I learned just how extreme the devotion to football was."

But on the court, Vander Wal and his teammates knew that they were beginning to see something special even though they didn't have many wins yet to show for it. They heard stories of how Riverside was transformed into a competitor by their coach. A few things just had to fall into place. It only made sense. Not only was the program the same but Coach Miller's dedication, along with his demeanor and quirks, was the same too.

Vander Wal remembers, "Coach was so focused. And you just knew he was there for you, whatever would happen. He wasn't overly sensitive and wasn't going to give you a hug if you were feeling down, but when someone packs his car—I can still see it. Little green thing with Miller hunched over the steering wheel, probably thinking up plays—with his players and travels to the Hill district in inner city Pittsburgh just so they can see some real competition. The guy must care for you. Right?"

Vander Wal remembers another story that happened during a time out. "Coach had us in our huddle and he was holding his clipboard. Brian 'Manhole' Mansell was in a time out and had his head down. Now Brian, who was nicknamed Manhole because his shoulders were as wide as one, was starting to lose focus or maybe he was feeling a little down.

I don't know. Anyway, Coach responded by whapping Brian on the head with his clipboard. It was something I'll never forget—Coach just rapped him on the head. Brian looked up and Coach went right on with the game plan as if nothing happened. That kind of sums his coaching up for me. Nike might have stolen their 'Just Do It' slogan from the way coach worked. He had a way of making you understand that even if you weren't the scorer, you had a definite valuable role to play for the team."

For Miller, it seemed that as determined and talented as he was as a coach, he was still going to need some help from the ones in charge to push the basketball program in the right direction. He was going to need some help from others to enable Blackhawk basketball to compete with the other sports at the school. This help finally came from three very different places.

The first of these three was former Riverside superintendent Ken Yonkee, who hired Miller at Riverside. He was now the superintendent of schools at Blackhawk. He knew and respected John Miller from his work coaching and teaching at Riverside a few years ago. When he heard about the negative talk coming from the community, he made sure that at the next quarterback club meeting, it would be made clear that the gossip and the false accusations were going stop. It is unclear exactly who was contacted or what was said, but it seemed that overnight the negative talk stopped.

Once the talk from the adults was put to a stop, the pieces quickly— and startlingly—fell into place for John Miller and his Cougars. In 1981, the team won its first section championship. In December of that year, John Lennon's swan song "Just Like Starting Over" was constantly on the radio and would have been an apt anthem for Miller's career and Blackhawk basketball. With this achievement, Miller got a fresh start. He had turned the basketball program around and would not look back. The 1981–1982 team was just five years removed from the anemic 1–21 first season, but to the kids and the Blackhawk faithful, it might as well never have happened. Since then, the team had been the hardest working team around. Miller made sure of that. Basketball went from a source of laughter to a source of pride for the community in just four short years.

By then, the Cougars' section had been renamed Section 2. No matter the name, the Cougars had become the champions of its section. Not only that, the team was a semifinalist for the coveted WPIAL title and a quarterfinalist for the Pennsylvania State title. You would have been laughed out of the room suggesting a chance of a state title in the late 1970s. Even in 1980–1981, Miller went 3 and 19 for the season. And here the Cougars were, in 1982 nearly achieving the feat. Miller's Cougars had been the doormat of the section since his arrival but had just gone 9–1 in section play and 23–5 overall. The team even defeated the hated Beaver Falls Tigers two times that season. This was a new accomplishment. Co-captain Dennis Maher shared his feelings, stating that, "to beat your arch rival is always nice, but to do it twice is especially satisfying."

And in the Miller's first postseason, his team's first opponent was the North Hills Indians, a school from the outskirts of Pittsburgh. The buildup to the game was fever pitched at the school. Since the school's inception, the school's basketball teams had never made it to the play-offs. This was a very big deal.

And then it finally came—the night of the event that many thought impossible. The Blackhawk Cougars, the farmers on the hill, was about to take the floor in the play-offs. No longer were the boys from the suburbs afraid of the big schools—the city schools. A team that eked out one win out of twenty-two games a few seasons ago had become a team to be respected and feared. It was an event that would be one of the first successful milestones on the road to greatness as a coach, a team, and a program. The years of preparing, planning, working, and sweating all certainly played a role, but the outcome of the game may have been determined by a teenager's miscalculation and gaffe in etiquette. The mistake, though, was ultimately turned into a tribute—the ultimate show of respect and affection for a coach.

As tradition went, Coach Miller let his captain, who at this time was a boy named Dennis Maher, determine what the team would wear to the games. The team wore the appointed wardrobe to school, boarding and coming off of the team bus, and ultimately in the stands waiting for the team's time to go to the locker room to put on uniforms and get final instructions. It was a silent understanding that though color combinations and choice of tie were at the discretion of the captain, the team was absolutely to be neat, clean, and business-like.

At school before the game though, captain Dennis Maher gathered his guys together and told them that this time would be different. This was special. This was a play-off game! His deluded teenage mind concluded that it would look so cool if the guys would all show up wearing blue jeans topped off with a green and gold Blackhawk Cougars sweater. He didn't realize that all of the guys didn't have jeans that were appropriate. Some showed up in jeans that were ripped and faded.

"When Coach saw us sitting in the stands with our jeans on," Dennis recalls, "he hit the roof. His face turned beet red. When we got in the locker room, he let us have it. He went on and on about how we looked like bums. He went over it again and again how we came off looking like trash. I've never seen him so angry. And it was about fashion! I don't even think his pregame tirade even included one word about basketball or the running of plays. When he finally left us alone though, the reality of what we had done slowly began to sink in. This was maybe especially true for me. *I* had hatched this idea to wear the jeans. I had, without meaning to, insulted the man who had sacrificed so many hours for us—the man that we owed this very opportunity to. We should have known, too. Coach always looked sharp. He never had expensive stuff or whatever, but he was always in a pressed jacket and tie for games. Even at practice, he was tucked in and sharp."

As the teammates sat in that locker room looking around, the feelings turned from shock, to embarrassment, to shame, and finally, to a resolve to make things right. And the only way to make it right was to play harder than they had ever played in their lives. And, as Miller had stunned the team with his pregame rant, so too would they stun Pennsylvania by blowing out the favored North Hills Indians.

"As we ran out onto the court, I was in a state of mind that I can't really describe," said Maher. "I went ape shit. The whole team played like they were possessed. Again, we were playing North Hills. It was supposed to be a close game, but we made the game a laugher. And it wasn't because of some great game plan. It was all because we felt, to a man, that we needed to please our coach whom we thought so much of. And we never wore ragged blue jeans to a game again. That was for sure."

And they didn't. The dress was strictly business as the Cougars pulled off a one-point victory over Penn Hills to get to the semifinals. They were a hair's breadth away from the WPIAL Championship when they lost at the Pittsburgh Civic Arena in overtime to a talented Latrobe hoop squad. Still, for the once hard luck Cougars, playing at the Civic Arena was a delight in itself. Any further play, including their final loss to the New Castle Hurricanes, seemed to be a bonus for a team that wasn't used to this type of success. This year, though, the 1981–1982 edition of Miller's Blackhawk Cougars would be a template for the next twenty-two years of basketball excellence. Assistant Coach Bob Amalia calls it the year that the Cougars "got over the hump." There was no looking back from there. John Miller and those who had the unenviable honor of trying to follow his act would use his model of laborious work and smart play to fill the trophy case embedded in the wall at Blackhawk High School; the community had been won over. Fans showed up in droves to cheer on the green and gold. "The fan support was excellent this year," player Dan Vander Wal stated at the conclusion of the year. "It was the driving force to keep us going in the play-offs."

On a note of trivia, that same year the first slam dunk in the school's history was recorded. Jay Irwin delivered a backboard-rattling blow near the end of the game to shock a struggling Butler team. Apart from seeing Moses Malone or Dr. J flying through the air on television, high schools, especially Cougars fans, had never seen anything like that before.

Television strangely enough would hold a key in the giant leap of popularity that basketball would take at Blackhawk and, on a larger scale, western Pennsylvania as a whole.

Coach waiting for the state play-off bus (1982).

Late night television personalities don't very often affect high school sports teams, but the second person to forever change the lives of John Miller, his household, and western Pennsylvania sports in general was much more famous than a local school superintendent. His full name was John William Carson, but when he hosted the most popular late night program of all time, he went simply by the name Johnny. In 1983, around the same time that John Miller was molding his early teams at Blackhawk High School, the *Tonight Show* on NBC would welcome a small, skinny hoops phenom from nearby Ellwood City and broadcast him into the living rooms of America. His name was Sean. This youngster was personable, entertaining, and could work magic with a basketball or two or three or four. He also just happened to be Coach Miller's son.

Almost immediately after the show aired, you could feel the popularity of high school basketball in Beaver and Lawrence counties climbing a bit. With the talk of the TV appearance spreading through the school, more and more kids were deciding to give it a try. Now more than ever, Miller had the clout and cooperation to assemble and form the powerhouse teams that would earn him and his team places in the record books. It wasn't a matter of finding kids to sign up anymore. The only question was who was going to make the cut. Actually, Miller never had to cut players. His practices were so intense that only the strong remained on the roster. But that will be addressed later in this book. For now, let's hear how John Miller turned his smallish six-year-old son into a ball-handling wizard worthy of a headlining appearances in half-time shows, movies, television, and beyond.

CHAPTER 12

TRAINING PLAYERS
THE MILLER WAY

"Fear not the man who has practiced 10,000 kicks … fear the man who has practiced one kick 10,000 times."

−*Bruce Lee*

Sometimes life's biggest challenges and trying times turn out to be the greatest gifts. Years later we look back and say "Wow. I get it now. That's why that struggle happened. It was just a step in the process." The beginning of John Miller's record-breaking coaching success that he would have at Blackhawk began with four years of stress, struggle, and plenty of second-guessing from many. Looking back though, these struggles happened at just the right time.

If Miller wouldn't have had such a rough start at Blackhawk, he may have come home from practice content to eat dinner, watch some TV, and happily call it a day. As it was, though, stress at school and worries about his coaching left him needing a diversion—something in which he was in complete control of the outcome.

Miller longed for something to counteract the constant stress of coaching a team that was not only struggling but also seemingly being sabotaged by others. So each night, after John's wife Barb prepared dinner for the family, John and then six-year-old Sean would enjoy the meal, clean the dishes, and head to the basement for a few hours of "basketball therapy." Sean and his dad shut the real world away and replaced it with one of dribbling, passing, and finally shooting into a makeshift hoop bolted to the wall of their modest basement. Playing with his kid wasn't just healthy bonding time for the two of them; the "pleasant distraction" was turning his son into a world-class ball handler.

It all began like it does in thousands of basements and driveways across the country. Messing around with the basketball, playing games like Horse and Make It, Take It. As a coach, though, John noticed that his small boy could handle the ball at a very advanced skill level for his age. Even in the very beginning, he never slapped at the ball or did silly stuff. The other noticeable difference between him and a typical six-year-old was that, while other boys his age would tire and ask to do something else, he only wanted more and more basketball and more and more challenges.

Beaver County Sports Hall of Fame Coach Ed Olkowski recalls these early days. "John would do anything for that boy. He worked him hard all right, but that was okay in my book because I saw firsthand that it wasn't a forced thing. Sean seemed to relish the workouts and even look forward to them." This was fine with John Miller, who is a self-proclaimed basketball junkie.

It seemed like in no time John's elementary school aged boy could do things with the ball that would cause to stare in amazement. Sean credits some of this ball-handling prowess to his distinct childhood advantage: having a quality coach for a dad. However, he also notes a disadvantage that actually helped him focus on what is an afterthought of the game for some: ball handling.

Sean recalls, "Back in those days they didn't have the adjustable hoops where you could put them up inch by inch and work on your shot. For little guys at the time, if you were serious, you had one choice: You had to learn to dribble. So for me, after putting in the work that I did, dribbling two, three, and even four balls at a time became routine."

To organize these practice sessions, John made charts to record how many repetitions Sean did in a night. John made it organized. It became a true regimen that was to be done daily. He gave the drills names to help keep track of which ones were which. He created a workout routine that was quick moving, fun, and organized. It focused on rapid transitions between brief drills. After a predetermined set of repetitions, the player knew that it was time to move on. This cut down on frustration, and with the constant charting of progress, the player could see visually that his work was paying off.

If John were walking through the living room and noticed that one of the kids was on the couch watching television a bit too long, he would use a little needling to get his point across. "He'd just start on us (me and my brother and sisters)," Sean remembers. "If we were lying around a little too long, it could be the middle of winter and he'd let us know about it. 'You talk about being a college player. You say that is your dream. But it's not far away. Guys will be bigger and stronger than you. You have a court out there in the backyard. What's wrong with shoveling the snow off and getting in some practice?' Half the time I'd end up out there shoveling. And I'd be mad about it sometimes. I'd say to myself. 'I'll show him. If he wants me to shoot 100, I'll shoot 500.'"

Meanwhile, that's what John wanted all along.

Years later, John would bring his motivation and teaching to the masses when he authored his own instructional book and video series *Drill for Skill*. It was based on the methods he learned from "Crazy George"— whom we'll meet momentarily—and some tweaks John developed on his own. It was an instruction manual that dared the reader to put in as much work as Miller's players.

Starring in the video was John himself along with help from a collegian Sean Miller. Also, elementary student Brandon Fuss-Cheatham high school players Mike DeMonaco and Adin McCann, along with Archie and Lisa Miller showed that these drills were not just for the high school athlete. If done slowly at first and with enough repetition, anyone could do these drills if they had the drive and the patience. These drills were performed at blazing speed to show the finished product and then broken down with slow motion film to show detail that was missed by the naked eye.

The video included an opening that showcased Sean progressing from childhood to all-time assist leader at the University of Pittsburgh. The opening voice-over would be the first for now veteran KDKA sports on-air personality, Rob Pratte. Next, a motivational introduction featuring Coach Miller sitting with none other than cousin John Calipari. At the time, Calipari was the coach at the University of Massachusetts. He explained his relationship with the Miller family and gave a wholehearted endorsement for the lessons and exercises that were in *Drill for Skill.* "I've known the Miller family for over thirty years," says the very young coach. "I've watched Sean practice and master each of the drills in this series as he's worked his way through the levels to become the all-time assist leader at Pitt. If there's one thing I've learned during my ten years as a coach is that practice does indeed make perfect. But it's not just how much you practice that's important; it's how you practice. I believe that Coach Miller's *Drill for Skill* can help you develop the skills you need to play the game of basketball."

The accompanying book and its methods were endorsed by basketball legends such as Coach Dean Smith of North Carolina and Stu Jackson, the former NBA vice president and current Big East president.

Jackson raved about the series calling it "the best instructional video of its kind. I would not only recommend that every elementary, junior high, and high school basketball player view it, but collegiate players as well." Tom Davis of the University of Iowa praised John himself, calling him "a hard-working, devoted basketball coach and his ball-handling tape is proof of that."

The late Dean Smith, who maybe felt like he missed the boat when he didn't land Sean Miller for the Tar Heels, traveled back to Pennsylvania when Dante Calabria, one of Miller's stars, was dominant. He wasn't going to miss another one. He saw the series at the time and had no hesitation putting his seal of endorsement on the product. John Calipari rounded out the back jacket endorsements, calling the series "the three-pointer of instructional videos."

Though the series featured step-by-step descriptions with illustrations of each drill that he used to train Sean, Archie, Lisa, and Fuss-Cheatham, the focus was on the phenomenal oldest son, Sean. As the video opened, the viewer saw a highlight reel of Sean through the years, ending with him escorting his mom onto the court at Pitt for senior night.

"Pitt's all-time assist leader"

127

When the video rewinds back in time to Sean's boyhood, his father's voice is heard. It seems to subconsciously tell the viewer that anyone can do this if he puts in the work. He says, "Ever since Sean was six years old, he wanted to play basketball."

The drills were separated into categories of beginner, intermediate, and advanced. They used stationary, eye-hand, and moving drills with one, two, and even three basketballs. One drill, for example, called Rhythm, sent the ball swirling around both legs only to percussively drop to the floor creating a duh-da-duh-duh-smack! Duh-da-duh-duh-smack! Over and over again the ball went faster and faster. Beyond being an instructional video, it was a fantastic vehicle to display just how talented Sean and the others in Miller's stable actually were. The film had to be slowed down to show what the ball was doing in some cases. The video proved too that Sean especially had mastered Pistol Pete classics like the Ricochet and the "impossible catch." He also perfected with blinding speed others like the Butterfly in which the ball is tapped twice in the front of the body then twice behind. Sean performed this drill at a speed that made viewers shake their heads in disbelief. The video showed how even watching television could become an excuse to refine some of the skills of the game. In the drill TV Dribble, a pint-sized Archie Miller was on the floor looking up at an imaginary TV show while he tapped at a ball so that it bounced so fast that it sounded like a drum roll. This drill not only developed touch but also got the player in the habit of keeping his head up while he dribbled.

But where did all these drills and methods come from? Miller invented some of them, but most were taken from elsewhere and then refined. From that point, they were to be performed over and over by dedicated players serious enough to proclaim that they were training the Miller Way.

Sean Miller in an interview with ESPN.

In 1980, an experimental new cable sports network called ESPN interviewed a twelve-year-old Sean Miller. In the interview, he explained how it was his dad that taught him his skills. "The way I got started is my dad was at a coach's clinic, and he saw a ball handler named 'Crazy

George' and he was the greatest ball handler in the world. Well, he saw him and afterwards he went up to him and asked him how he learned all his stuff and if you could teach a little kid to do it. And Crazy George he gave him one of his books, called *Keep the Ball Rollin.*"

The Crazy George that Sean was referring to was Cleveland native, George Schauer, and his book would change the Millers' lives forever. Though a member of the University of Minnesota Golden Gophers basketball team, he was mostly known for his dazzling pregame and half-time shows. Known by some fans as the Gopher Trotter, he put on a basketball show that, for fans, rivaled the actual game in popularity. Upon getting his college degree from the University of Minnesota, he toured the country putting on the altered versions of the basketball shows for school kids. These assemblies combined basketball and humor with positive messages about listening to parents and staying away from drugs and alcohol.

It was after a clinic presentation held by Coach Ron Galbreath at Westminster University that John Miller approached Crazy George and asked him if he thought that kids could be taught his tricks. George responded by offering John one of his books for $4. Sean, brimming with enthusiasm, would take the book and read and work out of it until the edges of the paper were tissue thin, dog-eared, and tattered.

When the same ESPN interviewer asked young Sean how much he practiced, he responded matter-of-fact and with a smile, "Right now I practice two hours a day. I'm on a basketball team and we practice an hour after school. Then I get home and go an hour with my dad." Next, without being prompted, Sean shares, "Right now I hope to be a college basketball player and maybe a pro. That's my goal right now."

Keep the Ball Rollin'
The blueprint for Drill for Skill

Listening to this interview almost thirty years later, it is evident that the hardworking attitude and goal-oriented mindset had already been passed on to Sean from his father. The tone of voice and body language of the youngster conveyed to the ESPN audience that this boy not only could achieve these goals that he so plainly spelled out but also truly had a plan to go after his dreams and was enjoying their pursuit. Ron Galbreath is retired after 634 victories. He credits John Miller with "putting basketball on the map in western Pennsylvania, and his kids were a big part of that."

Dribbling show (Patrick and Sean Regan also pictured)

Many of the neighborhood kids were also into sports, including basketball, when Sean was young, but they were a little baffled at the extreme lengths that their friend took when it came to his dedication to the sport. They remember Sean in the driveway at a young age practicing for literally hours. His father wasn't there cheering or prodding him on either. He was out there on his own, wanting to do it. He was buying what his dad was selling. The success he had at camps and playing against kids his own age felt so good that he began to hunger for more. Neighbors recall the sounds of dribbling and, every once in a while, the thud of the backboard well into many summer nights.

Former Miller player Dave Vetica remembers Coach Miller's theory on the whole ball handling side of the game. "Miller is a firm believer that if you practice ball handling to a large degree, it doesn't matter who you are, you're going to be a player. If you ask everyone at the school who the best dribbler is in the school, and they point to you, you're going to start. It doesn't matter how tall you are." That was surely the case with Sean, and later on with Lisa and Archie.

One childhood friend from Sean's Ellwood City days was Doug Tammaro. He remembers, "There were days when we were at the end of the street playing football or Wiffle ball, and Sean was dribbling around the entire block with his left hand, and we were like, 'Hey, give it a rest.' And now," Tammaro jokes, "Sean Miller's the highest-paid person in the state!" Ironically, that state is Arizona, where Tammaro is a director for media relations for the Arizona Wildcat's biggest rival, the Arizona State University Sun Devils.

"All the neighborhood kids had a built-in hobby growing up because of Sean's dad, John Miller," Tammaro continues. "All the guys in the neighborhood played basketball." To the neighborhood kids, it was always a source of fun to play with Sean in the driveway or around the block. It was a given that he'd be out practicing.

But not to be mistaken, for Sean it was a different kind of fun. It wasn't "mindless shooting around because you were bored" fun. There was a goal to it all. Miller clarifies, "We would joke around at times, but it was serious most of the time. The fun came in knowing that the work would lead to success. The more work, the more success. The better the quality of work, the more success. Nothing is more fun truly than knowing that you've achieved something that you've set out to do."

Getting ready for the shows and ultimately preparing for a life in basketball, whether playing or coaching, is a full-time job if you're doing it right. "It was every day," Miller recalls. "It was what we wanted to do. It was every single day, working out in the gym, working on it to the nth degree. Our motto was, 'We're going to be the hardest-working guys out there.' It just came back to the same old thing: every day shooting the ball, every day handling the ball, every day working."

In one legendary Blackhawk story, Sean and Archie were instructed by Coach Miller to dribble from their house to the high school before each game. The trek involved crossing Route 51, dribbling through Pappan's Family Restaurant's parking lot, down a small alley where Ray the janitor lived, and finally down Blackhawk Road to the high school gymnasium. The length of the trip was approximately two and a half miles of dribbling. It usually took about forty-five minutes. Once, one of the boys (the story changes with each telling) bounced the ball on the berm where it hit a rock and flew down into a creek below. It was never to be seen again. When Sean or Arch (the truth is murky) told their father what had happened, they assumed this tradition would be finished. What they got instead was another ball sitting on their bed with the word "Miller" written boldly across it in Sharpie.

Today, Sean sums it up as, "You know, as a dad he gave me the greatest gift that one can. And that is attention. I was around him all the time. There wasn't a game or practice or any event in his life that I wasn't good enough to go with him. A lot of myself now as a person and as a coach comes from me watching him as a kid."

CHAPTER 13

CAMPS, CLINICS, AND CONTACTS

There's winning and there's losing and in life both will happen.
What's never acceptable to me is quitting.

-Earvin "Magic" Johnson

It's one thing to work hard in seclusion. There is value in that, but John Miller was always looking for something to "keep his kids going." In other words, he was always on the lookout for situations that would continue to motivate them further. "Ever since Sean was six years old, he wanted to play basketball," was John Miller's quote that opened his *Drill for Skill* video series. It illustrated Sean's inner drive to play, but John discovered that his kids would begin to practice harder when they realized that people were watching.

Coach Miller wanted Sean to experience a higher level of play. The first place he thought of was the Pitt Panthers Little Dribblers Play Basketball in '78 Day Camp. It was one of the first basketball instructional camps in the area, and it was designed for kids ages seven and up. The old Fitzgerald Field House on the Pitt campus would be filled with little kids slapping

---

* Coach Miller coaching Kobe, Sean doing his thing, and camp instructors, Magic and Bird.

at the ball trying to dribble and others struggling to "oomph" the ball any way they could to try to make their first baskets. Back then, the Panthers Little Dribblers had a few of their more talented kids perform during the halftime show of the college games. These performers were called the Little Panthers, and Sean

76er T.J. McConnell

was picked to be one of them. In fact, Tim McConnell, father of current Philadelphia 76ers point guard T. J. McConnell, performed alongside Sean as a Little Panther. Their friendship began there, and their mutual love of basketball lasts to this day. Tim McConnell built a great high school basketball program at Chartiers Valley. He credits John Miller's coaching style as the blueprint for his success. From there, after a detour to Duquesne University, his son T. J. ended up at Arizona with Sean as his head coach. "He's the last piece of the puzzle for what could be a Final Four team," Sean would say as he wooed him away from the Duquesne Dukes. As predicted, young McConnell would be a star at Arizona, and Coach Sean Miller used the media to express his idea that T. J. would make an excellent NBA point guard. As this book is being written, T. J. is proving his college coach right. He is a definite bright spot on the 2015–2016 Philadelphia 76ers team.

Back to halftime in the Pitt Field House in 1978. None of the people there knew what to think when they saw little Sean Miller perform. He was polished, he knew the game, and his skills were dazzling. One of the first people to take notice was the then Pitt Panthers' coach Tim Grgurich. He had seen some talented little kids come out to dribble and shoot during the halftime of games, but he had never seen anything like this. He was so taken aback by little Sean Miller's prowess that he scanned the field house seats for someone with whom to share the experience. As luck would have it, up in the stands was one of Pittsburgh's most prominent sports promoters. His name was Bernard Regan, but everyone knew him as "Baldy." Besides being a sports promoter, he was also the district attorney and a member of the Pittsburgh city council.

Coach Grgurich's eyes widened as he waved a finger to Baldy and then pointed to Sean. When Baldy finally found Sean in the sea of little dribblers, he knew what the Pitt coach was so excited about. Baldy was absolutely dumbfounded at what he was witnessing. He immediately stood up and, navigating through rows of seats, found his way to the court and to Coach Grgurich. "Gurg," as Coach calls him, then pointed over to John. Councilman Regan half jogged, half limped over to him and knowingly asked, "Are you the dad? Is that your boy?" John responded affirmatively.

Regan continued, "He must have a lot of practice hours under his belt. How would you like to have Sean do some work with the Steelers?"

Miller wondered aloud, "The Steelers? What do the Steelers have to do with basketball?" And more importantly, how did that involve Sean? Regan explained that he booked the World Champion Football Steelers to play basketball during the off-season. The money raised by the appearances was given to area charities. It was a great way to give back to the community. In these games, the Steelers would play basketball games against the faculty of the high schools in the area. Baldy decided right then and there that Sean's act was perfect for the Steelers half-time shows.

Miller thought of how huge the Steelers were at the time. They had just come off of their third Super Bowl win. They were the kings of Pittsburgh. He knew that when Sean heard about this, he would take his practice to new levels.

Custom-made Steelers uniform for the half-time show

Once he told Baldy that they would do the half-time shows, Miller was thrilled. The very next day he ordered a special top-of-the-line beautiful black and gold shiny Steelers basketball uniform for Sean. You would think that the flashy uniform and the chance to play with NFL players would have pumped up Sean and made him practice more than usual, but you must understand that it just wasn't him. To this day, John insists that Sean practiced and prepared for these shows as hard and with as much heart as he would have for an ordinary Ellwood

City game. He simply wanted to be a top-flight player no matter who the audience was.

But John does remember and admits to the thrill of it all. "All of a sudden we were in the locker room, man, with Franco Harris, Mike Webster, Larry Brown; it was like walking into a live hall of fame."

Though most of the shows were in and around Pittsburgh, one of the first appearances that Sean did for a half-time show took him to Evansville, Indiana. It was a charity event for a town whose college basketball team was killed in a plane crash. The town was completely devastated at the loss. The coach of the team was from western Pennsylvania. The Steelers wanted to do something to try to raise money for the families and to just help out in general. They went to Evansville to do the event, and they brought Sean along. You have to remember that John had to prepare Sean for the gravity of the situation and the size of the spotlight; he was only in fourth grade.

It was finally time to perform for the first time, and the place was packed. Baldy did everything first class, especially for this event. The Steelers were playing all of these guys from the Evansville Alumni. The first half of the game ended. And the announcement was made to not go away and that a show for halftime was ready to begin. Just then, the lights were dimmed and a spotlight appeared. Into the spotlight strode a first grader in a tuxedo holding a microphone. It was Baldy's five-and-a-half-year-old son, Patrick. Baldy was a great promoter. He had practiced the lines over and over in the car with little Patrick.

"Good evening ladies and gentlemen! You're here tonight to see the World Champs play the greatest from Evansville's past. I'm here to introduce you to the greatest ball handler in the world! Here he is, Sean Miller!"

And out he came. John Miller's boom box blasted out two 1970s songs into the crowd as Sean did his thing. They were "Boogie Nights" by Heat Wave and the Bombers' "Dance, Dance, Dance." Miller was quoted in the paper saying that they were pretty good tunes to dribble a ball to, and they lasted just long enough for a half-time show.

The capacity crowd of thirteen thousand went crazy when they saw what he could do. They gave him three standing ovations. Baldy Regan was quoted afterward, "To walk into that gym that night and see those people open their hearts was something unforgettable."

Miller remembers these older gentlemen coming down to look at the basketballs. They were regular leather basketballs painted black and gold for the Steelers. Miller remembers them showing their appreciation but also giving some sage advice. "This is a wonderful thing you and your boy have done tonight, but one thing—you got to get the paint off of these balls," they told Miller. "That kid's so good, people are saying that he's using some sort of trick balls. Leave 'em plain leather. You're doing the kid a disservice."

From then on, John only used regular, store-bought orange leather basketballs for the act. Once the red, white, and blue ABA balls became commonplace, they were used as well.

The success of that evening's game was reported widely in Indiana, western Pennsylvania, and other places. The headlines read, "9-Year Old Steeler Sean Miller Dribbles His Way to the Big Time."

From those Steeler shows and the exposure that they brought, Coach Miller and Sean caught another big break. As it happened, they were invited to give a dribbling show at the most watched high school all-star game in the United States at the time. Sonny Vaccaro's Dapper Dan Roundball Classic was the original and considered by some the most prestigious high school all-star game held in the 1970s and early 1980s. Sonny Vaccaro, from the suburban Pittsburgh neighborhood Trafford, is most famously known for creating the Nike Air Jordan brand, but before that crowning achievement, Sonny was running the Roundball Classic. His story has recently been documented in the ESPN documentary titled *Sole Man*.

Conveniently enough for the Millers, the Dapper Dan Roundball Classic was staged each year just down the road at the Pittsburgh Civic Arena. The NHL Penguins fans more casually knew it as "the igloo," and with one of the world's only retractable dome roofs, it was one of the most technologically advanced structures in America. Only the best of the best of the high school basketball world were invited to show off their skills. Much of the proceeds went to the Dapper Dan Charity Program. The Dapper Dan charity helped and continues to help fund the Boys and Girls Clubs of America.

Playing in such a huge venue, Sean remembers, "I was so nervous. You'll have to remember I was about nine years old I think. But I went on and did my thing. I just remember that the whole place stopped.

They focused on me. I was eight or nine years old and I got a standing ovation. I wish there would have been cell phones back then because I could do stuff that if I told you, you wouldn't believe. But after that performance one thing lead to another. I could've gone anywhere in the country and done half-time shows. That's how I ended up at the Spectrum. And that led to the TV appearances."

1978 Roundball Classic Program

And Sean was right. The Dapper Dan turned out to be another night of standing ovations and great exposure. The arena was filled to its thirteen thousand capacity—and not just with casual fans. A who's who of basketball celebrities and businessmen were present. Miller made many contacts that would lead to new experiences and opportunities for his family.

Besides that, on the coaching side of things, John met, for the first time, his biggest influence as far as shooting the ball. George Lehmann was at the Dapper Dan doing some demonstrations and representing Pro-Keds. Lehman, a shooting specialist, played in the NBA and the ABA from 1967 to 1974 as a member of Atlanta Hawks and many other ABA teams. Lehmann's biggest claim was that he was the first professional basketball player to make more than forty percent of his three-point attempts in a season, which he did in 1970–1971. When he saw Sean, he was floored, along with everyone else in the arena. He approached his dad and booked them to appear in North Carolina at one of the biggest basketball camps in the country. Press Maravich, Pete Maravich's father, was going to be there. John Wooden was going to be the headline speaker. This was a fantastic opportunity.

Legendary Coach John Wooden and Miller

By 1978, Lehmann was now hosting Pony shoes

sponsored basketball clinics at his North Carolina alma mater, Campbell University. There were about a thousand dedicated high school players at this camp. They were split up into teams and bussed around to several different gyms in the area. Miller gives credit for much of his shooting expertise to George Lehmann. He got to watch this true professional teach the same lesson again and again because he was always the last presentation at the clinics before Sean gave his dribbling performance to each group coming in.

"I was fortunate enough to have seen him do his presentation maybe forty times," Miller says with reverence. "By the end, I knew what he was going to say before he was going to say it. I got to absorb all of that information and make it my own."

ABA's George Lehmann on a bubble gum card and in action

In the early years, Miller studied many local high school coaching legends like Ed McClusky and Ed Olkowski, but outside of that, no one had a bigger effect on his coaching and shooting in particular than George Lehmann. He had an uncompromising way of playing the game as a whole, but what stood out the most to Miller was how Lehmann shot the ball. It was a smooth, quick motion that was identical each time he shot. It was more refined than anyone John had seen before. Miller studied him a great deal at the camps.

Lehmann wasn't just a great player and instructor; besides doing his camp and representing Pony, he was there as a sales representative for Pro-Keds athletic shoes. Moreover, George would go around to schools and sell Pro-Keds to the school's basketball coach. An inventor, Lehmann also developed what was known as the Toss Back machine. It was a high-tension net similar to a baseball pitch return but was designed so that it could be placed under a basketball hoop for fast shooting drills or placed around the gym for passing drills. It allowed the player to use his time as efficiently as possible, and if need be, the player could practice alone. You needn't waste time and energy rebounding each shot or waiting for someone else to pass it to you. The machine shot the ball back to you following each shot. The bottom line was that you could significantly increase the number of reps that you did in a period of time whether it was shooting or passing. That was right up Miller's alley.

Miller remembers Lehmann as such a big influence on his way of doing things. "Lehmann, this former ABA/NBA guy sort of stumbled on to Sean and I doing our thing. I watched so many clinics from him at Campbell University down in North Carolina, and they were phenomenal. He's got some videos out there on YouTube or for sale, and I'd recommend them highly. I learned the proper way to shoot the basketball directly from him and used his exact techniques back in my coaching career at Blackhawk, and I still use them today with the Drill for Skill Academy, my AAU teams. I owe a ton to George Lehmann."

During clinics, George was a ceaseless fountain of energy and focused motivation. Miller remembered him as being startlingly intense. "You didn't want to be that kid staring off into space because he might have thrown a ball in the direction of your head. He would set up his Toss Back machines all around the gym and fire the balls full blast at them and catch them and sink shots from wherever he'd be standing. All the while he'd be shouting, 'How bad do you want to be a player? How much are you going to work? It's your right to try out for your school's team, but it's an earned privilege to be chosen to play. And you must honor that privilege with skills to prove that you are worthy to have that school's name sewn on the front of your jersey. You must earn your place on the floor! Practice keeps your name in the score book and off the cut list.' That's quite a far ways from the 'everyone has a right to play' thinking of today. But man was he good at what he did."

From the camp at Campbell University where Lehmann was the head instructor, word got around, and Coach Miller and Sean began to perform all over the country. With each clinic, they got better and better at what they did. John became a master teacher, and Sean became a master ball handler, despite his age.

At a clinic in Wilmington, North Carolina, Sean's amazing skills were not lost on Greg Stoda, who was, in 1983, one of the lead sport reporters for the *Wilmington Star News*. He caught Sean Miller and his father in action during a half-time show during the Wilmington basketball tournament in which Coach Miller's Blackhawk Cougars earned a third place showing. Like Crazy George before him, Sean Miller's half-time performances would take center stage and almost overshadow the actual games in the annual North Carolina tournament. People that came to see their team compete in the tournament were noticing that this little kid Sean, though not old enough to play high school basketball, had more superior ball-handling skills than the teenagers on the teams competing in the tournament.

Reporter Greg Stoda wrote a glowing report in the *Wilmington Star News*. "The tape deck that blasts out the accompanying music for his magical basketball routine is very nearly as big as Sean Miller.

"When I interviewed the perpetually smiling, Miller, who is thirteen years old, he told me that he still easily wanders into movie theaters for under-twelve prices and probably will for several years, maybe even until he's old enough to drive. The dark eyes and darker hair only add to his look of youth and innocence, and that same look only adds to spectators' disbelief when Miller goes into his act.

"Sean Miller is a wizard with a basketball. He dribbles three at a time, spins them on anything that's handy—a finger, a can, his head, another ball—and shoots with remarkable accuracy from spots just outside the free throw line."

Sean himself is also quoted in that article saying, "A lot of my friends don't even know I dribble. I just don't tell them anything. I won't tell them I went to North Carolina, and they'll never find out." When asked why he was so secretive about his skills, he responded with, "Well, a couple guys have seen me, but my dad and I just decided that this was the best way to do it. My dad's a big influence. He played basketball and got me interested. I guess my goal is to play Division One basketball and maybe play on my dad's team in high school. But first, we have to move. We live twenty miles out of the district and we're having trouble selling the house!"

The fact that John Miller instructed his son not to talk about how talented he was, let alone the fact that his performances for collegiate and sometimes professional athletes were making their jaws drop in amazement, had less to do with shyness or modesty and more to do with the business-like attitude that John wanted his kids to exude. He didn't want his children to be show-offs. Miller is a firm believer in "Pride goeth before the fall." Too many times a cocky flamboyant "showboat" will be humiliated or end up a sad story on some sports documentary in the end.

To explain his thinking further, Miller said, "One big influence as far as learning the skills to be able to compete in modern basketball went was LSU's 'Pistol' Pete Maravich. I wanted to help my kids to be able to do tricks and shots and perform plays in the game like he could. I believe Sean, Arch, and Lisa attained similar dribbling skills and some of the shooting skills. Where I wanted to make sure we diverged from the Pistol was in attitude though. I wanted all of my kids and my students, too, to know that being an excellent person was far more important than being an excellent basketball player." There would be no flash, showing off, or showboating in the Miller Way of playing ball. He wanted his children and any player on his team to behave with dignity and poise whether they had won or lost. "When you do something that you think is great, act like you've done it a thousand times before. I think that has a greater effect psyching out an opponent than celebrating like it's the first time it's ever happened."

He goes on. "As far as the family goes, one thing that we're all about is treating people right. We're no better than anyone else. I made it known to anyone that would listen that Sean, Arch, and *anyone* in our family that is getting notoriety or whatever was because it was the result of the hard work paying off. It's surely not because we're special or better than anyone else. We're nothing special. If you let the work drop off, you're going to lose. You let you're intensity down, you're going to lose. And you've got to show humility."

Dave Vetica, Riverside High School star under Miller, remembers this side of the Coach. He remembers one of the final practices of the year when Riverside finished second in the section. This was quite an accomplishment for the time. Coach Miller motioned to Dave to come over for a word. "With an arm around me, he pointed over to two guys on the opposite side of the gym. They were two of our substitute players. They were guys that had just barely made the team. He told me to go over to them and to thank them for all the hard work they had put in. He made it clear to me that they had put in just as much work as the starters had and they were just as responsible for our successful season. Never mind basketball. That was a lesson in life that I'll never forget."

You might be surprised, but one thing John Miller was particularly proud of is that, in eleventh grade, Sean was named his high school's prom king. He explains, "It wasn't that I was happy for popularity's sake or whatever. The thing about that honor that made it special to me was that it was the *kids* that voted on it. All the kids—the jocks, the smart ones, the outsiders—all of them. If Sean would have been cocky or arrogant, the average kid in the hall is not going to vote for him. They must've thought, hey, this dude's all right. And that made me really proud. It's the same with Lisa and her Lion's Club Award. That meant a lot."

Sean may have been brought up to emulate Pistol Pete as far as basketball skills went. But as far as attitude and respect toward his parents and other people went, Sean would be taught to be the polar opposite. Like Sean Miller, Pete Maravich was also a child prodigy. Born in Aliquippa, Pennsylvania, Pete is still the all-time NCAA point leader with 3,667 and an average of 44.2 per game. This feat is even more incredible when you take into account that all of his accomplishments were achieved before the three-point line was introduced. Additionally, he achieved his records in only three years thanks to a long since abolished NCAA rule that forbade freshmen playing on the college varsity team.

Unfortunately though, as fantastic as Pete Maravich was on the court, he caused his family great grief. The more fame he achieved, the worse it got. His mom eventually committed suicide. His was a tragic story. He was a lost soul whose life, in its first two acts, consisted only of basketball and basketball alone. After an injury forced him to leave basketball in the fall of 1980, Maravich became a recluse for over two years. During that time he battled alcoholism and lived hard before trying to search for an answer to his demons. At the end of it all, he said he was searching "for life." To find meaning in life after basketball, he dabbled in yoga and Hinduism. He even ventured further into the bizarre when he developed a fixation with UFOs, but he did eventually find peace near the end of his life when he became an evangelical Christian, but he only lived a short while longer following his conversion. He toured the country for a brief time with Focus on the Family to tell his story. It wasn't long after though that he suffered a sudden massive heart attack, ironically enough, on a basketball court in the arms of James Dobson, Focus on the Family's founder.

John Miller knew he didn't want any of his kids to end up like that, so respect and humility would be taught along with crossovers and jump shots. Lisa Miller remembers her dad telling her time and time again, "When you're good, you don't need to tell anyone that you're good. Just show it on the court and shake hands afterward. On the court, don't show your emotions. Let people remember how good you played, not how you ran your mouth about the fact that you scored forty points. There's nothing worse than a show-off."

When discussing this issue, Miller throws his hands up and declares, "And that was it. That was how we went about our business. You played, you shook hands, and you went home. Later on, when Sean and Archie would meet guys like Julius Dr. J Erving, Larry Bird, and Michael Jordan, they didn't mention it at school the next day. I had them under the mindset that this is just what we're doing, and it's no big deal. That, at the time, may have seemed like a fault of mine. I didn't take a lot of pictures. I didn't tell anyone, 'Look how proud I am of my kids.' Any photo opportunities were quick shots taken by someone else." In this day and age of Facebook and Instagram, parents battle over who can send out the most pictures and videos highlighting how great and talented their kids are. Miller unknowingly teaches the lesson that maybe it's more prudent to keep these things to yourself. Wait until people notice how wonderful your family or kids are. It has a bigger effect then anyway.

At this time, people began to notice just how successful the Dapper Dan Roundball Classic was not only for its charities but also for its promoters' wallets. Before long, copycat events began popping up. A man named Bob Geogan introduced the Millers to two of the best and biggest basketball venues, the Derby Classic in Kentucky and the Capitol Classic in Washington. The Capitol Classic would eventually be renamed the McDonald's All American Game. Once this happened, it became a magnet for all sorts of basketball stars and coaches from college to the NBA. The father-son Miller team was one of the first to be booked for this big event. At the Dapper Dan, the Derby, and especially the McDonalds All American game, they would meet and, in some cases, befriend a galaxy of big-time basketball stars.

The Millers learned from and performed for Isaiah Thomas, Phil Ford, Dean Smith, Magic Johnson, Michael Jordan—the list goes on and on. McDonald's pumped so much money into its event that it couldn't help being the most fantastic and top of the line. Even the bus rides from the event to the hotel were something to remember. The McDonald's busses were beyond plush for the time with televisions on the ceilings. No one at the camp had ever seen anything like it. And since McDonald's ran the event, the campers were fêted with Big Macs, fries, and so on at the end of each day. Miller jokes, "I don't know how McDonald's came away with a profit with the way these kids ate. They could *pound* massive amounts of food. Some guys would eat four Big Macs. For Sean, it was great. He's with Isaiah Thomas. He was having the time of his life."

Of the players on this team that Miller coached, Corey Benjamin, Mike Bibby, Mateen Cleaves, Jason Collier, Loren Woods, Richard Hamilton, Stephen Jackson, Jermaine O'Neal, Tim Thomas, and Ed Cota would go to the NBA. Kobe Bryant would become a legend.

Meanwhile, other clinics and camps continued for Sean and his father. One particularly memorable one was held in the summer of 1976. It was called B/C Camp (B/C stood for Bolton and Cronauer), and it rivaled the famous Five-Star Camps that were firing on all cylinders at the time. The location of the camp was at the home of the Bobcats, Georgia College & State University in Milledgeville, Georgia, right below Atlanta. If the mascot was chosen as a representative of southern Georgia, then bobcats evidently love extreme heat and big bugs. Miller remembers, "In August when we were there, the temperatures in Milledgeville averaged from nintey-five degrees to just plain unbearable. We had no air conditioning, but we didn't care. This camp down there had the best guys from all over the country. It was similar to the McDonald's All American Camps on television now. You got all these guys coming in from everywhere.

Twenty-four teams of ten boys were there, so there were probably about two hundred fifty awesome players to meet and watch. I remember current Celtics coach Doc Rivers was there. Atlanta Hawks superstar Dominique "The Human Highlight Reel" Wilkins was there. He was a high school senior, and he was the most spectacular player I'd ever seen. It seemed like in every game he'd have seven or eight slam dunks. Again, I'd never seen anything like this before. When I got home, I remember sitting in the teacher's lounge at the beginning of school just shaking my head back and forth. I told all the teachers at the time to 'write down the name Dominique Wilkins. He *will* be in the NBA, and he will be a star.'"

At this time, John Miller wasn't well known as a prominent high school coach. He got invited to the Georgia College Clinic because of Sean Miller, who was a fourth grader at the time. Those in charge at the camp invited them to be the entertainment after dinner. Coach recalls, "When I agreed to go, I twisted a few arms and made sure that I could bring along one of my best players at Blackhawk. His name was Johnny Maher. It would be a trip Johnny wouldn't soon forget, and he would bring home a treasure trove of stories and confidence to share with his Cougar teammates back in Beaver Falls.

"Everyone played four games a day. At the start of the camp, they had a meeting for all the coaches. They included us to these morning gatherings because we were the performers for the evening. As it turns out, on the first day one of the twenty-four guest coaches had a death in the family. They asked me if I'd like to coach in his place since I was going to be there all week anyway. Let me tell you, they didn't have to twist my arm. This would be a chance to coach the best in the country and against the best in the country. What a learning experience. One of the other counselors was Kevin McHale for crying out loud. He rode our bus and joked around with Sean when we'd travel to the different gyms. Looking back, it was like this fantasy basketball summer camp."

John Miller was assigned a group of boys to coach, and soon everyone at the camp would see firsthand what people up north already knew: Miller could build a contending team out of almost any group of kids.

Miller remembers the game like it was yesterday. "Anyway, on my team they gave me, I had West Virginia University's coach Bob 'Huggy Bear' Huggins' brother, Larry 'Hambone' Huggins. You've got to love those nicknames. Larry went on to become an Ohio State Buckeye, so obviously he was good and I got the rest to quickly buy in to my way of doing things and play together in a short time. The camp was set up like a tournament, and as it turns out, the team that I was coaching got to the championship at the end of the week. Me with all these big-time coaches that were hand picked from around the country, and we were in the championship. Unbelievable."

It wasn't all basketball that is remembered on these father-and-son adventures. Rolling his eyes up toward the sky and smiling, John offers one more memory from Georgia College & University. "It's funny. What I remember the most clearly out of the whole trip was Sean standing up on his bed in the middle of the night. I looked over, and I thought he'd seen a ghost. It was actually a little scarier than a ghost to us Yankees. There on the floor of our room was actually just the biggest roach any of us had ever seen. There was nothing like this guy up in Pennsylvania. I think he was wearing a backpack."

It was truly a gift to be able to be there. Every night he performed for and spoke in front of a virtual who's who of basketball. Michael Jordan was there. Seven-foot freak of nature Ralph Sampson was there.

Chris Herren: Then and Now

Besides that, the two guys running the camp with George Lehmann were two legends: UCLA's John Wooden and Pistol Pete Maravich's father, Press Maravich. John and Sean were able to hear the stories, good and bad, about Pete right from his own father. "Can you imagine us, two nobodies from western Pennsylvania sitting at a lunch table listening to and learning from Press Maravich and John Wooden, the 'Wizard of Westwood' himself?" Miller asks. I mean this man won ten national championships."

One of the toughest well-known guys that Coach Miller has come in contact with in his coaching travels was Chris Herren. Chris was a six-foot-two guard from Durfee High School in Fall River, Massachusetts. He played college basketball for Boston College and Fresno State. He played professionally for the Boston Celtics and the Denver Nuggets and for pro teams in Europe and Asia. He has gained new fame from the ESPN documentary called *Unguarded*. It documented Chris's struggles with drug addiction. He is currently dedicating his life to helping others battle drug addiction with his foundation, the Herren Project.

Miller always knew Herren as 'Chrissy.' He was a young player when he was just starting out in AAU, a supplemental league for unusually talented teens. Miller had been coaching a Pittsburgh AAU team called the JOTS for many years. Miller explains, "We were playing Chris Herren's Boston AAU team down in Florida. I had to leave a little early to teach a camp and wouldn't be able to be with the team, so I had to figure out how to beat them before I left. I sat down with my assistant coach at the time, J.O. Stright to see how we could beat these guys from Boston. When we looked at the Boston team, Herren wasn't ever mentioned as one of the guys that could readily hurt you with the three. So when we huddled up, we made sure that the three-point guys were really covered, but we forgot about Chris a little. He was already known as a great player, but he wasn't considered that serious of a threat as a long-range shooter. When I got home, I called J.O. to ask how the game was. He said, 'Coach, they crushed us. This kid named Chrissy Herron had fifteen threes on us! He lit it up.' And wow was he tough. He was funny too. You almost enjoyed watching him and his coach Leo Papile and how they interacted. It was always an interesting and entertaining two hours. We were good, but we could hardly ever beat them. He was so powerful and mentally tough. It never entered his mind that they might lose."

At a clinic in North Carolina, John Miller and son were able meet and learn from a man whose story is arguably the most touching to ever have been documented by ESPN's *30 for 30* series. *Survive and Advance* was a film produced by ESPN about Coach James Valvano. To his players and friends, he was known simply as "Jimmy V."

Jimmy V.

The Millers befriended Valvano during his magic 1983 season as coach of the North Carolina State. That year he won the NCAA basketball tournament as an extreme underdog. After winning the championship, he famously ran up and down the court looking for someone to hug. His inspirational 1993 ESPY Awards speech was given just eight weeks before he died of metastatic cancer. In this speech, he reminded us that if "you laugh, you think, and you cry, that's a full day. That's a heck of a day. You do that seven days a week, you're going to have something special." He could have been speaking about John Miller and the successes of his family when he made his other famous quote: "My father gave me the greatest gift anyone could give another person. He believed in me."

In 1983, John's brother Joe, who lived in Wilmington, North Carolina, was setting John up with a multitude of clinics and demonstrations with Sean at various colleges down south. They had been scheduled to do clinics at the University of North Carolina, Wake Forest, and a couple of other smaller schools, but they couldn't get a booking with the biggest prize of the era, North Carolina State. Joe Miller, who was a great coach in his on right, was a little upset that he couldn't get in contact with Jimmy Valvano. As luck would have it though, John told his brother not to worry, because Sean, who was still just a sixth grader, was going to help him do a clinic in the Poconos, upstate New York, and Jim Valvano was scheduled to be there as a speaker and a teacher. Miller had a feeling from watching Valvano interviews and the way that he coached that he would be interested in the Drill For Skill method once he saw it in action.

The Poconos Basketball Convention was set up at a big resort and, as luck would have it, when the schedule for events came out, Valvano was on the schedule to speak right after John Miller's Drill For Skill demonstration featuring Sean's dribbling clinic. John was sure to mention Jimmy Valvano and the great job he was doing at NC State in his opening speech. He saw out of the corner of his eye that Jimmy V and his assistants were off to the side watching the Drill For Skill portion of the clinic.

John Miller remembers, "I saw his assistant give him a nudge to kind of let him know, 'Hey, this guy's talking about you.' Anyway, after we did our thing, Valvano came over to me and asked if I was Sean's dad. In his infectious New York Italian accent, he blurted out, 'Hey Dad, this kid's amazing!' Next, he tells us that he wanted us to do two camps for his Wolfpack Camp upcoming in August. And he really went out of his way to treat us right. He didn't just try to get Sean and me down there. He put our whole family up for the week, all expenses paid. Just talking to the guy, you could see that he was something special. Talk about positive energy!"

After Miller did his clinics at NC State, he gave Sean some Nike shoes. Valvano talked about getting Sean a Nike endorsement via Sonny Vaccaro, but he politely declined. John was still nervous about the whole issue of accepting money as a high school student even if the money was in the form of shoes. Miller explains, "As a coach, I had a Converse endorsement at the time, but it was just myself, not Sean. This would have been both of us on the endorsement. It was really difficult, but we politely declined. Years later, Sean was recruited by the Wolfpack, but it wasn't to be, as Pitt was the place for Sean. But Jim Valvano? One of a kind—man—we need more guys like that today. Even with all the success he was having at the time, he was still so down-to-earth. It made you want him to succeed. That's how I tried to teach my kids to be."

Sean and his dad then went to demonstrate *Drill for Skill: the Miller Way*, now growing rapidly in fame, for Tom Davis's Iowa Hawkeyes and others. He dribbled and shot with perfection for the players at the University of Massachusetts. Cousin and coach of the UMass Minutemen, John Calipari needed his players to witness Sean's skill firsthand to see what people are capable of if they truly puts their minds to it. All over the country, college athletes were inspired by what they saw this father and son team accomplish in such a short amount of time.

Subsequently, Coach Miller took his son to perform at clinics and camps including the famous Five Star Basketball Camp. Michael Jordan was in attendance, and even his Airness had a "shake my head" moment when then young Sean and his dad took the court for their demonstration.

After an initial display showcasing tricks and skills at these camps and college practices, Sean and his dad switched gears and focused more on motivating the players in attendance. One of Coach Miller's favorite parts of Sean's routine was the foul shot demonstration. Sean would routinely complete impossibly impressive feats that included sinking forty or more foul shots in a row. Even seasoned players at that point would be looking in disbelief. They would ultimately raise their hands and ask, "How does he do it?" At this point, Miller, playing the part of a wise sage, would hold up a scroll that he would introduce simply as "the chart."

Today Miller explains, "I have always been a chart guy. I keep track of everything when it comes to my teams and my players." After this, Miller stopped and remembered that his dad sometimes used charts to map out his progress with his polio treatments. "Wow. I never really thought of it. Maybe that had something to do with how I am," he said shaking his head.

"So it was the same when I was training my kids. When Sean would do his workout for the day, I would track statistics like how many shots were made in a certain time period. I would record measureable things such as how many times the ball could be dribbled in a figure eight in a minute. Each day, little by little, the seconds he could dribble three balls at once without messing up would increase. Anyway, as it was for other parts of the game, for his foul shots, I would write how many shots it would take for Sean to make one hundred. I would do this every single day. When we would run out of room on the first sheet of paper, I would keep it and tape another to its edge. Two pages taped together became three and then four. By the time he was good, I had this insane looking scroll of paper and scotch tape that stretched out to about twenty-five feet."

This twenty-five-foot-long behemoth became known simply as "the chart." At the camps, Sean would sink free throw after free throw as the crowd counted them off. Many times the number would approach or surpass fifty. Inevitably then there would be a player on the bleachers who would ask what he or she could do to shoot with the accuracy that Sean had. The coach would casually say, "You know, if you want to be good you've got to get at it every day and. He would pause. Well, it would probably be easier if I showed you instead of trying to explain it with words. Here's a little chart that shows how much Sean practices his shot."

At that point John would unroll this scroll of ridiculously long, taped together sheets of paper. The players and coaches at the clinics would crack up when the paper would reach from the baseline to the foul line and then continue to stretch to midcourt. At this point the players, who already considered themselves pretty good, would then turn serious and give each other looks. Miller then invited them to walk around the scroll and study it. Sure enough, it wasn't just a prop, when closely examined, you could see, for example, that Sean was 100/125 on September 12,

1982, 100 for 112 on October 21, and so on. Walk another five feet and you could see that he was 100/143 on July 4 and 100/134 on December 25. "He didn't even take off holidays!" kids would point out while shaking their heads. What amazed them the most was pain staking way that everything from shots to drills was accounted for. No one did that.

To this day, if you visit the Drill for Skill Academy, you will see bookshelves. They hold binder after binder with Sharpie written titles such as *AAU foul shots: 2012* and *DFS (Drill for Skill) ball handling.*

Miller goes on, "Talking about the 'star' players and coaches we came in contact with, I knew that most of these guys just wanted to get out of whatever camp or locker room we were in and live their lives. I felt bad making someone like Larry Bird, for example, hang around a locker room and take photos with us. He was basically a nice guy, but he was reserved and just wanted to get in his pickup truck and go home."

When Miller had the opportunity to work a camp with Ervin "Magic" Johnson, however, it was a completely different story. Magic, unlike Bird, completely embraced the spotlight.

Magic rolled up in a limousine, got out, and did one of the most carefully thought-out clinics that Miller had ever seen. The hundreds of kids there hung on every word. He told his life story to the kids through the stages of his basketball play. He described growing up in a rough neighborhood in Lansing, Michigan. There, he would have to get up extra early to make it ten blocks to the courts to practice before the seedier element woke up and took it over. He talked about how he took his basketball with him everywhere he went including bed. The basketball was his teddy bear.

Next, he talked about his high school playing career. He really made the kids at the camp identify with him. He talked about how he went through the same school problems that they did. He got a big laugh when he was talking about his middle school team. Magic, with his big smile, looks around at the kids and said, "The best part, kids, was in eighth grade. When I came into the gym with my guys I looked to the sideline. And guess what I saw?" At this Magic slyly looked to his left and then right. "Cheerleaders! Real girls were cheering for us! Now I knew I had to do my best!"

At the end of Magic's clinic, he stood for a good half hour exchanging words and high fives with all of the campers. After that, he got in his limo with a personalized "MAGIC – 1" on the back plate and off he went. It was something that John and his son would never forget.

It was definitely beneficial for Sean and, later on, Archie to see these "stars" for what they were—just people. Some were shy, some were cocky, some were nice, some were not so nice, some were funny, and some were serious. For the most part, they were hardworking people who sweated like crazy to get where they were. These experiences may have shown Sean that it was possible for him to play near the high levels that people like Magic Johnson, Larry Bird, Isaiah Thomas, and Michael Jordan reached.

Similarly, John Miller advised his kids against the sports hero worship that is so prevalent today. "When it comes to sports, I taught my kids not to focus on getting so and so's rookie card. Focus on practicing making a good pass like the person on the card makes. Don't focus on getting such and such's autograph. Focus on practicing making shots over and over so that when the time comes, you can make a free throw under pressure just like he does."

That's exactly what Sean, Archie, and his dad did. They focused on their own game. Archie in particular was a deadly accurate shooter. And, naturally, when Coach Miller would bring his kids to the high school practices that he was running, they would practice off to the side. John noticed that when his high school players sneaked a peek at Sean's, Arch's, or Lisa's dribbling, they were not only amused by their skills but also motivated to do better and practice more. If Coach's little kid could control the ball like this, why not them? If this little guy was performing at camps all over the country, then they surely could step it up and do a few more hours a week on ball handling and proper shooting.

Importantly, Sean and his dad weren't allowed to accept a dime for all of this work at clinics and other performances. A couple places in Pittsburgh offered $500 for Sean to perform. Miller's concern was that if he took the money, it would affect Sean's eligibility in later years. NCAA rules specifically state that players cannot be paid for playing no matter what the circumstance. Doing things the right way was a difficult but important decision that the Coach had to make.

"People around me thought I was crazy. They were saying things like, 'Come on John, this is stupid! Take the money. He's only a little kid, and you need the money. It could help. You're trying to make it work with your teaching salary,' they would tell me. So I called the NCAA and the Pennsylvania Interscholastic Athletic Association (PIAA) offices a couple of times and tried to explain. No one could come up with a real answer, so they just always ended up saying no in the end. I even got a friend who happened to be a lawyer, to take a look at the situation, and he couldn't find a way. So we ended up just doing the stuff for free."

In the end though, what they were getting was way more valuable than $500. Sean, in fact, was being conditioned to have nerves of steel, even in front of massive audiences. Though these clinics and appearances were all unpaid, he was making invaluable connections with people who he and his father never would have gotten to meet otherwise.

John, to this day, credits these clinic experiences for how well spoken his boys are in front of a microphone. They are two of the most articulate, well-spoken coaches in the sport. They both are stars of talk shows and appear in commercials in their areas. The *Sean Miller Show* in Tucson and the *Archie Miller Show* are shown on television, heard on radio, and streamed on various Internet outlets.

And as it would turn out, Sean would need those public speaking skills sooner rather than later. He would shortly be expected to speak in front of millions of people on three different occasions. The audience he would be speaking to and performing for would include a couple hundred people in two different studios in California. Two of these performances would be taped and then broadcast into a couple million homes across the country. The first, though, would be filmed in nearby Moon High School gym, where his dad grew up. The images filmed would be shown in movie theatres all over the world. Little Sean Miller was about to go Hollywood.

CHAPTER 14

CHANCES OF A LIFETIME

PART 1:
THE FISH THAT SAVED PITTSBURGH

"If your ship doesn't come in, swim out and meet it."
—Jonathan Winters, costar of The Fish That Saved Pittsburgh

The fish that the movie title is referring to is the astrological sign Pisces. And in the film, Pisces would play a key role. So yes, you could say that success seemed to be in the stars for Sean Miller in 1979. Between performing with his father at clinics and half-time shows near and far, the young student then attending Ellwood City Elementary School was picked to perform in a motion picture called *The Fish That Saved Pittsburgh*. A sports fantasy film, it featured big stars of the day. Among the cast were Jonathan Winters, Flip Wilson, Stockard Channing, Debbie Allen, and Michael Gazzo of *The Godfather*, who earned an Oscar as mobster Frank Pentangeli. Despite the star power, the movie was a flop at the box office.

But even though critics deemed the quality of the script subpar, *The Fish* has enough basketball goodies in it that people still talk about it today. Made at the tail end of the disco era, the soundtrack is filled with wah-wah pedals and slick 1970s dance beats. The clothes that the characters wear are as funky as the soundtrack. In recent years, the movie has slowly garnered a sort of cult following. One of the most redeeming aspects of the movie is the identity of its lead character. For the first time, years before Michael Jordan lit up the screen in *Space Jam*, the main star of the film was an NBA player. It was someone who could never be considered a failure. After all, he was a doctor.

Julius Erving, more famously known as Dr. J, played an elite ABA star named Moses Guthrie. To succeed at this role, he simply had to be himself. Like the Buck Owens song "Act Naturally," that's all he really had to do. In one particularly memorable segment, the doctor showcases his real-life skills. In a memorable montage set to disco funk, he flies through the air to slam home dunk after dunk at a neighborhood basketball court. At last count, this playground sequence has garnered over 43,000 hits on YouTube.

The film itself features a storyline that follows Moses Guthrie, the star of the Pittsburgh Pythons, a fictional ABA team. Moses is the best and flashiest player on the team, but the team is the worst in the league. He is so superior to the rest of his team that the other players quit. They believe that Moses is hogging the spotlight of the media.

When a concerned water boy approaches a neighborhood astrologist Mona, he convinces her to try to solve the team's problems. She gives the following spiritual advice: form a team around the astrological sign, Pisces, the fish. It was in the stars that with that sign, success would come to Moses Guthrie and the rest of the Pythons, that would, of course, need to first change the name of the team to the Pisces.

Following Mona's advice, the Pisces hold open tryouts to find new players that have birthdays ranging from February 19 to March 20. In the only scene in which Sean Miller appears, a sea of players swarm to the Moon High School gymnasium where tryouts are being held. Comically, these players are mostly freaks and weirdos who have no chance of making the team. The pickings are so slim in fact that the coach (played by soap opera and *NYPD Blue* actor Nicholas Pryor) approaches an obviously too young and, hence, too short Sean Miller and asks, "How tall is your mother?" Sean is too busy dribbling four basketballs at once to answer. All the while, on the soundtrack, the Four

Tops perform a disco tune called "Chance of a Lifetime," which is pretty appropriate for young Sean in particular.

With that, movie audiences witnessed the beginning and the end of Sean Miller's movie career. In the process of filming his part though, he was able to meet Dr. J and a host of other stars.

As stated before, *The Fish That Saved Pittsburgh* has been almost completely lost to obscurity, but according to its director Gary Stromberg, it is ranked in many top-ten sports films lists. Shaquille O'Neill and Donovan McNabb are reportedly big fans of the movie.

The director was surprised to learn Sean Miller's whereabouts in 2014. "I remember that kid from the movie," Stromberg said in a telephone interview with the *New York Times*. "I didn't realize that was the Arizona Wildcat's Coach Sean Miller until just now. I had no idea he became a coach."

John Miller remembers the experience. "When they filmed Sean's part in that gym in Moon, it was just like when you see it in the film clips. All these people just showed up wanting to be in the movie. We were invited, a few others were invited, and a few other strange people just showed up. The craziest thing that I remember from the experience was that the movie producer wanted a real biker gang to be in the gym as if they were in line to try out for the team. Well, that's exactly what they got: a real, hardcore biker gang. There were about fifteen guys, head to toe in leather, chains, and tattoos. They were all on their Harley-Davidsons revving their engines as loud as they could *inside* the gym. It was nuts. After a while, they started getting out of control. They proceeded to peel out and do burn outs on the gym floor! Finally, the film crew threatened to call the police, and, after that, the bikers all left. They never appeared in the final cut of the film.

"But Sean was able to meet Dr. J, and it was a good experience and everything but that was the extent of it. It was merely a day trip. We went to the Moon gym, Sean did his thing for a few minutes while they filmed, and we went to lunch and back home. It took about a year to produce the entire movie, so we kind of forgot about it. And then about a year later, we went to the movies up by the mall and there he was, up on the screen. His part only lasted for less than a minute, but it was amazing. Imagine driving up to the mall theatre with your kid to see a movie that he was in. An Al Pacino movie is playing in the next theatre. Pretty cool."

But Sean's appearance in *The Fish* was a minor part. What was to come for the Millers was anything but minor. It wouldn't be long when arguably the most powerful man in show business at the time was going to announce Sean Miller on his show as the main attraction.

PART 2:
AN AUDIENCE WITH THE KING

"Talent alone won't make you a success.
Neither will being in the right place at the right time, unless you are ready.
The most important question is: 'Are you ready?'"

–*Johnny Carson*

You must not forget that John Miller was taking Sean to all of these clinics, camps, and practices, while at the same time teaching full-time and coaching high school basketball. For most people, they only have enough energy and time to *try* to make life work. For teachers, it's common knowledge that it is a struggle to make enough time for their families while still getting all of the work done at school. There were times when the obligations of being an educator or coach simply wouldn't allow John to take his son to every place that was clamoring to see him perform. For this, Miller had a close friend take Sean to the various gyms and schools that were on the schedule. It was at one of these sessions in which John was absent that a basketball and show business legend was blown away by the youngster's skills.

Fred Neal, otherwise known as the Harlem Globetrotters' "Curly Joe," was present at one of the 76ers' half-time shows and was astonished. He called a few people, and unexpected doors began to open for the Millers.

Back in March of 1983, you must remember that in the United States, people had perhaps six television channels from which to choose. In Ellwood City, the Millers' hometown at the time, people had the three big networks that served the Greater Pittsburgh area. The call letters KDKA, WTAE, and WPXI represented the three main channels. If you had an especially nice TV, you could pick up a few UHF stations and Channel 13 if you wanted to watch public television. Only a small minority had cable television.

With so few choices, an appearance on network television was a much bigger deal than it is now. At the water cooler and break room at work, or in the halls of high schools, everyone gabbed about the same shows. Memorable shows including *Dallas* and *Magnum P.I.* were dominating the prime time, and the undisputed king of late night television was Johnny Carson of the *Tonight Show*. Being the king, he summoned acts from all over the country to entertain him. Most would be Hollywood actors and musicians, but Carson still included some vaudeville-style variety on the *Tonight Show*. When his staff heard about Sean Miller, the young basketball wizard, the king of late night just had to have him on the show. That night over seventeen million people would see the show.

The appearance was unforgettable to those who watched. It seemed that everyone in western Pennsylvania had tuned in. Though Sean was an expert at what he was doing by now, he came off as down to

Johnny Carson: King of late night television

earth, polite, and likable. The first thrill was having his name announced by Ed McMahon while simultaneously appearing across the television screen. Doc Severinsen was on vacation, so Tommy Newsom led the *Tonight Show* Orchestra. The orchestra played its characteristic swing introduction as master of ceremony Ed McMahon opened the show. Abruptly, the music stopped and only a dramatic tympani roll remained. At this point McMahon used his baritone voice to trumpet the phrase that by then was a television trademark "And now, Heeeeeeere's Johnny!" Bam! The multicolored curtains parted, and out from behind them came the beaming and welcoming show business legend, Johnny Carson.

Back in the dressing room, Sean and the other guests could hear the muffled laughs Mr. Carson's monologue elicited from the audience. After an opening comedy sketch called "The Cycle of Nature in Los Angeles," it was Sean's turn to entertain the studio audience and the multitude of viewers tuning in at home.

Johnny, holding his standard small stack of cards, tapped them and introduced the thirteen-year-old Ellwood City native. "He's said to be a wizard with a basketball, and I think you're going to love him. He's the star attraction. Here's Sean Miller."

To the applause of the studio audience, Sean, dressed in an unassuming red polo shirt and khakis, smiled and walked over to the place that showed that you had "made it" in show business: the comfortable chair just to the left of Johnny's desk. Ed McMahon stood and moved to the adjacent couch as the king of late night invited Sean to have a seat. It was March 14, 1983, 11:43 p.m. and a dream was coming true. America was watching John Miller's thirteen-year-old son.

To start things off, Johnny and Sean talked about his background and the story behind his precocious talent. Sean drew a hearty laugh from Johnny and the audience when he told a story explaining how he learned to play so well at a young age. "Well, I have been doing this since I was six years old. And how I got started was my dad's a high school basketball coach. And he's just an ordinary high school coach. And he went to a coach's clinic."

At this Johnny smiles and interrupts to set the bait, "Now what do you mean when you said he was just ordinary?"

Sean nodded his head; he then smiled back and said, "Well, he loses more than he wins." And at this point in time, Sean was right.

Johnny loved that remark and repeated back, "He loses more than he wins." The audience was filled with laughter. "I guess that takes care of dad."

Sean continued to tell his story, including his dad's training him, the Crazy George stuff, and how he's been doing his routine at Five Star camps. "People see me at these camps, and they ask me to perform all around, and I guess that's why I'm here." For this, he was given more laughter and applause. One can tell watching that Johnny Carson and the audience were charmed immediately. After a commercial break, Johnny asked Sean one final question about his personal foul shot record. "Well, one time when I was in Wichita, Kansas, for a halftime at an all-star game, I hit fifty in a row."

Johnny, wide-eyed, leaned back and said, "Wow! Fifty!"

Very matter of fact, Sean came back with a dry response. "Yeah, it took a long time. The teams had to wait to come back on the court." Mr. Carson, with a wry smile, leaned back on his chair and chuckled at Sean's matter-of-fact answer. He then invited him onto the main stage by the band to do his dribbling show for America.

Dressed in white leather Converse high tops, khakis, and a red collared shirt, Sean began his routine. He pounded out a tempo with two basketballs, and soon, Tommy Newsom and the *Tonight Show* Orchestra began to follow by playing funky disco background music. Sean began by dribbling two basketballs first high, then low, then through the legs and behind the back. He lets one purposely drop only to spin it on top of the others. Ed Shaughessy, the *Tonight Show* drummer, played his high hat cymbals with a rolling beat pattern that mimicked the motion of Sean's manic but controlled moves. To the delight of the studio audience, and no doubt, the people watching at home, Sean continued with his routine by adding a third and a fourth ball to his dribbling routine. Lastly came a big finish that included juggling three basketballs and spinning two. The routine ended with a proud pose with one hand on his hip and the other spinning one single ball next to his obviously proud face. It all wrapped up in perfect time with the music as the *Tonight Show* Orchestra ended with one big note. The applause was thunderous.

Wide-eyed Carson was genuinely taken aback. "That's sensational. I don't believe it. Well, they told me that you were real good. You're better than that. That's sensational. Teach me one trick, just anything."

Sean obliged and warned, "Ok, but this is a dangerous one."

"This is dangerous?"

Sean had a big smile by now. "Yeah. Okay what you do is you put the ball like this, and you throw it through your legs. Be careful though." Bam! Sean slammed the ball precariously through his legs with both hands and caught it behind him. The display left no doubt in the minds of the *Tonight Show* audience what Sean meant by dangerous. Sean was a middle school boy, after all. They exploded with applause, hysterical hoots, whistles, and laughter.

After a pitiful attempt that sent the ball into the orchestra, Mr. Carson meekly asked, "What did I do wrong?"

Sean just shook his head and replied, "Just a little too hard. You gotta go soft at the end." Immediately, Johnny tried again and this time the basketball hit "home." This of course sent the audience into hysterics.

With a little grimace, Johnny looked toward the camera. "Ok, moving along then. Do you have another one I could try?"

"Sure. This one is for sound. You really hear this one." To round out the segment, he demonstrated a quick lesson on the impressive and percussive drill called "Rhythm." At the completion, Sean looked at Johnny as if to say, "Your turn."

In true Carson fashion, Johnny drew laughs by staring thoughtfully, yet cluelessly, at the basketball he was holding. He let out a sigh, smiled, and uttered a sarcastic, "No problem. Can you show me how to spin a ball? That looks easy." Failing at this feat as well, Carson asked if there's a hole in ball that he can use to hold it on his finger. He applauded Sean once again and extended an open hand toward him. "Sean Miller, ladies and gentlemen!"

The appearance on the *Tonight Show* was a success.

Years later John Miller remembers, "It's like it was yesterday. You don't forget an experience like that. I was lying in the living room floor with a couch pillow under my head. I was watching my boy on the *Tonight Show*. Unreal."

As far as Sean's basketball exposure, things were starting to snowball. The appearance on the *Tonight Show* was such a hit, that soon a new show titled *That's Incredible!* was interested in featuring Sean and his talents. Like Robert L. Ripley's *Ripley's Believe It or Not!*, *That's Incredible!* featured people from all over the world doing fascinating and unbelievable stunts along with stories of the paranormal and the just plain weird, *That's Incredible!* had a star studded cast that included

football legend Fran Tarkenton, Actress Cathy Lee Crosby, and actor, singer, and game show host John Davidson. This show was a big deal, even reaching number three in the Nielsen Ratings at the show's peak. The show would reach close to twenty million viewers each week.

Performing in prime time on ABC

Coach Miller remembers, "When people from our home town [Ellwood City] heard about this, they were really excited. The only person from there to make it onto TV before this was baseball hall of famer Hack Wilson, and he had been dead since the forties. It was one thing for Sean to go out to California for the *Tonight Show*, but this time Hollywood would come to little Ellwood City.

It was all so surreal when it started. Like in a dream, Sean was booked to do his thing at the Philadelphia Spectrum during the halftime of a 76ers/Bulls game. It was a thrill just to be doing that, and as if that wasn't enough, Hollywood agents approached the family about a TV appearance hoping that John would approve.

They introduced themselves as people who worked for the ABC Network.

Sean at the Philadelphia Spectrum

"First we're going to take him to California. With your approval, we're going to tape him in the studio with Fran Tarkenton, Cathy Lee Crosby, and John Davidson. He'll do a performance similar to the one he did on the *Tonight Show*, but that's only going to be the beginning. We want to show him in his element in Ellwood City and actually playing in a game," they explained to Miller.

In addition to the studio performance, the producers wanted to have Sean perform a few stunts in unusual settings to show how brilliant his dribbling actually was. It was the nature of the show to do the unexpected. They rented out the local grocery store Loccisano's Golden Dawn.

Rewind a month. Down the block and up the hill to Crescent Avenue is Lincoln Junior-Senior High School. Imagine you are a student here. The day begins as usual. The daily announcements begin to be broadcasted over the PA system. "Good Morning. Please rise and recite the Pledge of Allegiance." Nothing out of the ordinary was said. "For lunch today, we will be having turkey turnovers, mashed potatoes, salad, and a roll with butter." Then the secretary pauses dramatically. "One other announcement. I have some exciting news to share with you this morning. We will have an assembly in the gym in two weeks. Our Ellwood City Wolverines will be playing a basketball game against the Blackhawk Cougars."

Everyone looks at each other as if to say, "So what?"

The woman's voice continues, "By the way, ABC's hit television show *That's Incredible!* will be here to film the game. It will be broadcast nationwide at a later date." Needless to say, everyone went bananas. Cheers and applause erupted and high fives were exchanged. And that's just among faculty members. It's a few minutes before teachers can get everyone quiet enough to begin class.

After a couple of weeks, the wait was over. The TV trucks arrived with their cameras and bright lights. The kids were seated in the gym ready for the game. The people from ABC had to particularly drive home the point that they were there to film a real game.

John Miller recalls, "The people from ABC didn't want the kids to be making crazy faces for the camera. This was a big task considering the hyped up atmosphere. Everywhere you looked, there were television cameras. They had the camera guy on the roller, and the lights and all. It was supposed to look real *because it was real.* What a crazy day. It all worked out, too, because as the game is going on, there was a fire in the science wing. Kids would have been up there, but they were down watching the game. Everything happens for a reason, right? The game itself was pretty exciting too. You have to remember now that I'm coaching Blackhawk *against* my own son's team!

"Plus everything was a little weird with the game being played in the daytime at the school. And, of course, the television presence was getting to everyone. I remember one of our players at the time named Jimmy Peel coming up to me by the bench and asking, 'Coach, what do you want us to do? Should we go easy on them for the show? What?'

Sean plays in the That's Incredible! scrimmage vs. his dad's Cougars.

"I told him, 'No, c'mon. This is Cougars! This is a real game. Go get 'em. Play your best.'"

It ended up being a barnburner of a game with Ellwood City (Sean's team) losing by two points in the final seconds, but that was of no real consequence. The TV crews were there just to film Sean in an actual game. Even as his team ended up on the losing side of the scoreboard, Sean showed how well he could play.

Miller family friends, the Aloi brothers, Danny and Frankie had become bigger and stronger. They improved and were competitive during the *That's Incredible!* game, but they were even better now. In another Hollywood twist, Miller had moved his family to Blackhawk since the ABC televised game. Though he received grief from Ellwood City fans at the time, he naturally wanted to coach his own son. Sean Miller was a Cougar now.

John Miller speculates, "Some Ellwood people still are mad at me for that, I think. I know, and they know, that if Sean Miller was still on their team, they would have brought home the trophy, not Blackhawk."

Previously, though, the *That's Incredible!* film footage showed the Miller basketball family to the nation. When smallish Sean Miller brought the ball up the court with authority that was beyond his years, it looked peculiar and almost unreal when he made passes that threaded the needle between the much larger guys on his father's Cougar squad.

On the overdub, host Fran Tarkenton described fourteen-year-old Miller as running plays "like a seasoned pro."

Following the game footage segment, the program segued from the packed Ellwood City gymnasium to Sean and his father standing in the family's small basement. This portion of the show succeeded in illustrating the incredible amount of time that father and son spent together during his training sessions.

The camera panned out to reveal the homemade miniature gym that John created in the basement, complete with a smaller, but realistic hoop, called a "sharpie". The minature hoop complemented by a Blackhawk Cougar pennant (sign of things to come), a Dr. J poster, and a big painted sign from the cheerleaders that says "Sink It." Coach fed the basketball to Sean as he repeatedly went in for lay-up after lay-up. A few years later, this routine would be mimicked by Lisa and Archie. The camera then focused on how quick and strong Sean's fingers were. In a tiny four-inch span from the floor to his fingers, the basketball sprung vertically with blinding speed from the hands to the floor. At the same time, the ball moved around the basement floor almost hovering through the space. It appeared as though the film was sped up, but everything was in real time.

The audience then heard John Miller explain the scene while Sean continued his insane dribbling routine. Sean spoke for a few seconds about overcoming his age and size disadvantage. "If you work harder than the other guy, it doesn't matter how big he his. You can get around him."

Sean and dad train in the basement gym.

Elaborating, Coach Miller then went into greater detail about the daily ball handling and shooting workouts. "We spent the most intense

That's Incredible! John Davidson,
Cathy Lee Crosby, Sean Miller, and
Fran Tarkenton

workouts during Sean's third and fourth grade years. We would spend hours in the basement together developing the hands. If you can develop the speed and the strength of the hands, everything else comes a lot easier. It takes hard work and sweat, though."

The camera shot then opened up big for a panoramic scene of the floor of the Philadelphia Spectrum. John Davidson announced, "All of Sean's work has finally paid off. He is a star performer at NBA half-time shows and other basketball events!"

At this, the audience applauded and the viewers at home were brought into the studio for the final segment of the show. Sean was announced and came out to, as Tarkenton described "make some moves that will make your head spin."

Following a nearly three-minute-long dribbling display from Sean, former Viking quarterback Tarkenton quipped, "If I trained like you, I'd still be playing!"

Today, Sean really doesn't like to talk much about the whole show-dribbling thing. He likes to keep in the present, but once in awhile you can catch him dusting off his skills. In 2015, he was a minor YouTube sensation when he dribbled four balls at once for a kids' clinic at the McKale Center in Arizona.

Sean showing he still
has it in 2015.

PART 3:
THUNDER IN THE EAST:
AN ATTACK ON TOKYO AND A CHALLENGE BACK HOME

> *"I can hardly believe what has just happened.*
> *Now Tokyo has no defense."*
> —Joe Brody, Godzilla (1954)

That's Incredible! would be Sean's last appearance on American television as an exhibition trick dribbler. However, he would have one more appearance on overseas television before he made the conscious decision to make the jump from being a dribbling act to a team basketball player. More and more, the ball handling performances became more of a distraction than something to look forward to.

When John Miller was approached to let his son travel to Tokyo, Japan, to film a television program called *Amazing Kids of the World*, he knew it would be a learning and traveling opportunity for his son that he couldn't pass up. He also knew that it might be the last of the trick dribbling shows Sean would be on before he focused on the actual game of basketball.

Out of the blue, John received a call in his office at the school. On the line was an offer from NBC's Japanese television affiliate to book Sean on a variety show that was similar to *That's Incredible!* John remembers putting his head in his hands to try to process what he had just been told. Japan now? His next step was to see what Sean thought of the whole idea.

After school practice that day, John drove home, took his son aside, and asked him if he wanted to go to Japan to perform on a Japanese television program.

This time, Sean clearly did not want to go. He was worried about how his coach (Al Campman) and his team at Ellwood City would react. Even though he was getting to travel to the Far East, an opportunity that may never come again, he felt the tug of responsibility and accountability that goes with being a part of a team. In his eyes and his father's eyes, he should consider himself a member of the Ellwood City Wolverines more than the dribbling kid he was once so proud to be. In other words, he shouldn't go.

Ellwood City Coach Al Campman

Plus, he was worried how his new coach would react to his absence. Ellwood City's Coach Campman was known as a rabid perfectionist when it came to his teams.

He sometimes implied to his players that they'd better be dead or dying if they were planning on missing a practice or a game. Only the most pressing situations like a family wedding or funeral would do for a valid excuse for showing up late or missing a practice or a game.

As Sean's parent, John Miller ultimately had to wrestle with the decision too. On one hand, his son made a commitment to his team to be there. On the other hand, this was a big opportunity—one others could only dream of. In the end John realized that the best thing to do was to stop thinking like a head coach and think like a father. He couldn't let this opportunity pass his son by. Loyalty to his coach and teammates was admirable, but this was something special. If John held him back from this trip, Sean would be missing out on an experience in Japan that would broaden him beyond anything he'd seen so far.

This trip was an opportunity for his son to see another culture and would open his eyes to a whole other way of living. He began to see it as a chance for Sean to do what almost no one from the western Pennsylvania mill towns had ever done. He couldn't let anyone sway him from taking advantage of this opportunity.

Miller concedes with a laugh, "Once I got this take on the situation, it was over. He was going. He didn't want to go at first, but when he came back, he said it was good for him and he was glad he could experience it."

Luckily for him, Coach Campman supported his family's decision and agreed that an opportunity to appear on the Japanese network NHK was a good enough reason for missing a few practices.

It happened then that in late 1983 Sean boarded a plane that would make the twenty-three-hour TWA flight to Tokyo, Japan.

The Japanese television show itself was pretty eccentric and strange. It featured not only athletic feats like Sean's, but also stomach-turning bizarre and peculiar stunts. For instance, on the show a preteen girl from India was a featured performer. Her act involved her entering a room filled with writhing and crawling poisonous snakes. This girl had the ability to handle and play with the serpents without receiving one bite. Another featured performer on the show was a fourteen-year-old boy whose talent was the ability to support the weight of a car parked on his chest. Still another was a little tyke who could direct a symphony orchestra. It was a pretty eye-opening experience all around.

Nevertheless, the writing was on the wall. If Sean wanted to climb the ladder as a player, the dribbling clinics and shows would have to be put on the backburner, especially during the season. "How many great trick players can you name that are also real players that can play? I can't name one," Sean admitted in a 2014 interview on the Seth Davis Show in Arizona.

Around the time of these TV appearances, his mom Barbara was quoted in a *Beaver County Times* newspaper article written by the now

Pittsburgh Pirates beat reporter John Perrotto. It's main idea was that Sean Miller, at this point, was almost disinterested in trick dribbling and show business and wanted it to go away. It was titled "TV Appearance Not So Incredible to Sean Miller" and was printed two days after *That's Incredible!* aired on October 18, 1983. She said, "Sean didn't watch the show just yet. He was at a clinic in Ohio helping his father. He's just really not overly impressed with the television appearances. He'll eventually watch the video of it, but it didn't bother him that he wasn't going to see it tonight. He was more excited to be going to the basketball clinic." The article went on to shine a spotlight on Archie as well. Barb Miller continued, "He wants to help his little brother too. Ryan [five-year-old Archie] is starting to do some of the dribbling drills that Sean did when he was younger. He can dribble two balls now too."

Reporter John Perrotto went on to write, "Two basketball wizards in one family are what is really incredible." He couldn't have known how prophetic that statement would become.

In retrospect, the trip to perform on Japanese television served to continue to broaden Sean's horizons. It was with this experience that he and his family came to realize that there definitely were places outside of western Pennsylvania that they could one day succeed and thrive. Experiences like this, along with the *Tonight Show, That's Incredible!,* and all of the clinics and camps showed Sean that he belonged way beyond the borders of Beaver County. The Miller kids would hone their skills in western Pennsylvania, but it was becoming increasingly clear to everyone involved that the Keystone State wouldn't contain them or their talents.

Sean remembers, "I'll tell you, it was an exciting time, but it was also a difficult time in a way. I really wanted to be known as a player first. And to a degree, the trick dribbling helped me to become a good point guard. But really it was like a fork in the road. At some point you have to make a choice to either pursue the game for real or pursue being a showman. Two really don't mix. I was starting to be known as

'That halftime kid' instead of a good player. Kids would give you a hard time. You know, you get put into a category of 'He's just this dribbling guy. He can't really play.' That's like when little kids ask their dads, 'Why aren't the Globetrotter players in the NBA? They win all their games.' I juggled both roles for a while (being a player and performing shows), but I knew, and my dad knew, that I had to get on with playing. Even my dad will tell you that my first exposure to the game was with wanting to be a good player, not this half-time guy. But don't get me wrong; it was really good for me at the time. It opened a lot of doors. I think the lesson is obvious: If you spend enough time doing one thing, you can get really good at it."

For some perspective, in 1981, John Calipari was beginning his playing career at Clarion University, having just transferred from UNC Wilmington. *The Tonight Show* and *That's Incredible!* were still in the future. However, in Sean's mind, he had already wanted the roles of half-time performer and trick dribbler to gradually slip into his past. One of the main events that helped him move from a performer to a player was a nationwide

Take the Pepsi Challenge
Early eighties Pepsi slogan

shooting contest called the Pepsi Hot Shot Challenge. There was no flash and show biz in the Pepsi Hot Shot completion. Its focus was on speed and shooting precision from all over the court.

On February 20, 1981, Sean was a very busy sixth grader. He had a full day of school capped with basketball practice. That evening, he would skip his usual nightly home practice routine to go see his dad's team, the Blackhawk Cougars, take on the Beaver Falls Tigers at the high school. He was really thinking about tomorrow, though. He was going to be headed to Indianapolis, Indiana with his dad to compete in one of the most prestigious basketball individual skills competitions in the world. The Pepsi Hotshot Challenge would be one of the first chances that Sean Miller had to show off his *game,* not just his ball-handling skills.

In addition to Pepsi, the NBA sponsored the Hot Shot Challenge. With this in mind, there were divisions created based on the NBA teams and their locations. Earlier that year, Sean had won the title top "hot shot" of the Cleveland Cavaliers in the Central Division. This division included western Pennsylvania, all of Ohio, and southern Michigan.

John Miller remembers, "The Pepsi Hot Shot Challenge is basically a speed, endurance, and accuracy test. It's a conditioning drill where kids shoot from designated spots all over the court. They have to run as fast as they can so they can score as many points as they can in one minute. Points are accumulated by making baskets from five spots on the court—medium range corner shots are worth two, long corners are worth three, left wing is worth four, and the top of the key is worth five. Each contestant is allowed two lay-ups that are a point each. Back then, you were allowed to pick and choose which stations you went to. Now they changed the rules. To make it more exciting, more action packed, I think. But back then you could rack up points any way that you wanted to.

"There were three rounds. The first was at a Cleveland area gym in the morning. The second was at the same gym in the afternoon. All the while, you are racking up points. The final one is at halftime of the NBA game. In our case, our last round was done at the Cleveland Arena, the home of the Cavaliers. When it started off, both guys are back to back. Go! Sixty seconds. If you go to all of them, you get a little bonus. Four points. If you don't go to all the stations, then you were just awarded the points without a bonus. So our strategy was to just bang away at that corner that we were the best at."

To reach the finals, you had to score higher than thousands of other kids. Pepsi promoted the program in hundreds of schools in each state. If you won the competition in your school, you went to county competitions. It went on like that until you reached the regional and finally national finals.

In an interview with Mike Bires of the *Beaver County Times* just prior to the trip, John Miller tried to speak up for his son's wish to be known as a player first. "The big thing I'd like to get across about Sean is that his shows are okay but playing is what it's all about for him. When he plays for his grade school team, you won't see any fancy jive moves and dribbling. He comes to play. People tend to get the wrong idea about this hot-shot bit."

"Sean's a basketball player," added Miller. "He works extremely hard at it. He's always bouncing a ball or skipping rope. He puts in tons of hours. I know at this time he wants to be known not as a showy 'look at me' kind of guy, but an important part of his team."

That fact was driven home by his player statistics at Purification Catholic School in Ellwood City (Sean attended this school for one year before returning to Ellwood City Public Schools). At the time, he averaged twenty-three points a game, and the sixth grade team was in the Catholic league play-offs with a record of 15–1. Soon, though, unbeknown to Ellwood City fans, John Miller would be moving his family to the same district as he coached. Usually, a family moving doesn't make headlines, but on May 17, 1984, while the front page was announcing a rare MX missile reduction from President Reagan and the death of beloved comedian Andy Kaufmann, the biggest news in the sports section of the *Beaver County Times* and the *Ellwood City Ledger* was "Miller moving to Blackhawk, Sean to play for his Dad." The news set off a blaze of controversy in Ellwood City. Some were irate at the move. They had visualized, in advance, the championships that were sure to come when the boy wonder, Sean Miller, joined up with an already talented Ellwood team.

John Miller admits, "If Ellwood would have had the team they had which included the talented Aloi brothers and Sean, they would have been completely unstoppable. Most people, after they thought about it rationally, were good about the move and understood that it was the best for my family. It was tough because I was coaching in one place, and Sean was playing his heart out trying to make another place a winner. I think that going in one direction solidified everything. Having both allegiances frustrated Sean I think."

The small blaze of controversy in Ellwood did, however, also light a strong flame of hope for the basketball fans to the south across the Beaver River. In the Blackhawk area of Beaver Falls, they were licking their chops.

*

TIP OFF

CHAPTER 15

BLACKHAWK FINALLY CATCHES FIRE

"Set your life on fire. Seek those who fan your flames."
—Rumi, 13th Century Persian Poet

"I'll burn your house down!"
—Jackie Moon of the ABA's Flint Tropics 1976 to Fr. Pat the referee

With the addition of Sean Miller and a few other tweaks, the Blackhawk basketball program was about to go from an up-and-coming team with potential to a juggernaut that would rarely lose. Up until now, the Blackhawk Cougars under John Miller had occasionally reached the first round of the play-offs, but in the end, a stronger or more experienced team would always eventually snuff them out.

After the Section Championship of the 1981–1982 team, Miller would have a few lackluster seasons before Sean's arrival in 1984 and the WPIAL Championship season of 1986.

---

* Sean and John Miller (1987)

The 1982–1983 season held high hopes for Miller and his returning section champion Cougars. Despite losing some seniors, the team started strong. Ultimately though, injuries caused the Cougars to fizzle out with six straight losses to end the season. This year, though, wasn't all about the end result. Miller was still in the process of putting pieces together for a second run at a section title in the coming years. An important piece of the puzzle came a few years previous in the form of a talented up-and-coming coach named Bob Amalia, who was added to the staff in the 1980–1981 season as lead assistant coach. His sixteen-year assistant basketball-coaching career saw three PIAA State Championships, five WPIAL Championships, and nine section titles.

On a side note, it would be Bob Amalia's role as a baseball coach that would eventually land him in the Beaver County Hall of Fame alongside John Miller and his sons. Nonetheless, with Amalia added to his staff, Miller continued to build the foundation for the overpowering force that would become Blackhawk basketball.

Assistant Coach Bob Amalia

In 1983–1984, the team that came out showed progress by making the play-offs again, but bowed out early, losing to one of Miller's coaching heroes. Legend Ed McClusky and his Farrell High School Steelers squashed any hopes of a long play-off run. Miller, though, was building his machine with quality pieces. Seniors Jeff Sommer and John Dickinson along with Chris Kayafas and Eric Olson turned in consistent play throughout the season. Plus, important groundwork was laid for next season when junior Mark Kinger returned to the fold for his senior year. Local sportswriters would describe Miller's team as a bonfire that would catch fire and then go out. Miller could see some small flames and some smoke and then Farrell, Beaver Falls, or Aliquippa would walk by and rudely extinguish them. The smoldering embers were all there. The tinder was all there. Talented coaches were in place now to care of the fire. All that was needed was some real fuel to get it all going in a big way. Luckily, the needed fuel came over the hill, across the Beaver River with Sean Miller in the driver's seat holding the match. Actually, it was more like a blowtorch. Blackhawk was not ready for the fireworks they would witness.

-BREAKING DOWN THE DYNASTY-

The glory years of the John Miller era can be defined and neatly separated into four distinct parts. A point guard that went on to collegiate fame playing, coaching, or both leads each.

1985–1988: SEAN MILLER

1988–1992: DANTE CALABRIA

1993–1997: ARCHIE MILLER

1998–2001: BRANDON FUSS-CHEATHAM

In 1984, the Millers made the momentous move to Chippewa Township in the Blackhawk School District where John was teaching and coaching. To the dismay of the Ellwood City Wolverine fans, Sean Miller was now officially a resident and could wear the green and gold uniform of his dad's Blackhawk Cougars.

Row 1: Bryan Garrett, Jay Keenan, Jim Peel, Jon Caplan, Sean Miller. Row 2: Sam Stanchak, Dave Mazzei, Rod Thompson, Mike Smakosz, Eric Olson, Mark Kinger, Chris Kayafas, Jay Campbell, Kurt Jute.

1985–1986 Cougars

At first, the team wasn't too excited by the presence of Coach's son at practice. They were keeping their eyes peeled for how Sean would be treated and used. The first thing that the team noticed was that far from being favored or pampered at practice, he was treated the same as everyone else. In fact, Sean was sometimes held to a bit of a higher standard when he did something wrong.

Coach Miller explains, "You have to believe me when I tell you that I wasn't hard on Sean because he was my son. I was as hard on him as I was on any guy on any of my teams that was the leader. Most times if

---

FIRST QUARTER

SEAN MILLER:

THE BOY WONDER GROWS UP (1985–1988)

Key Point Guard #1, Sean Miller

1985–1986

FIRST TIME *WPIAL CHAMPS*
19 Wins–9 Losses

WESTERN PENNSYLVANIA CHAMPIONSHIP GAME
Blackhawk 71–Ellwood City 70

---

not all times, that guy is your point guard. They have to be 'the guy.' They rest of the team naturally looks to 'the guy' as an example of how to go about their business. I didn't just pick on Sean. Fuss Cheatham, Calabria, Archie, and all those guys knew that if they screwed up, they were going to hear about it worse than the rest. But they knew it was part of the job, and I hope that they took it as sort of an honor."

One of those point guards was Ohio State's Brandon Fuss-Cheatham. He played for Miller ten years after Sean had left Blackhawk to become a Pitt Panther. Brandon vividly remembers, "With the point guard, he expected more. He'd punish you a little more when you messed up. He needed you to know and the rest of the team to know that you were the model for them. He'd take you aside to explain that to you. That helped a lot."

John Miller explains, "I would never make Sean do anything because someone else on the team messed up. I think I was just holding him accountable that he was the leader and should give 110 percent. I wouldn't really single him out. They were just tough, hard practices for everyone. And when we began to win practically every game, it was much easier for the kids to buy into the work and the lengths that we needed to go to dominate like that. But again, I was hard on everybody. Dante Calabria, Jimmy Cantamessa, Brandon Fuss-Cheatham, Archie Miller, and Sean Miller especially; all those guys will tell you the same stories. Once you had that top guy in line, everyone else would just fall in line too. They just follow the leader. And usually the top guy would realize why you're being harder on them. Then it becomes like a source of pride. My leader knew that they weren't getting any favors. That's why they were the leader. They were the example to the rest."

The bottom line was, Coach expected perfection. Once during a game, the opponents believed that they had figured out John Miller's game and planned to extinguish Sean by running a triangle and two. If you know the game, then you realize that this meant that the point guard, who was at this time Sean Miller, would be double-teamed the entire game. It made no difference though. Sean put up thirty-seven points that game in which the Cougars would come away with a victory. If there had been a three-point line, the point total would have been much higher. The thing that his assistants remember to this day was that, after the initial happiness from winning the game, Coach went over to Sean to give him a little grief about missing three foul shots. Bob

Amalia remembers, "That's the way he was—just a total perfectionist. I remember his brother Joe was there, and he came over to me and told me to go over and calm John down. Again, he wanted total perfection, and that's what pushed his guys to try even harder. In that moment, it seemed harsh or crazy to onlookers, but when his players looked back, including Sean or Archie, I know that they were glad that their coach and dad was the way that he was."

Back in 1985 and 1986, Sean was already used to his dad's methods, so he took no offense when he had to run extra laps or suicides when he messed up. He may even run voluntarily when someone else messed up. It's what a leader did. His dad's successes in life had proved to Sean that his dad knew what he was doing. Sean was going to do what Coach instructed and emulate him.

With Sean, John Miller finally now had the perfect case in point to use to show proper shooting techniques and how practice and sweat was integral to success. The veterans on the Cougars' squad saw firsthand Sean's work ethic and knew that they would be judged against him. He made them all work harder and longer. And not just in the gym. The "dumb jock" stereotype certainly did not apply to Miller's team. Time at home was spent studying and finishing homework so that they could get shots in at the gym during study halls.

Basketball was not the darling sport at the district, and Miller was sure that no breaks would be given to kids who had slipping grades. John made clear that grades were to be the players' first priority. The point was taken, and grade point averages of basketball players were seen to rise to levels beyond that of the average student at the school. From there, the team set to work in the gym. Each player averaged hundreds of shots a day. And again, the actual practices were intense. Following Sean's routine that had been established when he was in primary school, they decided to follow suit and became practice machines. As a result, their hard work as a team gained them a reputation as a squad that could send devastating aerial bombardments accurately to the net.

The team improved week by week, and statistics showed that they were one of the very best shooting squads in the entire state. That, combined with a solid team-play attitude and a newly aggressive defense, made Miller's lineup more fearsome than ever before. By the end of the regular season, they had defeated every opponent twice and only lost twice. Both losses were to the league champion, Farrell High School.

Miller's team continued to win in the play-offs and made their way to the Final Four of the WPIAL Championship by defeating the talented Kiski High School Cavaliers. They had gone twenty-one in a row before meeting the Cougars. The team would eventually fall at the Pitt Fieldhouse, the home of the NCAA Panthers, to a very strong Baldwin High School team, but the writing was on the wall. The days of embarrassing lopsided losing seasons were over. And at Blackhawk, the more dominant sports were going to have to move over a little and leave a space on the throne for basketball. Patience was about to pay off. It would only be one more year before John Miller's first coveted WPIAL Championship would become a reality.

Game plan at Pitt Fieldhouse

Sharing the hardware with Principal Art Cornell

Where the 1985 team knocked on the door and came up short, the 1986 team finally kicked the door in. In fact, "short" was the word that sportswriters and donut shop experts were using to describe the team.

Miller remembers, "That year, 'little' Cougars didn't just describe the elementary program. My guys were small." But the undersized Cougars faced formidable enemies as they fought their way to a Section II second place finish. From there, the team really caught fire and won the first WPIAL Championship in the history of the school. And for this school, that had never won a championship, to do it at the NCAA's Pitt Panthers' Fieldhouse was a thrill as well for all involved.

Plus, the irony of the matchup was almost not to be believed. Ellwood City, the Miller's former hometown, was playing for the championship against Blackhawk, the school that, in its eyes, stole its star. One must remember that this was a rematch of the game that was played for national television cameras for the *That's Incredible!* show. In that game, Sean Miller was featured as the extraordinary point guard of the Ellwood City Wolverines. His father was, of course, coaching against his own son.

Now, of course, Sean was a member of his dad's Cougars and together they were expected to defeat their old hometown. Everyone involved knew that if the Millers had chosen to stay in Ellwood City, the Wolverines would have been completely unstoppable, and Coach John Miller would have the unenviable task of trying to stop his own son from winning a championship. To add to the tension and drama, even with the loss of Sean, Ellwood had improved so much as a team because of the talented Aloi brothers, Frankie and Danny. They had become division one athletes in Sean's absence. Coach Al Campton of Ellwood City had developed them and the rest of their team into a contender. It would be anyone's guess whether Blackhawk or Ellwood City had the greater advantage.

Miller remembers, "Ellwood was a great team with those two alone. If Sean had still been in a blue and white Wolverine uniform, he would have been an outstanding lead guard while opponents were distracted by the Aloi brothers. It would have been a nightmare for other teams. And if I hadn't moved Sean and the family out to Blackhawk, I would have been that other team trying to find a way to stop my own son. Ellwood in that situation would have been a state title team. There's not a doubt in my mind. Every game with them was down to the wire. In 1985 to 1986 every game against them was decided by one point. And of course, just like in the movies, it was a crazy close game again, and after all was said and done, Blackhawk finally won the WPIAL.

The 1986 WPIAL Champion team bus would be the first of many of Miller's teams that would receive a hero's welcome in Beaver Falls as fire trucks with sirens wailing escorted the buses past cheering residents to the high school. It was quite a ways from the one and twenty-one record in Miller's first year.

Miller's 1986 Cougars came painfully close to winning the state title, but like in the movies—this one being the 1984 classic *Hoosiers*—they lost by one point in the first round to a school (believe it or not) named Hickory.

The season was indeed a special one worthy of Hollywood. One of the most remarkable games of that WPIAL winning season was one that Miller engineered to surprise and defeat a much bigger and stronger opponent. And he almost pulled it off. It became known as the "Stall Ball Game."

Early in the year, the rival Beaver Falls Tigers soundly defeated the Cougars by a double-digit margin. Back in his Riverside days, Miller remembered a "Stall Plan" in which the players would be ordered to hold the ball, pass the ball, and no matter what, not to shoot the ball. With no shot clock, the passing back and forth could go on forever. Then during the last few minutes of the game, after the other team was asleep, the offense would explode and come away with a win. With Riverside, the plan didn't really work because they lacked the skill to pull it off when Miller attempted it. Miller said, "More often than not, back then the ball would be stolen or end up in the stands."

But with this polished group, the passes were crisp, quick, and always right on the money. If it was ever going to work, it would be now. It was February 15, 1986. People braved icy roads and subfreezing temperatures. They painted their faces and brought painted signs, anticipating an action-packed throwdown between two districts that had a post office in common, but not much else.

The Beaver Falls Tigers was a city school. The team players were big, tough, talented, and *tall*. Blackhawk was surely talented, but it had no one taller than five foot eleven on its squad. The team's big man Jason McCowen was six foot three but was out with a broken wrist. The Tigers on the other hand was starting a six foot seven named Darren Hopkins along with six foot six Andre Curry and an absolute monster named Mike Wagner who could bat away shots at will because he stood six foot ten.

Beaver Falls played a triangle-and-two defense with their big guys in a zone. Their coach Frank Chan instructed his two most skilled players Benny Carter and Tom Harriel to play man to man with Blackhawk's leading scorers Sean Miller and Kurt Jute. With that defense in place, Miller knew that rebounding would be almost impossible. The Tigers were just too tall next to the boards. And when Beaver Falls stuck with the zone it was using, Miller's players were told not to shoot. They stood still.

"If they had played man to man, we'd have played," Miller remembers. "What it came down to was that even though they had all the best guys, all the studs, why didn't they use them and play man to man? I thought that they would eventually switch to that, but they didn't. One of the things that I think it came down to was that they didn't want to deal with Sean."

This is not a hockey scoreboard: Stall Ball 1986.

The Tigers' coach answered candidly in the newspaper, "We have a lot of other defenses. We can play a two-three or a one-three-one. We can press. But do you think that I'm going to play a man to man when he has five midgets out there? I was thinking about going over and asking him what he wanted us to play. But I'd have gotten a technical, and two points is a big score in a game like that."

Beaver Falls led 6–0 with only four minutes left in the game. Sean Miller finally broke the ice with a smooth jumper. A minute later, the score was 8–4 when Blackhawk's Paul Mannix, normally an automatic shooter, missed a lay-up that would have put the Cougars down by only one score. Jim Peel leaped up high but missed the tip in. Miller remembers, "After that missed shot, big Curry grabs the rebounds and flies down the court for a one-handed tomahawk slam. 'The Air Curry' was the big play of the game. That was a backbreaker."

The Cougars made a game of it, though. Sam Stanchak drained two to pull his team within four (12–8) with two minutes left. Sean Miller and Jim Peel answered Beaver Falls scoring with baskets of their own, but after everything was said and done, it wouldn't be enough.

"It was one to remember, though," Miller said. "The gym was oversold. It was probably a fire hazard with people standing along the baseline. I remember a lot of the Beaver Falls fans were facing the wall instead of the game. Then they started tearing posters down. Some hecklers were yelling to Sean, 'Hey, tell your old man you want to go to college, so they'll let you play!' It was great."

Frustrated Beaver Falls Tiger Mike Wagner said, "I was seriously considering sitting down on the court. I'd have never done it, of course, but I was thinking about it."

After the Stall Ball Game, Beaver Falls would be unceremoniously knocked from the play-offs by a sixteen seed, Bishop Canevin. Miller believes that the

Sleeping Tigers

Tigers took that team too lightly, and he knows that, on paper, Beaver Falls was the best team in the entire state. "We were lucky not to have faced them in the play-offs that year. They probably would have won the whole thing. But they didn't. We did."

Many WPIAL Championship teams go undefeated or nearly undefeated in the regular season. The 1985–1986 Cougars would be the exception to this. The team that would go on to win the first WPIAL for Miller only ended up with a 14–8 record in the regular season. That is where leadership went a long way. In news articles, John Miller gave credit to many senior players for leading the team to victory.

He named senior players such as Rodney Thompson, Kurt Jute, Jim Peel, Jay Keenan, Rich Mattes, John Caplan, and Jay Campbell. Curiously missing from that list was his junior son, Sean. He was obviously the best player on the team. He was obviously going to go on to big things in basketball long after his time at Blackhawk, but John Miller made a point of publicly crediting the seniors on his team in the papers. This gesture was another subtle, yet effective, chance to show his team that everyone on this team was an equal no matter what your last name happened to be.

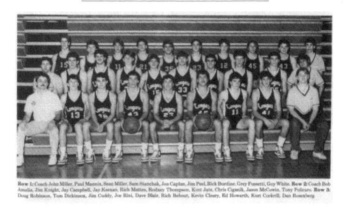

Row 1:Coach John Miller, Paul Mennis, Sean Miller, Sam Stanchak, Jon Caplan, Jim Paul, Rick Burdine, Grey Fussetti, Guy White. Row 2:Coach Bob Amelio, Jim Knight, Jay Campbell, Jay Keenan, Rich Mattas, Rodney Thompson, Kurt Juts, Chris Cigarik, Jason McCowin, Tony Policaro. Row 3: Doug Robinson, Tom Dickinson, Jim Cuddy, Joe Rizi, Dave Blair, Rich Bebout, Kevin Cleary, Ed Howarth, Kurt Cockrill, Dan Rosenberg.

The Cougars

As far as individual honors given by others, Sean Miller was a glaring stand out. He was awarded the Pennsylvania AAA Player of the Year honor. The *Pittsburgh Post-Gazette* named Sean a member of the Fabulous Five, a list of the best five players in Pittsburgh and the surrounding area. Another member of the Fab Five was Major Harris from Brashear, who became the quarterback for the West Virginia Mountaineers. John Rasp from Norwin, Tony Petraraca from Kiski, and Pete Freeman from nearby Rochester would round out the list. The best part of these awards for Sean and his dad was that Sean was finally being recognized as an elite player instead of just a dribbling act.

In the 1986–1987 season, Coach Miller would guide his team to another section championship. With footballer Sam Stanchak providing some beef and muscle on the court, the Cougars could look to Sean Miller to totally relax, displaying effortless domination from his point guard position.

The weather that winter was brutally cold and snowy. Many a school day was cut short with an announcement that a big snowstorm was coming. Assistant Mark Balbach remembers the contrast in the reaction of the basketball team to the rest of the students. "The announcement would come on, and as you'd expect, the kids would all cheer. That is everyone except the basketball team. They knew what was coming. Miller (and I guess he was right looking back) would hold the schedule as planned, but it would start as soon as the kids and other teachers had cleared out and continue until the snow let up. He told the kids that they were safe in the gym and that they were going to take care of business. By the time practice was over, the roads would be pretty cleared off and we had put in a lot of extra work. He was good like that. Some of the kids griped a little, but there were no complaints in March when the play-off wins started to stack up."

Thanks to the WPIAL Championship and the *Pittsburgh Post-Gazette* Fab Five exposure in 1986, home and away gyms were packed no matter what the weather conditions were like outside. Cougar basketball had become a hot ticket, and fans needed to arrive early if they wanted a seat. Besides Sean Miller, the star point guard, fans were treated to fantastic team play that featured precision passing, ball handling, and textbook shooting from the entire squad. With another section championship under their belts, Miller and his Cougars headed into the play-offs hopeful but lost to the Aliquippa Quips in the WPIAL Championship game and to Ellwood City in the state final four. At year's end, Sean was named again to the *Pittsburgh Post-Gazette's* Fab Five team along with future Pitt teammate Darrell Porter. Mike Yoest, Joe Nathan, and Ellwood's Dan Aloi completed the talented quintet.

The 1987 edition (Miller's second appearance)
of the Pittsburgh Post-Gazette Fab Five

The 1986–1987 run at the WPIAL and the state titles would not be the last Miller would get during the 1980s. In fact, his Cougars would finish in the state final four in 1989. For Miller, it had never been about the big trophy at the end. He never focused on the titles for motivation. To him, it was all about constant incremental improvement.

"When you inch closer and closer to the goal every day," says Miller, "you will eventually get there, even if there are setbacks. The idea is to keep plugging away no matter what. People tend to have trouble with the 'no matter what' part."

Even though there would be no gold returned home from the Pitt Field House for the WPIAL title or from Hershey for the state in 1988 or 1989, under Miller's leadership, the team went from one that was laughed at and pitied in 1977 to a perennial play-off monster by 1987 and beyond. That was quite a feat considering the tough section in which the team played. Miller's teams had become a feared-by-all opposition, not only because of their star point guard (it seemed they always had one), but also because everyone knew that as a team no one outworked them.

To this day, scores of former players from the opposition comment that Miller's replacements on the bench would often be better ball handlers and more developed shooters than most teams' starters. Also, by then it was common knowledge that, as a coach, no one was going to hold his team more accountable than John Miller.

He puts it this way: "There's nothing like the amount of effort you can get out of your guys when they're at the cusp of winning something big. They haven't really achieved anything yet, but they're so very close. Sean always told me that his teams at Blackhawk did the grunt work back then. In other words, his era built the foundation, and Dante Calabria's crew put the basketball program over the top. After Dante, Archie kept it going in a big way, and Fuss-Cheatham's guys carried the program successfully to its end. In 1985 to 1986, we were fighting to get to the top of that mountain. That's when you really find yourself doing your hardest, most intense work. And it paid off."

Tim Jones, one of Miller's players in the middle to late 1980s, now lives in Denver, Colorado. He is enjoying a very successful career as the owner of a Jeep dealership. His mom owned "Linda Jones Chevrolet" in Beaver Falls at the same time he was being worked out by Coach Miller in High School. He has cars in his blood. He remembers the grunt work he endured then but cherishes now.

"Coach Miller was a perfectionist," explains Jones. "And whether we knew it or not, his passion to get to be the best was rubbing off on us. It couldn't be helped. I had my work cut out for me when I was assigned to guard Sean Miller everyday in practice during his senior year. I, of course, was in tenth grade and had my hands full. My game reached new levels just by trying to guard him all the time. Plus, if Sean had an off day or bad day at practice, the whole team would run sprints with him. Not a choice. The practice would stop, and everybody was on the line. Blaine Cleckley, a brave teammate of mine, once stopped and, while shaking his head, blurted out, 'Coach, you mean to tell me that if Sean screws up, we all have to run?' Coach, in a stoic voice says, 'You got it brother.' That was Coach. He was teaching us about being loyal to the leader. He was also teaching us that one small part effects the whole."

But it wasn't just during Sean's era that individual lapses led to whole team discipline. Years before Sean Miller's time with the Cougars, former player Dennis Mayer experienced the same thing. He explains, "Miller encouraged all of us to do everything as a team, practice outside of school as a team, go to the movies as a team, hang out together as a team, and you'd better believe it, when one of us screwed up, we heard about it and paid for it, as a team."

In the war film *Full Metal Jacket,* widely quoted and profane US Marine Gunnery Sergeant Hartman, created unity and camaraderie and turned his squad into "killers" when he punished his whole unit because of the mistake of one individual. When the forever-bumbling Pvt. Leonard Lawrence (rechristened Private Pyle by Sgt. Hartman) decided to hide a jelly donut in his footlocker, he was made to stand on his overturned footlocker and choke down his forbidden treat while the rest of the unit was forced to do push-ups. Hartman chided, "They paid for it; now you eat it." Punishing the entire unit for the sins of the one is actually an ancient practice, long known to be effective in creating a deep, mystical unity in teams. The Roman army famously used the practice of decimation when a member of a military unit committed an infraction. The soldiers were lined up, and one out of every ten was executed.

Coach Miller created the same effect with his "troops," but unlike Sgt. Hartman or Roman Centurions, he did it with class, dignity, and minus the four-letter tirades. He proved that you can be tough, motivating, and a winner without stooping to a level that used to be considered beneath the dignity of an educator.

Blaine Cleckley is now a successful real estate agent and house flipper in Florida. He points to Coach Miller as one of the main reasons he

Blaine Cleckley

is where he is today. In the early 1980s, Blaine grew up a self-described street kid in a particularly rough section of Beaver Falls. His mother was one of fifteen children. Fights, crime, and drug dealers were commonplace in his neighborhood. Men came in and out of Blaine's life as a kid and, though none were outright abusive, he never had any meaningful father figure. As a typical kid on the streets, Blaine wasn't too fond of authority and police in particular. But in his early teens, to his dismay, his single mom married a local police chief named Earl Gardner. "I didn't like cops at this point. It was just my point of view coming from where I came from, the way my family was, and the way we grew up."

Blaine also wasn't too thrilled when he was told that he and his new family were moving to Blackhawk, where the only thing black was the first half of the school's name. When in Beaver Falls, he and his friends had heard of John Miller's success as a coach. He also heard of Sean Miller through his exposure on TV, but as he explained, "We didn't care about him or his team, we just wanted to beat them."

Whether he liked it or not in the beginning, the move to the suburbs would turn out to be a blessing in disguise for Blaine, because it was at Blackhawk High School that he and Coach Miller's paths would ultimately cross. When Blaine signed up for the basketball team, he knew that he would be the only African-American on the team. He had a kind of "I'll show them" attitude. He wanted to show (mostly the kids) that he could play.

As far as his new teachers, Blaine had experienced "slaps on the back" and attention from them and others who noticed and appreciated his basketball ability. But Blaine soon figured out that his athletic prowess was all they seemed concerned with if truth were told.

Blaine remembers, "One of Miller's assistants, Coach Mark 'Doc' Balbach used to be the gym teacher at Beaver Falls, so I always felt that he had my back, as did Coach Amalia, but what separated John Miller (the coach, of all people) from the rest of the teachers was that he seemed to be sincere about molding me as a person, and he wasn't just concerned with my play on the court. The best part of it all was when I realized that Coach was genuinely trying to improve me as a person. That meant my grades had to be up. If they weren't, I heard about it. And it wasn't like, 'Get your grades up or you can't *play* or be on time because you won't *play*.' It was, 'Get your grades up or you're going to fail at *life*.' And I knew that he was sincere.

"Once, I played for him at the big annual Christmas tournament. I played really well and made the list of All Stars. Tradition goes that they recognized the kids on the list over the PA at the close of the tournament. Well, for whatever reason, my name wasn't called. I was pissed and went kind of down to the locker room sulking. Coach Miller (not known for a sensitive, personal side) came down and congratulated me on playing so well and assured me that I'd be recognized at school as an All Star. No one has any idea what that meant to me as a kid. He's one of the main guys that made me the man I am today. You'll do anything asked for a guy like that. And that's what me and the rest of the Cougars did week after week."

"As far as basketball went," explains Blaine, "before Miller, I just got good at the game from playing it for hours and hours with my friends at school or on the playground." He hadn't really known anyone like Coach Miller who was a genuine student of the game, someone who was constantly trying to understand it mentally and methodically.

"He is someone that no matter how long he'd been coaching, or how many championships he'd won, he still tried to gain an edge with a new drill, or a new technique. It took awhile for me to fully buy in, but as time went on I became convinced that Coach Miller was something special and I eventually began to realize that I really wanted what he was selling. Once we started to see the results from his system and how tough it was, it didn't matter how tough it was. The results made you want to endure more and to buy into the system. And when the team and the Miller Way were firing on all cylinders, I'll never forget the pride I felt and the show that we put on during the games. It was something special to see."

There's no denying that those father-son Miller teams were a spectacle constantly leaving jaws agape. People from all walks of life can remember some of Sean Miller's performances like they happened yesterday. Teacher and coach Tom Lucchino is as pumped up today during his unique retelling of Sean's exploits as he was at the very moment decades ago.

Trying to dribble around Quiptown

Lucchino was bursting with enthusiasm as he recalled, "One time, late eighties, Sean Miller was a senior for Blackhawk High School. They were playing Slippery Rock High School. Well, I was in college as a sophomore at Slippery Rock University, which was right down the road. The buzz around the college was that we had to go check out this kid. He was the real deal, and he could play. So a big bunch of us pack in this car to go to the high school to check him out. Well, before you know it, the gym was packed with college kids waiting to see this kid play. Man, he came out and immediately began lighting it up, shooting the ball. Three after three after three. The thing was there was no three-point line then. I just knew he was hittin' them from downtown. He and his teammates were threading the needle making these insane passes. His old man was pacing the side like a field general. Everyone in the gym knew that he was running the show. And the college guys were going absolutely ape shit. They were jumping up and down high fiving each other; it was nuts. Pretty soon the whole crowd really got behind Sean. Rooting him on. 'Shoot the ball! Shoot the ball!'

"He'd run down by where the college guys were, and they'd really yell for him. 'C'mon Miller Time! Shoot that shit! Shoot that shit!' And right then—I will tell you this. He was *beyond* NBA three-point territory, and he launched a three, buried it, gave the college kids a look and a little smile and the college kids went berserk *again*. What a game. If I had to put a point total on it, I'd say he put up sixty that night. Scoring sixty points in a high school game? That kid could flat out play. And like I said, the whole time, his old man was running the show like it's no big deal. Strictly business."

John Miller heard the account of this story during my writing of this book, and his reaction was priceless. He smiled the whole time, but at the end he looked at me and calmly said, "It was fifty-two points, not sixty, but Sean had to sit a quarter and a half."

Playing for his dad in high school was just the thing to prepare Sean Miller for the national stage that was to become his home. The work ethic and businesslike demeanor that was instilled in him through his father mingled with his unparalleled personal talent. The results, achievements, and accolades were historic, and he adds to them each year.

John Calipari recruited this Pitt class in 1987 (Bobby Martin, Jason Matthews, Sean Miller, Darrelle Porter, and Brian Shorter).

After high school, Sean Miller took his talents and determination to the University of Pittsburgh and made an immediate impact with the Panthers. He was named Big East Freshman of the Year in 1988 and led the Panthers to the Big East regular season championship. This achievement was capped by an appearance at the big dance— March Madness. Just as he led his father's Cougars to new heights in high school, he would lead Pitt to two more NCAA tournament appearances. This, along with an NIT tournament selection, would seal Miller into the minds of Pitt fans as one of the greatest point guards in school history.

Sean started 124 of 128 games in college, including a Big East record 66 consecutive conference games. He graduated as the Big East's all-time leading free throw shooter and was Pitt's all-time leader in assists for a season and career. The casual fan may best remember him for his incredible pass to Jerome Lane on a fast break. Jerome would take the ball and vault airborne to make what would forever be known as "The Dunk." It was so powerful that the tempered glass backboard exploded and sent safety glass showering onto the court. T-shirts are still sold on the Pitt campus that feature an artist's rendering of a shattering backboard with the catch phrase "Send it in Jerome!" underneath. Send it in Jerome! were the words Bill Rafferty jubilantly howled while broadcasting the game for ESPN. John Miller later joked that in his family that play isn't called The Dunk, it's called "The Pass."

To cap his college career as a Pitt Panther, Sean's country came calling after his senior year. In the spring of 1991, he was honored with a selection to play for the United States of America in the World University Games. There he and his team won gold medals. In 2015, he would be the head coach for this team; his younger brother Archie would be his assistant. They would win the gold again. And the Team USA girl's team, led by Dori Anderson Oldaker, would make three Blackhawk kids and John Miller protégés representing Uncle Sam as coaches that year. Incredible.

Of course, following his graduation from Pitt, Sean entered the coaching ranks. Sean remembers how seamlessly he made the transition from player to coach. It was almost too simple. "I was watching ESPN and saw that Stu Jackson, who recruited me when he was an assistant under Rick Pitino at Providence, got the head job at Wisconsin. The next day, I went up to the basketball office and took the Blue Book out and called him up. Before I knew my playing days were over, I was coaching."

Right then and there, Miller became the restrictive-earnings coach on Stu Jackson's staff that also included current NC State coach Herb Sendek. When Sendek was hired for the head job at Miami of Ohio, he asked Sean Miller to join him as a second assistant, where he'd be heavily involved in recruiting.

"I knew what kind of a hard worker Herb Sendek was, and I knew what type of guy he was in terms of following rules and doing things the right way," said Sean Miller. "To be able to go on the road and recruit for a guy like him, it was an opportunity."

From there, Sean proved his abilities by working as an assistant coach at NC State, a short homecoming at the University of Pittsburgh, Miami of Ohio, Wisconsin, and Xavier University before getting the call to be the head coach at Xavier in 2004. There he reached seven NCAA tournaments in his first eight seasons on the coaching staff at Xavier. He led Xavier to six 20-or-more victory seasons including a school record thirty wins in the 2007–2008 season. It wasn't long after that that the University of Arizona made him an offer that he couldn't refuse. He accepted the job as Wildcats head coach in 2008 and hasn't looked back. T-shirts sporting the phrase "Sean Miller for President" are a common sight in Tucson.

Coming full circle in April 2012, Sean boarded a plane back to Pittsburgh and drove twenty more minutes to Beaver County where he made it clear to whom the credit was owed for all of his successes: his dad. He inducted him into the Beaver County Sports Hall of Fame. At the event, held annually at The Fez banquet hall, Sean told stories about his dad and the closeness that they had developed over all those years of training. He talked about what his dad taught him about life. And he talked about his WPIAL Championship with the Cougars in 1986 and how much it still meant to him. He reminded the crowd and his dad, who was of course in attendance, that it was the *first* of eight WPIAL Championships that his dad would bring back to Blackhawk High School in his career. He told the attendees that he relished in that championship then, and he still cherishes it now. The night was an experience that all present would remember. It's not often that a son joins his father in a hall of fame. A few years later, in 2015, his brother Archie would be inducted as well. At the hall of fame induction, the first WPIAL Championship may have been a fond, yet fading, memory for John and his son.

But, turning back to 1986, the WPIAL Championship was still fresh in the minds of Coach John Miller and his Cougars. They had achieved their goal but were determined to build on it. And build on it John did. Miller told his teams that the 1986 WPIAL was only the beginning. Miller believed; his teams believed. The community believed, and by now, everyone involved knew that they had something special. But no one, not even John Miller himself, predicted the amount of consistent winning that was about to happen.

CHAPTER 16

THE STREAK

"I hate losing …. I hate it. I hate losing more than I even wanna win."
—*Billy Beane, General Manager of the Oakland Athletics*

Unless you live in western Pennsylvania, you probably don't recognize school names like Aliquippa, Beaver Falls, Blackhawk, New Brighton, and others mentioned in the pages of this book. It is hard to overstate how unparalleled Coach John Miller and his Blackhawk Cougars' would be in comparison to the other schools. There are dynasties and excellent high school programs elsewhere that may come to mind. But regardless of how dominant those programs might be, very few can compare to the historic excellence of Coach John Miller and his Cougars in the coming years. At this time, I challenge the reader to do just that. Think of the best high school program in your area and see how it stacks up to this:

JOHN MILLER:
FOR THE RECORD

FOUR PENNSYLVANIA STATE TITLES

Year	Champion	Runner-Up	Score
1992	Blackhawk	Strath Haven	71–55
1995	Blackhawk	Pottstown	64–59

| 1996 | Blackhawk | Valley View | 67–55 |
| 1999 | Blackhawk | Holy Ghost Prep | 66–43 |

ONE PENNSYLVANIA STATE RUNNER-UP

Year	Champion	Runner-Up	Score
2000	Steelton-Highspire	Blackhawk	68–56

WESTERN PENNSYLVANIA INTERSCHOLASTIC ATHLETIC LEAGUE CHAMPIONSHIPS

Year	Champion	Runner-Up	Score
1986	Blackhawk	Ellwood City	71–70
1990	Blackhawk	Seton-La Salle	44–37
1991	Blackhawk	Seton-La Salle	84–52
1992	Blackhawk	Aliquippa	81–62
1996	Blackhawk	Chartiers Valley	65–61
1999	Blackhawk	South Park	48–44
2000	Blackhawk	Pine-Richland	73–50
2003	Blackhawk	Hopewell	66–59

WPIAL RUNNERS-UP

Year	Champion	Runner-Up	Score
1987	Aliquippa	Blackhawk	51–37
1994	Beaver Falls	Blackhawk	63–60 2OT
1995	Highlands	Blackhawk	58–56
1997	Chartiers Valley	Blackhawk	64–59
2001	Brownsville	Blackhawk	66–63

17 SECTION CHAMPIONSHIPS

1982, 1987, 1988, 1990, 1991, 1992, 1993, 1994,

1995, 1996, 1997, 1998, 1999, 2000, 2001, 2002, 2003

OTHER ACCOMPLISHMENTS

Coaching Record: 657–280 (.701); Post-Season: 104–29

WPIAL Record: 16 consecutive section titles, 1990–2003

WPIAL Record: 111 consecutive section wins, 1990–1999

Coached Kobe Bryant in the 1996 McDonald's All American game

The record 111 straight section wins has come to be known as the "Streak" in western Pennsylvania basketball circles. John Miller's unbroken line of section victories didn't just break the old record of eighty-two straight wins. It shattered it by surpassing it by almost thirty games. The old record was set in 1959 by Wampum High School. The Indians from Wampum won twelve straight section championships in the 1950s. The team became a national story when magazine articles that featured Coach Butler Hennon's unusual practice techniques appeared on newsstands. He, like Miller, would try anything to gain a fair advantage over opponents. His teams would practice while wearing weighted jackets, heavy gloves, thick boots, and special glasses to improve their skills.

The weighted-down Wampum Indians at work in the 1950s

By the time that Wampum's record was broken, it had stood for a quarter of a century, and the school district did not even exist anymore. Wampum splintered and was absorbed into the bigger Ellwood City School District. To bust this record wide open was an implausible feat that many saw as an accomplishment that might never be reached. Miller recognized the significance of beating that record as much or better than anyone. He was a player at nearby Moon High School when he would read about those incredible Wampum teams in the newspaper. At the time, the record to him seemed unbreakable. So it was quite a personal achievement to him when he was able to tie Wampum's 82-game win streak. The fans in the stands, too, knew the significance of that lopsided victory over Beaver Falls on that cold winter evening in Chippewa. The bleachers strained under the weight of the jumping fans that were celebrating history being made before their eyes. And the victory was particularly sweet to tie the record playing their archrivals, Beaver Falls. The Tigers had been the team that came closest to ending the streak a few years earlier. In that particular game, Beaver Falls had led the Cougars at halftime 41–34. But revitalized by their coach and led by their captain Steve Dickinson, the players rallied to lead 75–74 in the game's final ticks. And when Beaver Falls' Troy Nesmith rebounded an errant shot from Doug Yeager, the team called time out to plan a final, game winning shot. But that final shot hit the rim and then the floor. The game was over, and the Tigers had lost. Tempers flared, and both sides, including some fans, threw punches. The police had to clear the court.

But in true Miller fashion, after this record-tying win, the players knew better than to go overboard showing their emotions. There was no celebration or ceremony. Miller and his players, as prescribed, walked over and shook hands with the Beaver Falls Tigers and the coaches. They acknowledged a few pats on the back and made their way to the locker room under the gym. Wampum's win record had been tied at 82 and the aim now, besides winning the WPIAL, was to add on as many wins as possible. The addend would end up being the number 29 to bring the total wins record (that stands to this day) to 111. To put the significance of this 111-win record into further perspective, let's begin with a story that happened at the *end* of the streak.

-CUTTING THE NETS-

It has now become tradition that when members of a basketball team reach a particularly giant milestone, they step onto a ladder one by one holding a pair of scissors. They each take a turn snipping one piece of the top of the net until it falls from the hoop. The player who made the final cut then holds the net proudly high above his head for all to see. It has been seen on television with songs like "This Shining Moment" being pumped into the arena to really bring the emotion. Teams "cut down the net" after winning conference titles and important tournaments and after claiming titles like National Champion. These nets are then displayed with just as much pride in the trophy case as any trophy that may have been won in competition.

In 1999, the players of the Hopewell Vikings climbed a ladder to cut down the net at the end of one of their games. It wasn't for a championship. It was a just regular section game. So why would the coach of the Hopewell Vikings instruct his team to cut the nets after this seemingly inappropriate time? It was because he and his team had reached a milestone as rare in his eyes as a national championship. The Hopewell Vikings had finally succeeded in doing what no one had been able to do in almost a full decade. They had defeated John Miller's Cougars in a section game. So it was with reverence and respect that the Viking players strode up the ladder to claim the nylon prize for their trophy case. And in true Miller fashion, his team looked each player in the eye and shook each hand with an acknowledgement of a "good game." The players returned to stand quietly in front of their bench as they watched with respect as the net came down.

And now let us rewind the film twelve years.

1988–1989

23 Wins–8 Losses

"Guess who just got back today
Them wild-eyed boys that had been away.
Haven't changed that much to say.
But man, I still think them cats are crazy."

–Thin Lizzy

The 1985–1986 squad would be the first Miller era Blackhawk team to have its own official song. Thin Lizzy's "The Boys Are Back in Town" would blare from the public address system during warm-ups and introductions before each and every home game. This song drove home that the Blackhawk faithful were aching to see a return to basketball and missed it during the April through October absence. The song kind of became a theme for that entire era of Blackhawk basketball. And in 1989, even though the boys were indeed back, one notable boy wouldn't be back; he would be playing about an hour's drive to the southeast for the Pitt Panthers instead of for the Cougars. But despite Sean's absence, fans would see a Cougar squad return to the Final Four for both the WPIAL and state championship series. His presence was still felt. The team still worked out and prepared just as it always had. The ladder was still being climbed little by little. If the formula was followed, the season would be a success, and it was. The team took the section once again, but everyone could feel that something bigger was on the horizon.

SECOND QUARTER

DANTE'S INFERNO (1989–1992)

Key Point Guard #2, Dante Calabria

1989–1990
WPIAL CHAMPS, Section Champs
25 Wins–3 Losses

WESTERN PENNSYLVANIA CHAMPIONSHIP GAME
Blackhawk 44–Seton-La Salle 37

1990–1991
WPIAL CHAMPS, Section Champs
30 Wins–1 Loss, 0 Section Losses

WESTERN PENNSYLVANIA CHAMPIONSHIP GAME
Blackhawk 84–Seton-La Salle 52

1991–1992

PA STATE CHAMPS, WPIAL CHAMPS, SECTION CHAMPS

32 Wins–1 Loss, 0 Section Losses

WESTERN PENNSYLVANIA CHAMPIONSHIP GAME

Blackhawk 81–Aliquippa 62

PENNSYLVANIA STATE CHAMPIONSHIP GAME

Blackhawk 71–Strath Haven 55

Though Dante Calabria played many positions, for the sake of this book we'll call him the point guard. This was the time period when Miller's teams truly became Miller's teams. John and his assistants decided to abandon the zone defenses and began running man-to-man, quick inbounds, North Carolina breaks, and dead-on outside shooting that would kill the competition with threes. It would be the best coaching decision in his career. It wouldn't be until the 2000s and Mike D'Antoni's Phoenix Suns when even NBA teams recognized the built-in statistical advantage of a three-point heavy attack. But, as usual, John Miller was ahead of his time. Once in three-point territory, Miller's Cougars were, like the 1991 Tom Petty song says, "Into the Great Wide Open." Not many opponents would be able to stand in their way in the decade of the 1990s.

In 1990 the starting lineup included seasoned players such as Jason Stanchak, Matt Gray, Christian Bell, and Jamar Shegog. These guys were conditioned, fundamentally sound basketball machines who knew the Miller system like they knew their first names. When future North Carolina Tar Heel Dante Calabria was added as the final piece, they became almost unstoppable. His three-point shot and ball handling were unmatched among fellow high school players. In fact, his point total at the end of his time with Miller was ranked second all time at 2,252. Many consider him the best basketball player to ever play in western Pennsylvania. That is most definitely high praise. After a great career under Dean Smith at University of North Carolina at Chapel Hill,

Dante would continue playing ball at the professional level in Canada, France, Greece, and Spain. He spent the most time playing for the "Serie A" in Italy. He capped his career playing for the Italian national team. But before all of that, he was key point guard on John Miller's high school juggernaut, the Blackhawk Cougars.

With a system in place that Miller and his staff knew would be hell on the competition, the team's confidence grew. That made Miller, and his assistant Amalia, confident that they could push their players harder than ever. The practices were sweatier and more intense than ever before. It worked though, because the whole team was "all in." Everyone from the assistants to the water boy believed that Miller had the blueprint on how to win. His players were well schooled in learning the blueprint. They had been trained in the program since Little Cougars. All that was left was to condition the players so that they could outlast any opponent.

Practices and game strategies were drawn out wherever and whenever. John started his day almost religiously by stopping at the DeAngelis Donut Shop, about a five-minute drive from the school. Mark Balbach, former Blackhawk physical education teacher who shared that duty, would also share a table at the long-standing shop. The original store boasted a gigantic, plastic, rotating glazed donut outside that actually spun atop a large steel post, but the Chippewa location had no such extravagances. It was just a counter with some stools, a few tables, and strong coffee to get you going in the early morning.

John would arrive there early to begin planning the day, to catch up on the sports page, and to wait for Balbach to arrive. Once he was there, the schemes and plays were hatched and played out on the table before trying them out for real at practice.

"Everybody knew that DeAngelis was where to find John," said Balbach, who shared a real office with Miller under the gym at the school. "Some days, let's face it, a lot of days, the planning got so involved that we were ten minutes late for school. Everyone knew that, too. Some of them have said that they were

The "office"

going to hook up a loud speaker at the doughnut shop so that we wouldn't miss the morning announcements. But hey, we were technically working. Right? We were planning the practices for the day. And they were pretty involved."

Dante Calabria remembers these hardcore practices vividly. "We were actually relieved when game day rolled around. The actual game was way less intense than our practices. Kids were pumped up and really cared about the team and took things personal. Practice was an intense, intense, almost emotional experience every time. We had guys go to blows at a practice they were so fired up. Coach Miller blew the whistle and told them just to go battle it out in the locker room and to come back when they were done. That would be unheard of today, but that's the way it was back then."

Those passion-packed practices would lead to a fantastic season. The only loss of the 1991–1992 season was a one-point defeat in Aliquippa. That 79–80 game was decided by a foul shot awarded after a very questionable penalty. On the positive side, that was probably one of the only games played in the Aliquippa gym that year that was a close game to the very end. As tradition had it, at "Quip" the away team was usually pretty far behind by the fourth quarter. Around that time of the game, the Quip fans would turn to the visitors section and begin to clap and stomp in rhythm with the chant, "Get your hat, get your coat, and LEAVE!"

By the end of the decade, the Cougars were such a fundamentally sound and solid team that the guys from Quip town were about the only thorn in their sides. Blackhawk lost only two times that year. And both times were at the hands of the Aliquippa Quips.

Losing to Aliquippa was nothing to hang your head about. The Quips were loaded with talent. They were faster. Especially at the beginning of the season, they were just plain better in every facet of the game. The Quips would end up beating the Cougars soundly in the play-offs and by double digits in section play. And again, they would beat them by one point in the final game of 1990. It would be the only section loss of the season.

But something special was about to happen. By the end of the 1989–1990 season, the Quips no longer were blowing out Miller's Cougars. In fact, following the loss to the Quips at the end of the season, the Cougars would not lose to Aliquippa or any other section team for a very long time. The WPIAL's 111 straight section wins record—John Miller's crowning achievement—was about to begin.

It is a bit difficult to put in perspective just how often Miller-led teams won in this era and even for a time just prior to the actual winning streak that set the record. Former North Carolina Tar Heel Dante Calabria put it this way: "Just like a kid will do, at the beginning of fifth grade, I started counting the number of losses I had in basketball. I continued this all through high school. At the end of my senior year, I believe the total of losses was at six. Our team just worked and worked and worked so that we became untouchable. We were taught to make it a habit to ask ourselves if someone somewhere could've worked harder than us on that particular day. If the answer were yes or maybe, then we would get back to practicing a little more. The group that I was with, to say the least, was hard-nosed and all about basketball. Of course, Coach Miller loved us for that. He knew he could count on us to work just as hard as he did. And that was saying something. We wouldn't practice to get off five hundred shots each; we would practice to make five hundred shots each. And we would record everything on his charts. We knew that seeing the results on paper would inspire us to work even harder. It was all about beating personal bests. It drove us.

"What really made the difference in the amount of wins was the fact that we were his first era of three-point shooters. I believe we're ranked the third best high school team ever as far as the three-point line my junior and senior year. It got to the point where defenses would purposely give up lay-ups so that we wouldn't hit them with the three. Coach Miller was smart enough to adapt his coaching plan to suit our strengths. That meant that he went from a one-tempo coach to up and down tempo coach. All we did was press full court and we ran and transitioned and shot threes. We won game after game that way. And when we finally won the WPIAL for coach that first time, I gave him a big hug, and it was almost to say that we helped to bring him to the top of the mountain, but we kind of knew that he was going to be up there for a while."

By 1989, this Cougars team was one of the best units to ever have been coached by John Miller. The starters included Jason Stanchak, Matt Gray, Dante Calabria, Christian Bell, and Jamar Shegog. They had been indoctrinated since elementary school in Miller's methods, plays, and work ethic. They were five that worked as one. They had given Miller a second WPIAL trophy to put in the case, and it was still only the beginning.

Dante Calabria rises above sea of Quip defenders.

The 1990–1991 campaign started right in the middle of the two-month-long Gulf War. At the same time that US forces showed complete domination over their inferior Iraqi counterparts in Operation Desert Storm, John Miller's Cougars completely destroyed its competition each and every week of the season. This team was another steamroller that was built for flattening any team in its path. Dante Calabria led this edition of the Miller machine that included Kim Niedbala, Andy Gray, Christian Bell, and Jermaine Simpson. They averaged no less than 92 points per game in the first half of the season. The team's specialty was the three-point shot. Honed through hours and hours of repetitions before school, during study halls, and after school, these guys nearly wore out the "Shoot Away" and later the "Gun," shooting machines invented by John Joseph that John Miller helped to perfect. His high school teams were the first to use the devices that are now commonplace in NCAA and NBA practice facilities. They would handily beat the Seton-La Salle Rebels for the WPIAL title and would be stopped just short of the Pennsylvania State Championship by a Pittsburgh city school called Perry by a score of 75–68.

In the 1991–1992 season, always looking for a challenge, John Miller scheduled his team to participate in a tournament at the very beginning of the season. No ordinary tournament of local teams, this one was played a two-and-a-half-hour bus ride away at the Johnstown War Memorial, and it featured top teams from around the entire country. There, Miller's team clawed its way to the top again to face Dunbar High School from inner-city Baltimore. The team would fall in defeat, but Miller's real plan was to give his team a chance to feel what it was like to compete with the elite of the sport. Following a very competitive loss to Dunbar, his boys felt invincible. Dante Calabria, a senior by now, would inspire the players around him to greatness. Fellow starters Hal Koenemund, Andy Gray, Ken Newman, and Kim Niedbala would go on to roll over all competition in the WPIAL at an average pace of 95 points per game. The cherry on top was to finally defeat the mighty Aliquippa Quips for the WPIAL crown. The future NFL great Ty Law and his team had been a thorn in the side of the Cougars for years.

The "thorn in the side" Quips featuring Ty Law (#5)

That great victory for the western Pennsylvania crown would be followed up with an almost anticlimactic state title a few weeks later. That's not to say that the 71–55 victory in chocolate town wouldn't be sweet for Miller. In fact, it was one of the most memorable times in his life.

"It's a time to celebrate and be happy. I'm just so fired up," the normally reserved Miller would bellow at the end of regulation. Calabria, Coach Miller, and Assistant Coach Bob Amalia would appear in a huge picture in the *Pittsburgh Post-Gazette*. In the article, they spread the praise around the whole team for a cap on the top of a mountain of hard work. Forward Ken Newman, guards Hal Koenemund and Andy Gray would agree that it was a

NO. 1 IN THE STATE

lackhawk gets sweetest win in Hershey

Calabria, Miller, and Amalia

night they would cherish forever. And the look in John Miller's face when someone mentions any of his teams' achievements shows that he cherishes it as well. But as much as he prizes moments of victory, anyone who knows him will tell you that from the top of the mountain, he scans the horizon for the next one to climb.

1992–1993
SECTION CHAMPS
20 Wins, 8 Losses, 0 Section Losses

With Dante Calabria in North Carolina and only one returning senior from the last season, many predicted the worst, but they were proven wrong. The section win streak remained intact, and John Miller led his team to within one game of the western Pennsylvania championship. A rebuilding year for the Cougars ended up being much more. The starting five players (Doug Yeager, Pat Cutshall, Adin McCann, Jim Peterson, and Steve Dickinson) were average to above-average players who used what they'd learned from their coach to succeed as a team. Nothing fancy this time, just a strong relentless defense and rebounding prowess led to three pointers at the other end. The only returning senior that year, Doug Yeager, recalls, "We didn't expect to have such a good year, but through Coach Miller's work and determination, we achieved some pretty lofty goals."

John Miller remembers, "The team that year was an overachieving one. With seven of our best guys gone, we had our work cut out for us. It was supposed to be a rebuilding year, but with guys like Steve Dickinson, Jim Peterson, and Doug Yeager coming on strong, we had another dominant year, especially in our section. With Dante gone, there were no real stars, but what a team."

Jeff Weaver, one of the role players of the era, remembers a particular play that encapsulates Miller basketball as far as he is concerned. "We were working on stalling the clock at the end of a practice game in the high school gym. My team was up one point with thirty seconds left on the clock. The point guard, Doug Yeager, was running a 'stack' set and popping out the get the ball. Well, I popped out and got the ball, then passed to someone else. Yeager got the ball back with about twenty seconds still on the clock. Without hesitation, he launched a three-pointer, and made it!

"The whistle blew, and Coach Miller said, 'Doug, What the hell are you doing? We are up one point with thirty seconds, and you launch a three?'

"Doug's response was, 'But Coach, now we're up four points with twenty seconds.'

"Miller responded by telling us to all get on the line and to run suicides for five minutes. I'll never forget that. That's when I knew it wasn't about just a game and just a score. It was about playing within a system. And we all realized sooner rather than later that his system was genius. He didn't say a word explaining why the three pointer was the wrong thing to do at the time, but while we were sweating it out running, we all thought about it and figured it out on our own."

–A VIEW FROM THE VISITOR'S BENCH–

To look at things from a fresh perspective, it's instructive to get a different view. The following is an account of Miller and his fearsome Cougars from the bench at other end of the court.

If Dante Calabria had any rivals during his playing time under Coach Miller, it was six foot four New Brighton star and Butler County Sports Hall of Fame player Gabe Jackson. During his time with the New Brighton Lions, he scored 2,011 points in western Pennsylvania scholastic play. Only four others had done this since 1959. Calabria remembers that "Gabe could choose to play football or basketball, or whatever in college. It wouldn't matter. His athleticism would take over no matter what the situation. When you'd put him in any type of a game, he was sure to excel."

After high school, Gabe did indeed use his athleticism and dunking ability to dominate on and *above* the court for the Robert Morris Colonials and for professional ball in Europe. Nowadays, he is back home in Beaver County giving back in a big way as a drug counselor at Gateway Rehab Center in Aliquippa. He still teaches kids basketball and hosts an annual camp in New Brighton each summer to teach the game he loves to neighborhood kids.

One thing that is great about sports is that, years later, the players and even the spectators can joke, reminisce, remind, and especially needle each other about events that happened years ago. How many events in life can you remember and it's just like it was yesterday? Not that many. Gabe remembers a game like that from 1990 like it was yesterday.

Gabe Jackson

"One reason why I remember the game so well is because [John] Miller will remind me about it every time I run into him," Jackson says with a laugh and the obligatory high five.

Gabe and his brother Chris Pipkin were a lethal tandem for the rival New Brighton Lions back then. "We felt so good coming into that game, explains Gabe. "We had our music particularly loud for our warm-ups. I can still remember, Run DMC, Kurtis Blow, Fat Boys, and the list goes on. And it was a tight game the whole way, back and forth. By the end, we ended up in a tie, and then another, and then another. Triple overtime. I had some dunks, my brother had some dunks, and it was tied with only a few seconds on the clock. I could have ended it, but you know, I had to be 'showtime' and I took off with one leg up for the Tomahawk dunk and bam! That thing bounced clear back to half court. I tried to tear the roof off and slam the dunk and be the hero, but no, they get the ball back and score.

"My brother then gets the ball. He takes flight and slams one home. So we think it's a tie score. But no, there's one of their guys under the hoop. The ref looks up and signals for a technical for hanging on the rim. Aaaaaaaggghh! But the rule is if there's a player underneath, you got to give the offense room to land. He never did. Anyway, there was a loose scramble for the ball at the end. Blackhawk's Matt Gray, and I tease him when I see him, picks up the loose ball and knocks down a jumper to beat us. John teases me, Andy teases me, and I'm a good sport about it, but guess what? We beat 'em later in the play-offs so, hah!!" Gabe let's loose with his infectious laugh. "And that's what I tell John. We got you back! We got you back! We got you real good at the play-offs at Robert Morris!

"But that just goes to show the competition in that conference at the time. Some of the games now aren't bad, but back then it seemed like every game, no matter what town you went through, there was a game and it was bangin'. We were like rock stars. Once I saw two grown men fighting about tickets to get in to one of our games. And it was all over a high school basketball game. That's the kind of passion the game brings. And love him or hate him, that's the kind of thing John brought to the game. Anyone that says John Miller wasn't good for the sport around this area is a fool. Just look at the excitement his teams created. Just look at the record books. Look at the lives of his players after basketball. No matter who you were, he made you believe that you belonged out on that court. And guess what? He passed that on to his own boys Sean and Arch. Same thing."

Gabe's brother and New Brighton teammate, Chris Pipkin, echo's those sentiments. An intimidating presence, Pipkin is now a police officer in the Pittsburgh affluent suburb of Cranberry Township. Back in the late 1980s he was a four-year starter who was called by many, a man among boys. To this day he holds the record for scoring in Miller's Blackhawk Christmas Basketball Classic. As a high school senior, he led the WPIAL in scoring, was section MVP, was first team All-State, played in the Dapper Dan Roundball Classic, and was named an All-American. Like his brother, Chris went on to play college ball and travel to Europe and Asia to play professionally and win awards all the while.

But in high school, Chris names Coach Miller as a main source of inspiration and motivation, and he wasn't even the coach of his team. He was his rival's coach. Chris was amazed each time his team went up against Coach Miller and his Cougars. He was used to playing against incredible talent. Beaver County was known for teams that were as daunting as they were talented. The Aliquippa Quips, for instance, were loaded at the time that Gabe and Chris were playing, but somehow they weren't as scary to play as Miller's crew that were all short on height and God-given athleticism.

Chris explains, "When you look at other teams we played, they had guys like Sean Gilbert, who went on to a great NFL career, and Myron Walker, who is the all-time leading scorer at Robert Morris University who played briefly for the Cleveland Cavaliers. They had Chad Askew went on to Pitt and future NFL hall of famer Ty Law. The list goes on and on. It was amazing that I had no fear playing against those guys. But I'll tell you what, before playing against Miller and Blackhawk, I had nightmares. My most miserable times playing was against them because they were so prepared, like a machine, organized."

Chris remembers the same Blackhawk game that Gabe does. "We were undefeated, running through teams like they were nothing. And then on a Tuesday night we play these little guys at Blackhawk. I swear, they didn't have a kid over six foot one, and we were playing 'circus' basketball, dunking over people and whatnot. But I'll never forget Miller later on telling me, 'No matter how spectacular that dunk was, our lay-ups that we made were still worth the same two points. And they just kept making those lay-ups over and over and over. It was strange. They beat us that night, and I don't even remember barely anyone on that team. They all looked the same. They could all dribble. They could all shoot the ball accurately. They could all defend. And they all played hard. And that was because of him. It wasn't about their abilities, or lack of them. It was because of him. Some of the most amazing stuff I've ever seen."

Chris Pipkin

Later, a newspaper reporter quoted Chris saying, "I'm so embarrassed that we lost tonight."

Chris states now that though he wasn't misquoted, he thinks the quote was misunderstood. "It sounded like I was embarrassed that we lost to a bunch of short white dudes. That wasn't it at all. I was more embarrassed that they did so much with the talent that they had. If we had worked as hard as them prior to the game, we should have won by fifty. And that's the lesson I learned from Miller. After that game, my practice schedule increased tenfold. I rallied my team to do the same. That is the only reason we finally ended up beating them in the play-offs. I was set on fire by just watching how he got his team to play. They were a team. We were individuals. From that moment on, I knew that we had to change."

And they did. With a renewed commitment to the team concept, they did beat the Cougars in the play-offs. Later on, Chris would be offered a scholarship from Eastern Michigan University. Some big name latecomers like Florida State, Villanova, and Georgia Tech called Chris to try to steal him away from his commitment. Who did Chris call for advice? Coach Miller. His answer spoke volumes. "Stick with your commitment. They're the ones who brought you to the dance."

HALFTIME:

"JOTTING" DOWN SOME MEMORIES

Danny Fortson played in the NBA for ten seasons. He was a Seattle Supersonic, a Denver Nugget, a Boston Celtic, and a Golden State Warrior. Before his professional career, he spent his time breaking a number of school records at the University of Cincinnati. St. Louis Billikens coach Charlie Spoonhour once said of Fortson, "I could do a chin-up on his arm, and it wouldn't affect his shooting. He was best known as a Seattle Supersonic, but Coach John Miller knew him when he was a JOT, Miller's Pittsburgh AAU team.

Kenyon Martin's college career as a Cincinnati Bearcat was highlighted with two first-team All-Conference appearances in 1999 and 2000, and he was named the National college player of the year in 2000. Once in the NBA, he stayed for fifteen seasons making an appearance in the All-Star Game in 2004 as a member of the New Jersey Nets. Later that year he would be traded to the Denver Nuggets. Before all of that though, he was a JOT. Kenyon went to high school in Texas. At the time, AAU didn't restrict where kids could come from. Cincinnati's Bob Huggins was recruiting Kenyon from his high school near Dallas. From there he played for the JOTs before becoming a Bearcat and beyond.

LaVar Arrington played in the NFL for six seasons. A three-time player in the Pro Bowl, He was named one of the eighty greatest Washington Redskins of all time. Back in Happy Valley, Joe Paterno fielded LaVar with confidence from 1997 to 1999. One of many spectacular plays now has been immortalized as the "LaVar Leap." On that particular play, LaVar jumped over the offensive line to tackle an Illinois running back in the backfield. He was heralded as a possible Heisman candidate when he appeared as the cover boy for the *Sports Illustrated* 1999 College Football Preview. He was a member of the Redskins, but John Miller knew him as a JOT, and he played basketball.

Those guys, along with the many staples of Miller's career at Blackhawk—Sean Miller (as his coach), Dante Calabria, Jim, Brandon Fuss-Cheatham, Archie Miller—were all JOTS.

So what is a JOT? Webster defines it as "a very little amount" as in "He didn't care a jot," but somehow most don't believe that's what J. O. Stright was thinking of when he christened his basketball team, the Pittsburgh JOTS in 1986. When asked what the strange name stood for, he replied tongue in cheek, "I really don't want that printed in a book. You have to be one to know one."

Clockwise: J. O. Stright, John Miller, LaVar Arrington,
Danny Fortson, Kenyon Martin

In reality, JOTS simply stands for John Orville Team Sports. The team is part of the AAU, or Junior Amateur Athletic Union, and J. O. himself has been called the most influential basketball man in the football crazy area of Pittsburgh and other parts of western Pennsylvania. He has been called the "go to" man when it comes to recruiting star basketball players from Pittsburgh and the outlying suburbs. You only need to ask big name coaches such as Bob Huggins, Rick Pitino, Herb Sendek, and John Calipari to verify that notion. The late, great Jim Valvano went to college with Stright and used to stay with him in his small Pittsburgh apartment when recruiting in the area.

In 1995, Stright was put under the microscope a bit when he took in two players, Tino Hunter and Danny Fortson, when they needed a place to stay. J. O.'s son Justin played point guard for Shaler High School, and Tino and Danny were allowed to play since they resided with the Strights. People, of course, cried foul, but J. O. insists that his heart was firmly in the right place. "My main reason for taking the boys in was to put them in a position to make a life for themselves. I truly wanted them to succeed and to do the right thing. Some people won't want to hear that, but that's the truth of the matter. I used sports as a way to work my way out of a situation I didn't particularly want to be stuck in. Why shouldn't I help others do the same?"

Stright, now a wealthy man, grew up lower to middle class as the son of a steel mill worker. He saw athletics as a way to dream his way out of a steel mill job that seemed to be his and his classmates' destinies. He worked and played three sports hard at Hickory High School and was named the best athlete in his yearbook. He went to Rutgers University on a basketball scholarship and earned a degree that would put him on the path to the massive success that he enjoys today.

While playing for the Sonics in 2006, Fortson, who went from the Altoona slums to a multimillionaire NBA player under Stright's guidance, had this to say about him: "People will say what they want, but J. O. is really there to help the kids, and a lot of kids need help."

The JOTS started in the 1987–1988 basketball season in cooperation with the Pitt basketball program. Panther players such as Charles Smith, Demetrius Gore, Jerome Lane, and Sean Miller got involved to coach AAU teams like the JOTS during the summer to gain experience and earn college credit. Coach Roy Chipman was completely on board and thought that it was a great idea all of the way around. He knew J. O. when he played at Rutgers and brought him into practices to help some of the guys learn the plays. He was known as a tough guy who could also teach.

In 1992, John Miller entered the world of J. O. Stright and his JOTS. At that time his son, Sean was about to graduate from the University of Pittsburgh. Sean had been coaching the JOTS to earn credits for a class at Pitt. Upon graduation though, Sean was headed to an assistant coaching job with the Wisconsin Badgers. Sean immediately thought of his dad as the perfect replacement and suggested the idea to J. O.

Stright's son, Justin, knew the Miller's from visiting them over the summer. He told his dad how awesome it was at their house. Stright remembers, "Over dinner one night I asked Justin about it. He responded with, 'Dad, it's great. We just play basketball. We watch film. Archie's mom makes dinner, then we go out and play some more.' Once I saw the enthusiasm he got out of Justin, I knew he would make a great choice for the new coach of the JOTS."

Sean, though, had a small stipulation before handing his team off to his dad. He went to J. O. and told him, "You gotta take care of this group. My dad is going to be a great coach for them, but you have to sit on the bench with him."

J. O. was puzzled and asked Sean why would a seasoned coach like his dad need him to sit on the bench with him. Sean spoke up, "I know my dad. In the heat of battle, he's going to start running these complicated Blackhawk plays and these inner-city kids are used to street ball. They aren't going to know what he's talking about."

Laughing, J. O. shakes his head, "And damned if Sean wasn't right. A few times the game was getting intense and down to the wire and he starts calling out, run this and that, and he got some blank stares back. I had to remind him a few times to keep the Blackhawk out of the JOTS, but man, what a coach, what a teacher. You always learned something just being around the guy."

Future Pitt stars Darrelle Porter and Sean Miller at a JOTS practice

Players came to the JOTS in many ways. LaVar Arrington happened to be walking down the sidewalk one summer in Mount Washington as J. O. Stright and another famous Cincinnati coach Bob Huggins were sitting on Stright's deck having a drink. They were talking about how the JOTS were going to travel to Las Vegas the next day for a tournament. J. O. was distraught over the fact that his two "big guys" were hurt and that they were going to get their "butts kicked" in Vegas.

More than just a big guy, LaVar was an incredibly huge physical specimen. He was, as J. O. calls him, a Helmet Head, meaning his main focus was football. Earlier that summer, Stright told LaVar not to even waste time on basketball. He told him that he should focus completely on football as far as his future was concerned. That all changed that day when as if on cue, LaVar walked past just as the two coaches were lamenting the need for a big strong forward.

"Hey LaVar!" Stright called out. "L-A-V-A-R! Do you want to go to Vegas tomorrow with me and play some basketball for the JOTS?"

A little shocked, LaVar turned and answered, "Sure Mr. Stright! I'll go."

"Well then, call your mom and tell her you're going."

And it was as simple as that. The next day at the airport, Stright shows up with monstrous LaVar walking behind him with a suitcase, and Miller's face lit up. They ended up being really competitive at the tournament to say the least.

And don't forget, Archie Miller was on that team with LaVar Arrington. With Arch running the point, the team did great in Vegas. A few years before maturing to be the point guard for the JOTS, Archie, smaller than the others, was a great bench coach for his dad and the JOTS.

Tongue in cheek, J. O. points out that he went with Archie and Sean to their first ever recruiting trip. Archie was still in middle school when he asked J. O. if he'd ever heard of a boy named Tommy Pipkin. He's now seen as one of the best players to ever play at Valley High School. When Tommy went to play for Duquesne University, he wore number twenty-three and dunked a lot and his coach once called him a miniature Michael Jordan. He may have gone on to a pro career had it not been for a knee injury. Archie heard of this kid before he was in high school and thought he would be great for the JOTS. The only problem was, he was already on an AAU team in Penn Hills. J. O. told Sean and Arch to get in the car. And they drove to Tommy Pipkin's house. They explained about what kind of a coach John was and how Sean was involved and at Pitt, and the next thing anyone knew, he was a JOT.

All in all, during those years, the JOTS could compete with any AAU team in the country. They played guys like Chris Herron and his Boston crew, Allen Iverson, Tractor Trailer out of Michigan, and Randy Livingston out of Louisiana.

But each year, when summer ended, the JOTS also ended. That meant starting up the season for the Cougars. And in 1994, the point guard position on Cougars now belonged solely to Archie Miller.

THIRD QUARTER

ARCHIE'S OPERATION (1993–1997)

The new Fab Five included #11 Archie Miller, the third key point guard of the Miller Dynasty.

1993–1994
SECTION CHAMPS
26 Wins, 6 Losses, 0 Section Losses

1994–1995
PA STATE CHAMPS, WPIAL RUNNERS-UP, SECTION CHAMPS
30 Wins, 3 Losses, 0 Section Losses

WESTERN PENNSYLVANIA CHAMPIONSHIP GAME
Highlands 58–Blackhawk 56

PENNSYLVANIA STATE CHAMPIONSHIP GAME
Blackhawk 65–Pottstown 59

1995–1996
PA STATE CHAMPS, WPIAL RUNNERS-UP, SECTION CHAMPS
29 Wins, 3 Losses, 0 Section Losses

WESTERN PENNSYLVANIA CHAMPIONSHIP GAME
Blackhawk 65–Chartiers Valley 61

PENNSYLVANIA STATE CHAMPIONSHIP GAME
Blackhawk 67–Valley View 55

1996–1997
WPIAL RUNNERS-UP, SECTION CHAMPS
19 Wins, 3 Losses, 0 Section Losses

WESTERN PENNSYLVANIA CHAMPIONSHIP GAME
Chartiers Valley 64–Blackhawk 59

By 1993, it was getting more and more difficult for Miller's teams to live up to the reputation of the previous year's team. But in the eyes of Miller and those who bought in, each team was its own separate entity. If the hard work and dedication are the same year after year, then the results should be the same regardless of what has been accomplished in the past.

And in basketball, like all sports, the level of success can depend on one second, one inch, or one point. Such was the case with this version of the Cougars. Three points at the end of a double overtime game against the old rival Beaver Falls Tigers kept them from grabbing another WPIAL title. Consolations included another perfunctory perfect section record and another trip to the quarter final of the Pennsylvania State Championship.

Starters Adin McCann, Jim Peterson, John Koenemund, Steve Dickinson, and Alex Cantamessa were talented by anyone's standards. The section championship in 1994 was a primer shot for the championships to come once Archie Miller was added to the mix.

In 1995, for the second time in a decade, Miller's team had won the Pennsylvania State Championship. With only one returning senior, the Cougars rolled over the competition, but a broken foot would sideline that senior, Steve Dickinson, in the first weeks of the season. He would return twenty-seven games later to play for the state championship game in Hershey.

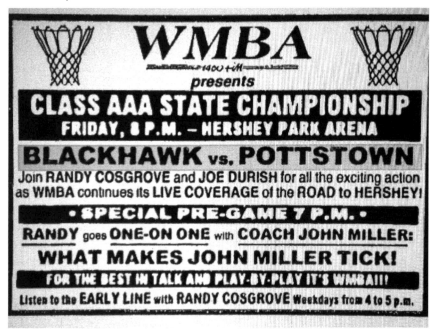

Pottstown's challenge was to contain the six foot six forwards Dickinson and Jim Cantamessa. Miller's challenge was to counter against Howard Brown, a six foot five guard who had already accepted a full ride to Villanova. At the half, Pottstown was ahead by a score of 30–29, but after some halftime adjustments, the tide would turn.

In the end though, the team just did what it had done time and time again all year. The players ran the plays they knew in their sleep, and by the next day, the *Pittsburgh Post-Gazette's* headline read, "Dynasty Continues for Miller and his Cougars."

This time around, even more so than in 1992, Coach Miller was able to relish in the victory. Miller was quoted after the game: "It was probably more fun tonight. I probably smiled a lot more. I actually helped cut down the net. I couldn't remember anyone cutting the net down when Dante and the guys won it. I think I was a little too stiff the first time because I was scared to death. You know, the first time ever getting there, so, this was more fun."

BLACKHAWK vs. VALLEY VIEW

PIAA PLAYOFFS: Class AAA final.

RECORD, DISTRICT: Blackhawk, (28-3) WPIAL champion. Valley View (26-6) District 2 runner-up.

TIME, DATE, SITE: 8 p.m., Friday, HersheyPark Arena, Hershey.

STARTERS: BLACKHAWK: Jim Cantamessa, Sr., C, 6-7, 17.1 ppg; J.T. Haskins, Sr., F, 6-1, 15.3; Ryan Miller, Jr., G, 5-9, 16.1; Jeremy Huber, Sr., G, 6-2, 8.7; Steve Lodovico, Sr., G, 5-10, 6.3. **VALLEY VIEW:** Jeff Ricketts, Jr., 6-1, 3.6; Dave Chekan, Sr., 6-6, 5.8; Mark Celuck, Jr., C, 7-0, 19.0; Mark Sakson, Sr., 5-11, 21.5; Mike Krupis, Sr., G, 6 6.

In these teams, Archie Miller would be the leader and the catalyst. Assistant Coach Bob Amalia remembers a few state play-offs where, with precision and cool, Arch would hit a devastating shot right at the buzzer to snatch games away from opponents. People mustn't forget that he helped to win back-to-back state championships for his father and his team. But beyond the marquee players such as Sean and Archie Miller, Dante Calabria, and later on Brandon Fuss-Cheatham, some of the best stories to come out of John Miller's coaching come from the players who were on the second or third team.

In 1995 and 1996, Jason DeRose was one of these players. Surely a starter on any other high school team, Jason was on the second team at Blackhawk. He is now the head of a business called simply, FASTER. It is one of *the* premier fitness facilities in western Pennsylvania. It is owned and run by DeRose, someone who admittedly needed to get "faster" and better at the beginning of the 1995–1996 basketball season. Young Jason was a great friend of Archie's. He had witnessed John Miller direct his sophomore son and the rest of the Cougars to a state title in the spring and had decided that he needed to be a part of something like that. Because of what he saw, in the fall he signed up for the basketball team. It would be a decision that would forever change his life.

"Hey, DeRose!" a short, mustachioed Miller yelled from across the gym. "It took you long enough to get to the line. And was that a chest pass? My grandmother could hit me with a harder chest pass! And she's dead!" That is one of Jason's clearest memories of Coach Miller.

Twenty years later, Jason DeRose remembers, "When I signed up for basketball, I expected what you see on movies where the cut list comes out and you nervously rush over to the bulletin board to look and see if you made the team. It wasn't that way at all for Coach Miller's teams. Miller never cut anyone. He would let you cut yourself from the team. The players from the previous year would absolutely dread the first few weeks of practice because they would be absolutely brutal. By the end of the first week, kids would start quitting. No one ever needed to be cut. If you weren't in insanely good shape, you would hate these practices.

"Suicides. You can't even probably call them that today," DeRose continues. "We ran suicides like any other team back then. You'd run to the foul line and back, to the half and back, to the opposite foul line and back, and to the baseline and back. But Miller would time us. If one didn't hit that line by the time he'd stated, we'd all have to go again. We had garbage cans set up at the baseline for the puke, but it made us strong. It made us proud we'd stuck it out where others quit. It made us feel like we could defeat anyone. And then we did."

Why would anyone put up with that kind of punishment? DeRose echoes the same sentiment of players from decades past. "I first became attracted to Coach Miller's personality and what he was all about because he

Archie as a Blackhawk Cougar

really was the first coach I'd known that would take an interest enough in me to really challenge me. It was far from being just a job to him. You knew he was in it to draw the best out of all of us. Everyone signed up for basketball, but after a week or so, they'd be gone. But after a few guys at practice shook their heads and laughed at me at the beginning, I noticed that Coach gave me a look as if to say 'How's this guy going to react to this?' I decided to stick around to spite them, and I think Coach respected me for it.

"Next thing I knew, a month of the hardest practices imaginable had passed and I thought, 'You know what? I'm going to bear down even more and make this team.'

The Archie Era

"I was encouraged further when Arch and some other guys, whom I had then earned their respect by now, began peppering in my ear. They would say things like, 'C'mon man, if you fight through this it will change your life.'"

That's a pretty prophetic thing for a teenager to tell another teenager. You could confidently say that, with the reputation Miller had made for himself since 1976, the players on his teams knew by now that what he was selling them was worth any price. This idea has been proven true time and time again. Former player after former player has translated the "hardships" at Miller's practices to real life lessons that have made them succeed in life.

"And he didn't care who you were either," explained DeRose. "One guy on the team, great guy, Jimmy Cantamessa, happened to show up late for practice one morning—Thanksgiving morning. Now Jimmy was one of the best players in the *state*, let alone the team. But, anyway, he was really late.

"Coach's rule for the team was that you had to run a suicide for each minute that you were late. Without hesitation or fanfare, he looked at Jimmy and looked at his assistant Bob Amalia. 'Bob, you got J. C. on the sideline. Run him for 110 suicides. One for each minute late.'

"And my man ran for what seemed a week. It was like a marathon or something. Occasionally he would bring him in for a pattern or to run a play, but then he would be running again. But then you knew. You respected him because the star was getting the same treatment that you would have gotten. It made you want to run through walls for this guy. I know for a fact that Jimmy made it big for himself later in life, and the trials he had to go through at practice had to have been a big part of what he's made of himself. Coach was of the mindset that you were either going to try to be really good or you weren't going to get along with him. There was no such thing as just trying to get good."

DeRose credits Miller and his insistence of excellence as one of the main reasons he is where he is today. He was inspired to create FASTER from all of those experiences at practice when he thought that he couldn't go on, only to find out that when he pushed himself, he got to another level physically and mentally.

MILLER'S DYNASTY

Following is John Miller's record as a head coach at Riverside and Blackhawk high schools.
1970-76 at Riverside – 74-58

BLACKHAWK

1976-77	1-21	1986-87	21-6
1977-78	14-7	1987-88	16-7
1978-79	6-16	1988-89	23-8
1979-80	13-12	*1989-90	25-3
1980-81	5-18	*1990-91	30-1
1981-82	23-6	*+1991-92	32-1
1982-83	11-12	1992-93	20-8
1983-84	13-15	1993-94	26-6
1984-85	19-8	+1994-95	30-3
*1985-86	19-9	*+1995-96	29-3
Blackhawk total			**376-169**
Miller total			**450-227**

* WPIAL champions.
+ PIAA champions.

When DeRose entered college, he went out for the college team and found that it wasn't challenging enough. From there he decided to create FASTER and inspire others to do their *very* best. He notes the word "very" because it signifies pushing to another level that's almost beyond what you think that you can do.

That's how the stories go for so many of the players who were coached by John Miller. By the late 1990s, winning had almost become an old hat to the fans at Blackhawk, but if you just ask a Yankee's fan, winning never really does get old. Once, following yet another World Series Championship, announcer Tim McCarver pondered aloud, "Could you imagine how terrible it would be for a Yankee's player that didn't like the taste of champagne?"

That was a little like how it was getting for John Miller and his Cougars. The only difference was that the taste in question wasn't champagne. It was Hershey's chocolate, the treat of choice in the central Pennsylvania city where the state championships were played.

FOURTH QUARTER

FUSS-CHEATHAM FINALE (1997–2001)

Fourth key guard: Brandon Fuss-Cheatham

1997–1998
SECTION CHAMPS

1998–1999
STATE CHAMPS, WPIAL CHAMPS, SECTION CHAMPS

WESTERN PENNSYLVANIA CHAMPIONSHIP GAME
Blackhawk 48–South Park 44

PENNSYLVANIA STATE CHAMPIONSHIP GAME
Blackhawk 66–Holy Ghost Prep 43

1999–2000
STATE RUNNERS-UP, WPIAL CHAMPS, SECTION CHAMPS

WESTERN PENNSYLVANIA CHAMPIONSHIP GAME
Blackhawk 73–Pine-Richland 50

PENNSYLVANIA STATE CHAMPIONSHIP GAME
Steelton Highspire 68–Blackhawk 56

Pure adrenaline. That is the way Cougar sophomore Daren Tielsch described the way he felt when he was being pelted from the stands by Hershey Kisses. Throwing the silver foil-wrapped chocolate treats at the players upon clinching a trip to Hershey for the state championship is a tradition in Pennsylvania. So is the crowd's chant of "We smell chocolate! We smell chocolate!" Those words are only heard when the game begins to feel as if the team you're backing has it in the bag.

Greg Huston proving "a lay-up is worth the same points as a dunk."

In 1999, the familiar smell of chocolate was indeed in the air both in the gym at Midland when Miller's Cougars defeated South Park and in Hershey when they completely destroyed Holy Ghost Prep for the state championship. Tielsch, Mark Franitti, Greg Huston, Matt Moye, and Dane Helsing were key players this time around. Daren Tielsch played a particularly strong part in the Holy Ghost victory, but Miller, always looking to mold his players into his image of what it means to be great, still had some "suggestions" for him to work on for next season. "I always tried to drill into my players that they shouldn't show their emotions on the court whether they be high or low. Daren would scream after a blocked shot for instance, and I had to break him of that. But that went for everyone."

And it truly did. Jim Deep, an assistant that year, was the head coach at Aliquippa earlier in the 1990s. When the Quips won an AA title, Jim ran around the court like a madman celebrating the win. This time around, he was calm and collected. When the *Pittsburgh Post-Gazette* asked Miller about the change, he replied, "He's a Cougar now. That's the way we do things."

Someone well aware of how Miller "did things" was the captain of those late 1990s Blackhawk teams—Brandon Fuss-Cheatham.

Today, Brandon Fuss-Cheatham is the owner of a highly profitable and successful Columbus clothing company called Lamp Apparel. It caters mostly to the Columbus college town and fans of its beloved Ohio State Buckeyes. One baby bib available at the store proudly claims that the wearer is a "Young Buck." From 2001 to 2005, Brandon was a star point guard at OSU. A fantastic shooting guard, he drove the "Buckeye Nuthouse" at the Value City Arena crazy for four years. When he gave my son and I a tour, you could still see the thrill in Brandon's eyes when he asked Ben, "Can you imagine running out on the court with this place packed and screaming your name?"

OSU Buckeye,
Brandon Fuss-
Cheatham

Brandon's skills and work ethic that he picked up at Blackhawk High School from his coach propelled him to play to packed houses in the Big Ten. He fondly remembers Miller using every opportunity to teach. On trips to clinics and games, there would, of course, be pit stops for food and gas. The booth became a classroom. The salt and pepper shakers became power forwards; the sugar became the guard. Full plays would be mapped out around blocking the syrup. Aunt Jemima got a full ride to Michigan after all. Brandon was Miller's point guard and main guy on his side when he played for him, but one of the ways that Coach Miller got him ready to compete against the best was to put him up against Miller's best.

"I guess one of the best things that Coach did for me to prepare for competition was how he would purposefully stack the deck against me in practice. In the summer, our team would be broken up so that we could play each other just to get in some game experience or whatever. It would be on the courts right next to the intermediate school, the ones that coach built. Coach Miller would always split up the teams,

and I would be by myself on the worst team. It would be second team and me versus all of the starters. So and it would be our seventh, eighth, ninth, and tenth man and me versus the starting four (all Division I Division II guys) plus the fifth guy. Those are great odds, right? Anyway, those were challenges that he would put up for me. He was trying to stack the deck so that my team was awful, but I would have to try to make the team better. How can you win with this team? The answer was that I had to teach them. And when you teach, you learn better than you ever had before.

"One main key that he taught me was that, if you were the point guard, you should always know the score, and you should always shout the score out after each and every bucket. If you don't know what the score is, you were immediately kicked out of practice. If you didn't shout out the score, he would stop play and ask me what the score was.

"If I said the words, 'I think the score is ...,' he would lose his mind and flip out. 'How are you going to lead your team if you don't know the score?'

"And he was right. The score for the most part determines what you do on each individual play. If you're down forty-eight to forty-seven and you need a two, then why risk it and shoot a three? Everything had a reason, and if you didn't know the score, that to him meant that you didn't care enough to know. And that's when you were in trouble. To this day, if I'm playing for fun, I still yell out the score after every hoop. It's just a habit now.

"In my life now too, I still think of myself as the point guard. I have to know what is going on around me in order to make the right decisions. I owe that all to coach."

The fact that the 111 game section win record was broken under Fuss-Cheatham's watch was one of the only disappointing things to occur during his time at Blackhawk. It had to happen sometime, and even the Hopewell Vikings didn't expect the record to be broken by them. It was just one of those things. Nothing lasts forever. This is especially true in sports.

So it was on January 26, 1999. Coach Joe Faletta of Hopewell stood in front of radio microphones and *Fox Sports Pittsburgh* TV cameras. He told the media that he didn't expect it to happen, and it was something that you just dream about. He went on to say that he really didn't think that his team could beat the Blackhawk Cougars. And then, the next thing he knew, as if it were the championship, the nets were cut down. Ultimately though, Miller and his Cougars were able to cut the real championship nets down in Hershey, Pennsylvania, for yet another Pennsylvania State Championship.

There would be a few more highlights in Miller's career after that night in Hershey. Runner-up for the state championship in 2000 and for the WPIAL in 2001 was among them. But in 2005, Miller decided to call it quits for good as a high school coach.

Miller, at sixty-two, left with a career record of 657–280 in thirty-five seasons. His eight WPIAL titles are second only to his one-time hero Ed McCluskey who won eleven at Farrell from 1956 to 1976. His teams made the play-offs an unbelievable twenty-one times in a row, and his record in the play-offs of 104–29 is even more impressive. On top of that, the sixteen section crowns, the thirteen consecutive titles, and the 111-section victory streak are mere side notes in his awesome career.

As far as the naysayers who point at his dealings with the JOTS as a recruitment tool and the few high-profile transfers (there were only two), Miller acknowledges that when you win big, a lot of people are going to search out the negative. Hopefully, this book disproved some of that.

At the time of his retirement, he still left the door open for basketball. "I can never really leave the game altogether. I probably need to spend more time with my grandkids. I still love to coach, and I'm still going to run my Drill For Skill camps. I'm not ready to put the ball down just yet."

That was a very true statement. He may be even busier now than before retirement. His induction to the county hall of fame in 2012 seemed to only be a breather for the coach to look back at his past and plan and chart the future.

Millers: Sean, Tim, John, Joe, and Archie at John's HOF induction

★

CHAPTER 17

ALL IN THE FAMILY

"Hopefully, we can build a rivalry and we'll be able to do this a lot.
Make a legacy, then retire champions."
—Serena Williams speaking of her sister Venus

When speaking of Archie Miller, former coach and current analyst Pete Gillen remarked, "He has the game in his blood. His dad was a great coach—his brother—Archie Miller probably was born with a basketball in his crib." Ryan Miller earned the new surname Archie early in life when his dad kiddingly began calling him Archie Bunker. He noticed that his little boy had a salty personality that reminded him of the cantankerous but likable 1970s TV character, but one thing is clear. His gratitude to his father and his family is real, despite his cranky public persona.

He set the record straight publicly at his Beaver County Sports Hall of Fame induction. "When it comes to my basketball and coaching career, my dad and Sean, they blazed a big trail for me. I was very lucky in that way because when it came to basketball, I had the early answers to the test. I was able to follow what they did and just stay on their path. That accelerated my game and my opportunities in the game like you wouldn't believe."

At Blackhawk under his father, Archie would win two back-to-back Pennsylvania state championships before being recruited by a number of Division I schools. Playing the game the Miller Way and "having all the

★ Ryan "Archie" Miller: Head Coach of the 2016 A10 Champion Dayton Flyers

answers to the test" in that sense took Archie all the way to North Carolina State University to play for the Wolfpack. And no one shouted nepotism when, in 1998, Assistant Coach Sean Miller recruited his brother to come play for the Wolfpack.

Around the time that Archie declined Pitt's offer of a scholarship in favor of North Carolina State's, reporters asked his father if he thought that NC State was recruiting Arch because of the relationship with his brother. He responded quickly with, "They don't want him there just because Sean is there. They want him because they feel like he's the best point guard they can get."

No one really did seriously suggest it, but if someone would have, all Sean would have had to do is point to Archie's spectacular high school stats to dismiss that idea. Plus, Archie was proving himself worthy of being there every day at practice. Thinking back to his playing days at NC State, Archie said, "Sean wasn't soft on me because I was his brother. He coached me harder than he did anyone else. It was sort of like with my dad. There were no free passes. But when he left, I was mature and could go up against anyone."

Sean was the perfect fit as far as coaching his brother. He was demanding but knew when to use

Archie calming the
New Castle Hurricanes

some encouraging feedback when it was needed. Archie recalls, "In addition to making us work, he was also a kind of helping guy who gave positive reinforcement all the time. His teaching came more from a player's perspective, but he knew when to put the pedal down to drive a guy, especially with me. He always knew how to hit the right button to get me in gear."

Archie remembers his arrival at NC State. "When I got there, it didn't take me long to realize that if people looked at just me, they would surmise that I really wasn't supposed to be there. I wasn't fast enough, didn't have the quickness. I wasn't tall enough. But what I did have was my family and the background with my dad to guide me and help me to succeed. Again, the answers to the test."

At NC State, Archie Miller proved that he did indeed belong in the storied basketball Wolfpack. He will always be remembered as one of the all-time greats at the university. He finished his career at NC State in 2002 with an eye popping 84.6 percent free-throw percentage, a 42.9 three-point field goal percentage, and 218 three-pointers. All of those achievements place him in the top ten in all three of those categories in NC State history.

Archie Miller proving he belonged.

And in return for all he did for the Wolfpack, North Carolina State University would be the place where Archie would first find the blessings that would be the basis for his life. For one, he met his wife Morgan there. They have a little girl named Leah. She is his pride and joy. He laments a little, though, that being a college coach comes with a bit of a sacrifice. He doesn't get to spend nearly as much time with her as he got to spend with his dad growing up.

Professionally, too, NC State was responsible for giving Arch his first

Arch

chance at coaching. "It was my last year. I didn't really set out trying or even wanting to be a coach. But Herb Sendek, my coach at the time, asked me the question, 'Well, you're going to graduate. What are you going to do now?'

"I responded at first that I didn't know. But what I did know was that the only thing that I was really good at was basketball. I guess I realized that my career was going to have to do with basketball and coaching. I followed up my response with, 'I guess I'd like to coach.'

"Coach Sendek shook his head and shot back, 'Why in the world would you want to do *this*?'"

Miller admitted, half joking, that he didn't know how to do anything else, so he'd better do something with the game.

It wasn't long after that that Herb Sendek handed him a great opportunity. He offered Archie a graduate assistant job right out of college. It came with a great amount of responsibility. Miller had to travel around, recruit players, and be involved with practice everyday. Archie found that he really enjoyed working with the players as a coach and not a teammate.

"It was different. And that is where I got hooked on the coaching and the coaching staff side of the game," Archie reflects.

This was quite a job for a man not yet in his mid-twenties. The trust Sendek showed when he gave the graduate assistant job to Archie was not lost on one school that was hunting for assistants. First-year coach Darrin Horn from western Kentucky would hire Archie for the 2003 season. At twenty-three, this would make him one of the youngest college assistant coaches in the country. Being that young, he had to overcome unexpected obstacles.

Archie jokes, "People don't realize, but I'd go to rent a car for recruiting, and I wouldn't be allowed get one without a cosigner. You needed to be twenty-five years old to rent a car on your own. That really drove home the idea that I was indeed blessed to be in the position that I was in at such a young age."

Archie Miller, without a chance to catch his breath, was off and running in the world of college coaching. Beginning with the graduate assistant job, things were moving fast and have not let up to this day. Things were fast and furious at first, and Archie and his wife Morgan had to learn the realities of having to move repeatedly, ultimately coming back to where he began. From western Kentucky, Archie was hired back at NC State as an official assistant coach under his old coach Herb Sendek. "I was back in my element. I was back where I went to school and played. I was in heaven. That's where I met Morgan, that's where I started my family."

As blissful as it was to be back in his old surroundings with his old coach, it wasn't meant to last. At the end of the 2006 campaign, Herb Sendek abruptly left to take a job as the new coach of the Arizona State Sun Devils. He wanted to take Arch with him.

"I was all settled," Archie remembers, "and now I was going to move to Arizona? What's in Arizona? Cactuses? What? I'd never been to Arizona. I didn't know anyone from Arizona, but I had to go with it. That is a big part of college coaching. Moving. My family and I packed up and moved across the country to Phoenix. It was a larger school, a bigger job, a bigger step."

All along, Archie was sniffing for something that would lead to the real prize: a head coach's position. If he was going to have the crazy schedule that went along with being an assistant NCAA coach, he might as well go for the whole thing. His next step toward that was a move to Ohio State University. He got a job offer after just six months at ASU. When the Buckeyes' coach Thad Matta came calling, Archie and Morgan packed up for their second cross-country move in less than a year. They unpacked, explored, and found that they liked Columbus and Ohio State.

Archie laughs, "My family and I liking Ohio State made perfect sense, because the next thing you know, my brother Sean gets hired as head coach of the Arizona Wildcats. Naturally, he offered me the job as his assistant. I told Morgan to get the suitcases back out. I knew my brother and I would be perfect working together. I knew because he'd always include me since I was little. He taught me to dribble alongside my dad. At Pitt, he'd included me when I was still a little guy in school. On Fridays, I can remember staying with him in his dorm room for the weekend. I really idolized him as an older brother. I trusted him and would always do what he said. It didn't matter. So I knew I had to move there. It was obvious."

And it was clearly the correct move. Imagine two coaches both trained under the same master. Sean and Archie had done just that. Being brothers,

Sean and Archie teamed up at Arizona

they had been raised, coached, and groomed by John Miller. They wouldn't even need to consult each other in most situations. They would know what to do. They both had the same direction sheet, if you will. And if all else failed, their father was just a phone call away. Archie became second in command of the Wildcats. And working with Sean at Arizona, Archie frequently spoke his mind.

"Sean learned to figure out that his brother was pretty good, so he'd let him have his say," John Miller said. "He knows he's a good coach."

The learning experience at Arizona was perfect for Archie because, at the end of the day, he looked up to his brother. At his Beaver County Sports Hall of Fame induction, Archie made it known. He said, "Sean is the one I'm the most like. He's the one I always wanted to be like. If I wanted to be a head coach, he's the one that I'm going to do it just like."

In 2009, Arizona was an ideal situation in which to be. Sean Miller had inherited seven players from the outgoing Arizona coach, and six of them were good enough to be scholarship athletes.

"It felt like it was a dream," explains Arch. "I had a contender right away. Within two years of my move there, we had a shot at the Final Four. Though we lost, it was quite a ride. And I'll never forget. That loss was on a Saturday. Four days later, I interviewed and was hired for the head coach job at Dayton. A few days later, I was in a plane and here we are. I never went back. It happened just like that. I'm so grateful for all those people and places that got me to where I am now."

Once Archie got to a certain age, some healthy competition was beginning to mix in with his respect and admiration for his older brother. Most brothers are competitive, but for Archie Miller, he seemed to have his work cut out for him. His brother's name was a household word in Beaver Falls, the town where he was born. He always felt like people were referring to him as "Sean's brother" rather than just Ryan or even Archie.

"I always felt that someone was looking at me and saying, 'He's not that good, he's not that big,'" Arch admitted. "I felt that all the time growing up. I wasn't as friendly. I didn't go out of my way to make conversation. I always felt like I had a chip on my shoulder."

His teachers could see that their personalities were different. Blackhawk teacher Nanette Boggs remembers, "They were both really nice kids, but where Sean was the outgoing personable one, you never really knew what Ryan was thinking."

Jack Fullen is the president of the PIAA and was the athletic director of the Blackhawk School District for many years. He concurs, "Archie was always a little ornery. He was a good kid, but he surely didn't march to the same drumbeat as Sean."

No matter what Archie's personality quirks might have been, on the court he was a positive force for his team.

John, Leah, and Archie

Air Archie

It is a fact that his qualities and statistics as a player and a coach stand alone no matter what his last name is or what family he comes from. Rating Archie as a player, Archie's coach at NC State, Herb Sendek, put it plainly when he said, "When he's on the court, he makes everyone else at least ten percent better."

Archie makes it clear, though, that even though the sibling rivalry does exist, his brother Sean was more mentor than rival because of the age difference. As the years have gone by, they continue to become closer as brothers and more similar as coaches.

One striking similarity is the amount of wins each of the brothers has. Since arriving in Dayton, Archie and his Flyers have already appeared in a Sweet 16 and an Elite 8. Those are feats that many college coaches dream of doing after years of sweat. Archie has been at Dayton for less than five years. In those years, Dayton has won five times in the NCAA tournament. The only other teams to do that are Kentucky, Connecticut, Michigan State, Wisconsin, and his brother's Arizona Wildcats. In 2015, he was a finalist for the Jim Phelan National Coach of the Year Award.

Archie has indeed come out from under any shadows his brother or father may have cast. He has made a name for himself. Just go to Dayton, Ohio, or any other Atlantic 10 town and ask someone if they know who Sean Miller is. Someone is likely to reply, "Oh him, that's Archie's brother."

Arch and his dad after a big win versus Duquesne in 2016

CHAPTER 18

DRILL FOR SKILL ACADEMY

REACHING THE NEW GOAL

"We don't stop playing because we grow old;
we grow old because we stop playing."
—*George Bernard Shaw*

Miller's student from forty years ago Brad Brown visited his old coach in 2015. Miller's current domain is his brand new Drill for Skill Academy. After sitting awhile and watching Miller run a practice at the new facility, he said, "When I asked his assistant about him, he said, 'He's been here for ten hours now. I'm half his age and I can't keep up with him. He's a machine.' Basketball isn't what he does. It's who his is."

Following retirement from coaching, it didn't take long for John Miller to realize that he wouldn't be able to simply leave behind what had become his passion.

The gym at Drill for Skill Academy is a representation of Miller himself. From the outside, it is not even recognizable as the state-of-the-art basketball training facility that it is. There is no signage on the building to alert anyone to what is held within. There are no billboards around town to draw people to sign up for the lessons and camps taught there. There are no commercials on television and no radio spots to entice parents to sign up their kids to indulge their hoop dreams either. Only just recently was Miller convinced to create a Facebook page and website to help current and potential customers navigate through all of the choices for instruction. On the outside, for all anyone knows, Drill For Skill is nonexistent. It is simply Beaver Valley Auto Mall. The gym is tucked away quietly in the back.

You know now that his children were taught that their play on the court would speak much louder than the words they may have spoken about themselves. This adage can now be used to describe the work and play going on at the academy. It speaks for itself. Despite the lack of advertising and signage, the place is packed daily with players honing their skills the Miller Way.

It all started when John Miller was a customer at the auto mall. The owner, P. J. Latsko, knew John because of his local legend status. Latsko told Miller that there was a pretty sizable stockroom in the back. The building used to be a Circuit City electronics store. Latsko was thinking of converting the space into a gymnasium that he could rent out. He knew Miller would be a reliable tenant, so he offered it to him first. Once the terms were set, Latsko set to work contracting the $100,000 facility.

"When P. J. tapped into this place for the Auto Mall, he told me about his idea to build a basketball court," Miller said. "So I came in, looked it over, and decided to give it a shot."

The gym is open to anyone wanting to elevate his or her game. The gym has also become home to sixteen AAU teams that need a place to practice. All year long since the gym first opened, players of all ages have been streaming in from all over. "I have kids coming in from everywhere," Miller said. "I got kids from Ohio, West Virginia, and all over Pittsburgh making the trip up here. They make the drive, and I work them out. They like the workout, so they keep coming. And they are telling other people to check it out. We've got a really good thing going here."

In the late 1990s, Tess Zufall, a great player in the 2000s for Cleveland State, used to make the hour-long trip every day after school from Slicksville, Pennsylvania, to Blackhawk to be trained by Miller . She's not surprised that today people drive all kinds of distances to make it to the academy.

The gym is beginning to churn out the basketball talent for area fans to enjoy and Miller's AAU team, the DFS Wildcats (an obvious tip of the hat to Sean), is dominating play in just about every tournament that they travel to across the country.

"I guess you could call it a second career," says Miller. "This keeps me active in basketball." And that is the understatement of the century.

Though his lessons and drills are basically decades old now, he does have to tweak them to fit the times now and again. His assistant at Drill For Skill Tim Kolodziej loves to tell the story of Miller announcing to a group of third and fourth graders that it was time for the "typewriter" dribble drill. "All the kids looked kind of dazed and didn't know what to do. I had to clue Coach in as to why they were confused. Right then and there, he changed the name of the drill to the 'computer dribble.' They knew what he meant immediately."

Everyone involved with Drill For Skill and its programs agree that the amount of work that this now seventy-three-year-old man puts into the program is the envy of people of all ages. His long-time assistant Bob Amalia explains, "What separates John Miller from any other coach is his work ethic. He's twenty years older than me and he outworks me on a day-to-day basis. He will outwork any coach in any league no matter what their age. That's the big difference. We had a twenty-five year old coming in to help, and he was outworking him."

The other part of his success that Amalia and others mention is his single mindedness. He was and is always thinking of the goal and nothing else. It didn't matter that people were jealous. It didn't matter that people were talking trash in the community or saying  things that really weren't true. He was able to shut all of that out and focus on his goals. That may be why he reached so many of those goals. There was no being sidetracked. No stopping to think and worry about what others were saying or what others thought about him. John did not need their approval. He proved his worth with his achievements, his family's success, and the achievements of his players.

Many have approached Coach Miller and asked, "What's your secret. Really? Clue me in here. What can I do to succeed?"

Coaches Tim Kolodziej and Miller today at the DFS Academy

His answer and advice is as simple as it is difficult to actually follow. "Put in the work every day." That is dedication. To stay dedicated, we must be motivated. To stay motivated, Coach Miller recommends to "devise a daily workout schedule to develop self discipline. Be creative with workouts. They should be fun and should change every so often. Buy two or three different basketballs to add variation to each workout. Keep a notebook and progress chart. There is something about seeing one's progress on paper that is gratifying and motivating."

"Don't go crazy," explains Miller. Do a few half-hours to one-hour workouts a day instead of marathon multi-hour sessions. Don't get frustrated over a certain drill. After a few attempts, move on and try it again later.

"Variety is key. Mix in shooting, strength, rope skipping, juggling, and coordination drills with ball handling throughout. Play different types of music while you're working out. It can bring about subtle changes and improvements to your drills. Keep your workout areas decorated with posters and motivational items. Change them often to keep things fresh.

"Work out with a partner, but stay away from group sessions. Groups tend to break down and make it difficult to concentrate on individual goals.

"Accept no self-made excuses. Some of the best workouts are done inside when the weather is bad. Or grab a snow shovel and clear off a place to practice! Don't let anything like weather stop you.

"Take advantage of excess time and space. Many dribbling drills can be done while watching TV. In fact, the act of watching TV ensures that the player has his head up and not looking at the ball. Malls and doctors' offices parking lots make excellent practice areas.

"If practices become routine, try speed workouts. Time yourself and chart it each day. Concentrate on keeping your head up while performing each drill smoother and faster.

Maybe most importantly keep some type of workout going *every* day, even if it's for ten minutes."

As far as moms and dads trying to help their kids do better at the game, Coach advises to make practice time productive, but more importantly, make it a fun. While they're young, it should be "fun time with mom or dad." And when they become teenagers, hand them off to a good coach.

But parents will be hard pressed to find one like John Miller. It seems that the mold was broken, but the original continues to shape the game his way. The lessons that were taught at little Riverside and Blackhawk high schools and that are still being taught in the small gym behind the Beaver Valley Auto Mall are echoed in Arizona, Dayton and Kentucky and in the various arenas where March Madness is advertised on their marquees.

Furthermore, all that were influenced by Coach Miller will continue to keep the ball rolling the Miller Way.

CHAPTER 19

FOR THE "HOOP GUYS"

JOHN MILLER'S COACHING PHILOSOPHY

The following is an updated version of Miller's philosophy on coaching, which was written in the 1980s.

This is an open letter to entry-level coaches. This is not about plays, patterns, and diagrams. After years of coaching basketball, I believe that having a philosophy, motivating players, being enthusiastic, and earning the respect of a squad are the major keys to a winning program.

What factors determine success on game night? Many people believe it is talent, size, or even some luck, but I choose to believe a coach can overcome many deficiencies in these areas. You're not going to be a consistent winner by simply having good patterns and a lot of plays. This chapter contains my random thoughts regarding my coaching philosophy. Technical knowledge is very important, but only a phase of the coaching world.

It is extremely important that a coach develops a philosophy. Coaches must take a good look at what they believe and decide what style that they would like to pursue. Your squad will be an extension of your personality. Are we conservative, or do we like to attack and gamble. My philosophy evolved over the years into a pressure man-to-man defense along with a pressure quick in bounds attacking offense. My teams really enjoyed coming right at the opponent on offense and defense!

It's not what you teach, but how well you teach it. It took me decades to become really comfortable with my philosophy. In my early coaching years, I would study and attend clinics and found myself constantly trying new techniques. But as time moved on, I found myself reverting to the technique that best fit my personality: the fast paced, pressure game.

AN OVERVIEW OF:

BLACKHAWK'S
BASKETBALL PROGRAM

BY JOHN MILLER · HEAD COACH

Develop a mental picture of what a good basketball team should look like and how its players should perform. Many coaches never seem to develop a feel or acquire that insight of how a team should play. Visualize the perfect game and coach towards that end. Break the game down into parts and put it back together. Total pressure on both sides of the ball should be the goal. Your teaching should be a progression of simple skills and concepts that begin in the second and third grade. Basketball is a game of reaction, and you should want the offense and the defense reacting to *your* team's pressure. You should try to keep your players in a disciplined, mentally tough mode. Your system should keep the opposition from running their offense. It should wear them down. It should frustrate them into making mistakes.

Your team should want to dictate the tempo for the entire game. The intensity should not change even if you have a big lead. Make it known to your players that when it's their turn to play, they should be with all their intensity for as long as they are in. At the high school level especially, a great mental attitude will overcome physical ability and take a team to the champion status.

Over the years, I had very few "stars" or "horses," but I managed to succeed through teamwork, mental attitude, and tremendous desire. I always stressed "in your face" team offense and team defense.

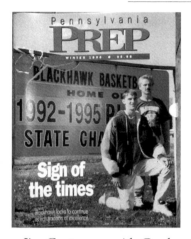

Jim Cantamessa with Coach

Many coaches tend to make the game too complex. If you keep it simple and know exactly what is to be taught, success will follow. Basketball is a game of errors, forced and unforced, and plays the percentages. If your team limits its errors and takes more higher percentage shots than their opposition, you will win plenty of games.

My yearly objective was always to get the maximum out of the total squad. That meant the junior varsity as well as the varsity. Each link in the chain was molded to feel important to the entire squad. I love to take the average player and develop him or her to the fullest potential.

ABSOLUTE ESSENTIALS

Here are some absolutely essential ingredients to producing a successful basketball program:

- The players must have discipline.
- The team must be organized.
- The team must believe in what they are doing.
- The coach must use simplicity
- The coach must communicate with the players.
- The players must communicate with each other.
- The coach and players must be enthusiastic.
- Good players and luck will help!

COACHING CONCEPTS

1. The goal for the season should be to work hard at every practice and at every game.

2. Try to stay away from talking about winning. The emphasis should be on working hard every day.

3. Do not key in on big games. Keep an even keel. All contests are important.

4. Do not get the team overly "fired up" before the game. You are not a football coach.

5. Captains are not a big thing to the coaching staff. Pick the captains. They shouldn't make decisions regarding the squad.

6. Do not embarrass a player in front of his peers. However, not hustling and playing hard on defense in unacceptable.

7. Say positive things to the players before you comment on weak areas. It will soften the blow.

8. Keep in mind that every player is not going to give you the same amount of effort.

9. Be careful of overly harsh criticism. A sharp tongue will turn off many competitors. Sometimes we dwell too much on the 20% lack rather that the 80% effort.

10. Develop a powerful positive attitude with the J.V. Squad. The importance of their role should not be overlooked. They should be developed just like the varsity. Work them together with the varsity when possible.

11. I usually subbed four minutes into the game. A post and a perimeter player will enter. The sub will not lose the game in the first quarter. If the sub sits the entire game and then enters the contest down the stretch, he will not be productive.

12. Constantly talk to your team about the fans enjoying the fast up-tempo style of play. Emphasize enthusiasm, hustle, and having a class attitude on the floor.

13. Scouting reports are basically for the coaching staff. High school players have a difficult time concentrating on video. I did not stress that the team watch video.

14. My team's attitude on a loss was that we would be back. They learned that as they left the floor, they should be thinking about the next encounter. It's on to the next game. Move ahead.

15. When things look bad, do not take things too seriously. The sun will come up the next day.

16. Each squad has a different personality. I tried to read the squad to find out when to go hard and when to ease up.

17. Going all the way to a state championship will put a tremendous strain on a coach! Stay in shape mentally and physically in order to withstand the demands of the season.

PERSONALITY OF THE COACH

1. Study the top coaches at every level. Adopt ideas from each one of them. Remember to always be yourself. Do it the way that you are going to be comfortable. By coaching this way, you will have confidence and the team will be an extension of you.

2. Maintain discipline without being a dictator. Be fair and earn the trust and confidence of the squad.

3. Do not hand out praise readily. It must be earned. After working hard, players appreciate it more when it finally does come.

4. Do not get personally close with your players, fans, and boosters. You need to run the show your way.

5. Do not try to make your players happy. A player should be happy to make the squad and to compete.

6. You will be successful with players that genuinely love the game and work at it daily.

7. You must correct mistakes immediately in practice. Waiting until afterward to talk about it does no good.

8. A coach cannot worry about what others think of him or her. A coach must handle his character and not worry about reputation.

9. I always tried to be 100% positive in the off-season. My personality became more workman-like when the regular season approached.

PERSONNEL: MAKING THE CUT

I was always concerned with a player's attitude and if he possessed the characteristics of an outstanding attitude. Some players come to play while others want to win.

1. Look for players with class.

2. The players determine success or failure. You can motivate and get solid play from a good kid.

3. Do not tolerate a complainer. You need the bench to be enthusiastic. Everyone on the squad has an important role.

4. Cutting the squad is a tough task. It is very important that the staff really studies the situation. They should not just go through the motions.

Proofreading Miller Time

5. As the coach recognizes the player with inadequate skills and abilities, he or she should make these players aware of their status leading into tryouts.

6. The head coach should post the list of members making the squad and then speak individually with the personnel being released.

7. You need to choose kids that have mental and physical toughness. Getting through our two-hour practices was a test.

8. Play the five that will win. Many times that will not be the best five players. You need to have the right combination on the floor at all times.

9. Your sixth, seventh, and eighth man should get plenty of playing time. It is important that they understand their roles.

10. Just liking to play the game is not enough. A successful player must love the game.

MOTIVATION

1. If a coach really loves the game, motivating players becomes easy. I work hard to continually improve. I try to lead by example rather than by words.

2. All athletes have the potential to be successful. It is the coach's job to motivate and develop this potential. The coach must utilize and devise a means of helping according to his own personality.

3. I do not believe in a lot of talk and gimmicks. I am more of a "nose to the grindstone" type of motivator.

4. I believe that players should write down off-season workouts. Set small individual goals and build on these.

5. An ultimate objective of a player should be to become a dependable, consistent basketball player who gives 100% effort.

6. Your team should win and lose with a class attitude.

7. Act like a champion, and you'll be a champion.

8. A coach should try to handle difficult player problems on a one-on-one basis rather than as a group.

9. Show the same qualities of dependability you expect from the team. Always be on time.

10. Your players shouldn't criticize each other. Your team does not have time for nit picking or anger in basketball.

11. Make a big issue out of certain little things as they happen. This usually prevents players from making major mistakes later on.

12. Don't play favorites or hold grudges. If a player deserves punishment or praise, give it because they expect it.

13. A coach must understand that players fall into several categories. They are either one sport hoopsters year round, two sport players that must split up their off-season time, or multi-sport players that really can't train in sport-specific skills.

OFFENSIVE PHILOSOPHY

1. My teams push the ball up court quickly! We need players that can go at top speed. I love this fast style of basketball.

2. I develop my post players to react quickly to the made shot and quick inbounds. One of the postmen inbounds.

3. We attack with the fast break, secondary break, and then our set offense.

4. To develop this, we drill constantly on converting from defense to offense.

5. We attack quickly taking the open shot and slide into the triangle 1–1 rebound slots.

6. Our main attack is a motion offense. We do a lot of back screening for the passer.

7. We try to force an up-tempo style of play. Pressure on defense and attack upon possession of the ball.

8. We are constantly taking the slash to the hoop.

9. We want and will get unselfish play and solid teamwork.

10. Build your offense according to your personnel.

11. Teach the proper way to set a good, solid screen.

12. Teach how to V-cut when shaking the defender.

DEFENSIVE PHILOSOPHY

1. My team's defense is a progressive teaching of man-to-man fundamental team defense.

2. I believe that players must learn the basic techniques of the defense over a period of years.

3. Each year the fundamental skills are reinforced and strengthened. After several seasons of instruction, the footwork becomes instinctive.

4. Outstanding defense will win championships.

5. Defense is the one phase of the game that remains constant. It's the same home or on the road.

6. The ability to convert from offense to defense quickly is extremely important in stopping the opponent.

7. Good defense requires that the offense takes good shots, not turn the ball over, and maintain proper floor balance.

8. We want to disrupt the ball with our aggressive play. We want to dominate the ball and make it react to our defense.

9. We want to force the opposition into mistakes, prevent them from running their offense, attack them, wear them down, and force them to use the bench.

ASSISTANT COACHES

Your staff must blend together. Someone has to be different than the head coach. Assistants must be loyal to the program. Be reasonable in the amount of time the assistant has to put in. The assistant should be closer to the players than the head coach is. The staff will always discuss situations at time outs and halftime. Each staff member starting in the grade school follows a progressive system of play. The head coach must outwork the assistant coach. A head coach cannot expect the staff to do the majority of the work.

BENCH COACHING STRATEGY

1. Use 8–10 players every game.

2. Substitutes are put into the game in the first quarter.

3. Play hard without fouling. That's our motto.

4. Look to run at every opportunity.

5. Look to pressure the ball.

6. Do not call many time outs!

7. Do not get sky high or tight before a game.

8. You need the bench in the game.

9. If the opponent calls a time out, change up your defense.

10. Go after a team early if you have the better team. This keeps the opposition from holding the ball.

11. Press the pressing team. It can change the tempo.

12. Test the opponent's young player. Let him shoot and see if he's cold.

13. When going for the last shot, start the play with about 8 seconds left. The shot should be taken with 4 seconds so you can get a tip in or a rebound put back.

14. Make sure you get out early after halftime. Get ready for the second half.

15. Never foul the jump shooter.

16. On the last shot at home, drive. The official will blow the whistle.

DRILL FOR SKILL ACADEMY CORE VALUES

1. Every child is an athlete. And every child can become a better athlete.

2. Talent is never enough. With few exceptions, the best players are the hardest workers.

3. We are teachers. And the court is our classroom.

4. Relentless focus on the fundamentals is the pathway to mastery.

5. We know we're not important enough to change the world, but we're important enough to change someone's world.

6. Our lives are a series of habits. It's important to develop good ones at an early age.

7. Trust. It's everything

SEE YOU IN THE GYM

Best Swishes,

John Miller

Coach Miller

MILLER GYMNASIUM PETITION

Sign the petition and make a difference.

Many gyms, stadiums, and auditoriums are dedicated to accomplished people. Why not rename the gym at Blackhawk High School where so much basketball history has taken place?

Rename the Blackhawk High School gymnasium in honor of the nationally recognized Miller basketball family. Visit http://www.ipetitions.com/petition/miller-gymnasium.

Blackhawk High School gymnasium today

And while you're at it, contact the Naismith Basketball Hall of Fame and nominate Coach Miller for membership. Visit http://www.hoophall.com/contact-us/.

WORKS CITED

Benjamin Miraski, "Dayton Coach Archie Miller on Hot Dog Stand Cup," *Mid-Major Madness*, 28 February 28, 2015, http://www.midmajormadness.com/2015/2/28/8127181/dayton-coach-archie-miller-on-hot-dog-stand-cup

"Dynasty Continues for Miller and his Cougars," *Pittsburgh Post-Gazette*, March 21, 1995.

Gary Parish, "Is Arizona's Sean Miller the Best Recruiter Not Named John Calipari?" *CBSSports.com*, July 14, 2014, http://www.cbssports.com/collegebasketball/eye-on-college-basketball/24620444/is-arizonas-sean-miller-the-best-recruiter-not-named-john-calipari.

John Perrott, "TV Appearance Not so Incredible to Sean Miller," *Beaver County Times*. October 18, 1983, https://news.google.com/newspapers?nid=2002&dat   =19831018&id=hWYuAAAAIBAJ&sjid=qdoFAAAAIBAJ&pg=4072,3308985&hl=en

Mike Bires, "Hot Shot Sean Miller," Beaver County Times, February 18, 1981.

Mike Bires, "Miller's Hoops Heaven,"Timesonline.com. May 12, 2015, http://www.timesonline.com/sports/local_sports/miller-s-hoops-heaven/article_e5e41c25-3602-5408-b6bb-8749d796dcad.html.

Mike White, "Western Pennsylvania Basketball Bursts onto State, National Scene," Pittsburgh Post-Gazette, May 25, 2014, http://www.post-gazette.com/sports/high-school-basketball/2014/03/25/

Western-Pennsylvania-basketball-bursts-onto-state-national-scene/
stories/201403250060.

"Miller Resigns After 29 Years at Blackhawk," Pittsburgh Post-Gazette,
April 7, 2005.

Pat Forde, "A Hardcourt Life: Sean and Archie Miller Have Their Father
to Thank for Relentless Work Ethic," Yahoo Sports, January 31, 2013,
http://sports.yahoo.com/news/ncaab--a-hardcourt-life--sean-and-
archie-miller-know-only-one-avenue-for-college-success-150944816.
html.

Rik Xander, "Miller Moving to Blackhawk," Beaver County Times,
May 17, 1984

ABOUT THE AUTHOR

David A. Burhenn was born in Beaver Falls, Pennsylvania. He has earned a Bachelor's and a master's degree in education from Indiana University of PA and Gannon University, respectively. Fascinated with the overwhelming success of the Miller family in basketball and in other pursuits, and especially after witnessing the positive effect that Coach John Miller had on his son and others, he decided to try to uncover the secret to the coach's success. Thus, his writing career began.

David and his wife Kristi live in Aliquippa, Pennsylvania, and have two children, Brooke and Benjamin. David is a teacher at Central Valley School District.

WA